Ruth R~

Ruth Roman

A Career Portrait

DEREK SCULTHORPE

McFarland & Company, Inc., Publishers

Jefferson, North Carolina

ALSO BY DEREK SCULTHORPE
AND FROM MCFARLAND

*Claire Trevor: The Life and Films
of the Queen of Noir* (2018)

Edmond O'Brien: Everyman of Film Noir (2018)

*Brian Donlevy, the Good Bad Guy:
A Bio-Filmography* (2017)

Van Heflin: A Life in Film (2016)

Frontispiece:
Signed photograph sent from Ruth Roman to author's father, circa 1950

**ISBN (print) 978-1-4766-8824-4
ISBN (ebook) 978-1-4766-4630-5**

LIBRARY OF CONGRESS AND BRITISH LIBRARY
CATALOGUING DATA ARE AVAILABLE

Library of Congress Control Number 2022027107

Front cover: Ruth Roman publicity still, circa 1949

Printed in the United States of America

*McFarland & Company, Inc., Publishers
Box 611, Jefferson, North Carolina 28640
www.mcfarlandpub.com*

Acknowledgments

With grateful thanks to Budd Burton Moss for his invaluable help and enthusiasm. Thanks also to Aaron Schmidt at the Boston Public Library. Thanks as always to my family for their forbearance and encouragement.

Table of Contents

Introduction

"I never did the greatest picture in the world. Maybe you can't be better than your material, but you can do a good job. When you start believing in yourself as a great actress and when you're looking for Academy Awards, you're in trouble, brother."
—Ruth Roman interviewed, 1954[1]

In many ways, Ruth Roman was "the nearly girl" of 1950s cinema. She seemingly had everything going for her: she was sexy yet wholesome, capable yet vulnerable with a good sense of humor. Behind her were the long years of trying, since the days as a child when she had dreamed of following in the footsteps of her heroines, such as Bette Davis. At one time, it all seemed to be falling into place. Voted the Most Promising Newcomer in 1950 and lauded as the "Sexiest Girl in Hollywood," she had a string of good roles and was consistently one of the most popular actresses. After her second marriage fell apart in the middle of the decade, her career too fell away. Success, as she might have said in one of her endearing mixed metaphors, was a horse of another opinion.

In the late 1940s and early 1950s, my dad, like many other young boys of his generation, used to send away to Hollywood studios for signed photos of the stars. The dusty side streets of a northern industrial city in England were thousands of miles away from the glamor capitol of Hollywood and, metaphorically speaking, the two were light years apart. The magic of cinema was a great escape for that generation from the mundanity and drabness of ordinary life, not to mention the privations of war and the lingering effects of rationing, which did not end until the mid–1950s. It was always exciting to see the postmarks stamped with the studio logos from Culver City. Among the many pictures he received by return of post, only a few were actually handwritten. Of those, only

Introduction

one or two were inscribed personally. One of those that was came from Ruth Roman (see frontispiece). It was a small thing, maybe, but I noticed it, and whenever I saw Ruth in a film, I would think of her as essentially a kind person who never forgot her early struggles and was always grateful and attentive to her many fans. This is something that was confirmed by the way she interacted with her fan club.

There have been few studies of Roman and certainly none of any great length. She was one of the subjects in the entertaining and collectible volume *Dames* in 1969 but has appeared in only a few books and magazine articles since then. Cineastes no doubt concur with the prevailing orthodoxy which consigns such second-tier actresses to oblivion. Even though she worked for many of the leading directors of her day, including Alfred Hitchcock, Nicholas Ray, King Vidor, Henry Hathaway and Jacques Tourneur, to name but a few, she has never been seriously thought worthy of discussion. Regardless of her ability as an actress or her undoubted glamor, the real interest lies in her own personal story of her struggle to get where she did and the tenacity she showed when repeatedly told she was not good enough. Hers is as much a tale of Hollywood as anyone else's and as such deserves to be told. This is not intended as a biography but a portrait. I hope to put her in context and shine a light on the experience of a neglected star of classic film. By extension, her story stands as a typical one of the myriad would-be stars who followed a similar path, who achieved half success or no success. Included is an extensive appendix with details of her credits across all mediums.

At her best on screen, she had a strong presence, with often a hint of danger about her. Seemingly tough and cynical, she had a withering gaze that any man or woman would do well to withstand. With a sudden flash of her dark eyes, she could register deep anger, hurt, sadness or sundry other emotions. Kirk Douglas once remarked that acting opposite her you knew there was someone there, that she was no featherweight. The characters she played were often sassy, down-to-earth, and relatable. They would brook no nonsense. They could as easily be disillusioned and world-weary. The feeling was that they had suffered some mighty disappointment which nothing in the world could ever assuage. There was a sardonic humor there too, as a saving grace, and beneath the hard exterior a deep well of banked-down emotion, often untapped. She strove so long and so determinedly for stardom, but, when it came, it proved elusive and soon slipped away again. Doggedly she kept on, true to herself. It was curious that even when she reached the heights of stardom, she still seemed to have to strive to stay there.

I must thank Budd Burton Moss, Ruth's third husband, for his kindness and encouragement in this project. Before I met him, I was all set to abandon it, after suffering two computer crashes in the space of as many months and the loss of crucial backup files. Without him it is likely that the book would never have been completed. His enthusiasm, good nature and optimism are infectious, and he is a true inspiration. For someone of 90 he retains a remarkable memory and faculty of observation. I would urge readers to seek out his memoirs of life in Hollywood, during which he met everyone and became friends with many of the greats.

Ruth's obituary writers were somewhat kinder to her than Hollywood had been. (One is reminded of that line in *Sunset Boulevard* when the corpse of Joe Gillis observes, "Funny how gentle people get with you once you're dead.") They mostly agreed that she could play good and bad with equal conviction, being both worldly and wholesome at one and the same time. It was an unusual combination, and this in itself made her a valuable asset to any film. Perhaps it was her underlying insecurity, which might have been a hangover of her early years of poverty, that kept her from being an all-out star. Perhaps it was her personality and the fact she spoke her mind in a town not built for honesty. It might even be a case of trying too hard and wanting something too much. Maybe it was just bad luck that she never hit the big time, although she came as close as anyone. She was always there or thereabouts for almost ten years from 1949, which in itself is no mean feat, considering the competition. However, the early promise she showed remained unfulfilled, and the roles she could have played to prove her worth mostly never came her way. She was striking and had a robust quality, tough, but tender withal; hence, she worked effectively with an array of virile leading men, including Errol Flynn, Gary Cooper, Sterling Hayden, James Stewart and Richard Burton. Her work had subtlety, which might explain why she was not always noticed. Her performance in the bizarre psycho-horror *The Baby* seemed out of character in some ways, although it was entirely apt for the film, which was rendered in the Grand Guignol style. In any event, her Mrs. Wadsworth was not a woman to trifle with. From the 1960s onwards she put her energies into her television career, and it was for this that she was ultimately rewarded with a star on the Hollywood Walk of Fame. Whether such baubles are important in the scheme of

Introduction

things is a moot point. Although her 40-year film career never hit the heights, it seems churlish not to give her a star for that too, at least for effort, because she added glamor and years of striving to make it on the big screen, and if she fell short of her own dreams, it was not for want of trying.

❖❖ 1 ❖❖

The Carnival
on the Beach

"Until I was seven, I was brought up in a carnival in an atmosphere both glittering and tawdry. An atmosphere of hot-dog stalls, barkers and
merry-go-rounds, candy floss and side-shows.... To
this day I can't look at a merry-go-round without a
few tears."[1]

Ruth was born December 22, 1922, the youngest of three daughters
of Anthony K. Roman and Mary Pauline (nee Gold). She was born at the
Lynn Hospital in Lynn, Boston, Massachusetts. Her parents were Jew-
ish and were both born in Vilnius in Lithuania. Like many, they came to
America with their families at the dawn of the century. She was initially
christened Norma, but a fortune teller supposedly told her mother that
Norma was a name that would only bring bad luck, so she was called
Ruth instead.

The Romans had long been established in Lithuania, where Jews
had settled since the Middle Ages and were known as a distinct group,
the Litvaks. Anthony's father, Charles Roman, first arrived in the
United States in 1905 and worked as a carpenter in a factory. In 1907,
Charles was joined by his wife, Martha, and son Anthony, who was
then about ten. Millions of Jews left Russia and Lithuania in the late
nineteenth and early twentieth century to flee pogroms, the threat of
them, or simply to escape from grinding poverty, overcrowded hous-
ing and rampant disease. Like the Romans, the vast majority settled in America. The family had suffered great personal tragedy in
their native land. Charles and Martha had married in 1894, but of
their six children born alive, only Anthony survived to adulthood.
Charles Roman later worked as a skilled man for the New York, New

Hampshire & Hartford Rail Road (N.Y.N.H. & H.R.R.) at the Readville Car Shops in Boston.[2]

On October 2, 1916, Anthony Roman and Mary Gold were married by Rabbi Hyman Glaser at his address, 323 Blue Hill Avenue, in Boston. At the time of the marriage, they were living at 60 Chambers Street in the West End of the city.[3] Anthony described himself as a shoe worker. Mary was a dressmaker. She was the daughter of Jake Gold, a tailor, and his wife Esther (nee Bycofski) of East 45th Street in New York. They came to America in around 1909 when Mary was about nine. Ruth had two elder sisters: Ana, born in 1918, and Eva in 1920. When Ruth was born, her father was working as a laborer, and the family was living at 72 Centre in Lynn.[4]

As the family grew, Anthony decided to switch to a more lucrative business of his own. He invested in a carnival pitch on Revere Beach, a popular holiday resort about five miles to the northeast of Boston. Revere Beach was first established as a resort at the turn of the century. Before the First World War, it was already beginning to attract holidaymakers from Boston and environs. The establishment of a light railway link made it a popular destination. In its heyday in the interwar years, it was a magnet for tourists, and the beach was packed for much of the day in the height of the holiday season. There were funfairs, rides, amusement arcades and all the usual paraphernalia of a seaside town. It was a hive of activity then, and it was only after the Second World War that it fell into something of a decline with the change in tastes and the rise in air travel.

Anthony and Mary ran the carnival between them. Anthony managed the whole shebang and was the barker or spiel man. He was also once described as an electrician, and it is probable that he had to be a jack of all trades. It was as well to have some skill to fall back on in the lean times or the off-season. Mary, always known as Suky, was a dancer, and a good one, according to Ruth, who thought she might have made a career in show business had things been otherwise. The family's time working in the carnival in the 1920s might have been relatively short but assumed great significance to Ruth, and she remembered it clearly and with great fondness. It was an uncertain existence and heavily dependent on the seasons, but she certainly took to the life which gave her a taste of what might be. She later spoke of the carnival, "It wasn't a very big one or a very fancy one, but it was the most exciting thing in the world to me. I would hang around it hour after hour. I even hated taking the time to go to lunch."[5] Her father's tent was next to the carousel,

6

1. *The Carnival on the Beach*

Postcard view of Revere Beach, Massachusetts, in the 1920s.

and she loved the music of it which always had a strange piquancy to her. Ever after she felt a surge of intense melancholy whenever she heard fairground music. As she often remarked, "I still get weak with nostalgia whenever I see a merry-go-round." Perhaps it was her early memories of a life on the peripheries of show business that inspired her to pursue her chosen field. Her first good memories were of the carnival and the beach, which she must have seen at all times of the day from morning until night in changing seasons. She was always drawn to the ocean. Unconsciously perhaps the twin fond memories of her early life, the sea and the carnival echoed her later love of the ocean and her career in Hollywood. After all, her earliest childhood companions were from the ranks of show-folk, the knife-throwers and small-timers of the sideshow. As she once reflected, "I soon realized … that those freaks and midgets, acrobats, barkers and small-time performers were as much a part of show business as the stars shining on Broadway. For them, there was no chance of making the big time. But for me, why not? They can't tax dreams can they."[6]

That happy part of their life ended abruptly when her father died suddenly at the age of around 32 in about February 1930, when Ruth was only seven. She barely remembered him, and her mother hardly ever spoke about him except to say that he was an educated man.[7]

7

Ruth Roman

After Anthony's sudden death, they left Revere Beach and the carnival. Suky sold their carnival interest, and the family went to live in an apartment block in the less salubrious part of town. Life was hard for them, and they changed addresses frequently because they often got into arrears with the rent. Suky tried all kinds of manual jobs and variously worked as a waitress, cleaner, charlady and laundress to make ends meet. The West End of Boston was home to successive waves of immigrants from the Old World. Among the most prominent were the Italians, Poles, Irish and Russians. Each brought with them their own language and culture, and English was rarely spoken. The warren of built-up streets and old apartment buildings often housed families of several generations in cramped living conditions. However, there was a genuine sense of community. Years later, in the late 1950s, practically the whole of the West End was designated a slum area and was swept away wholesale except for a few odd survivals such as a Catholic church, which stood as one of the only recognizable landmarks. In its place, huge office blocks and high-rise flats were constructed. The destruction of the neighborhood and its way of life caused great upheaval and rancor among the people who called it their home. Many felt, and still feel, that it ripped the heart out of a crucial part of the city without any proper consultation with those affected. Even today there remains a lingering resentment at the way in which it was done, and the whole episode has been held up as an object lesson for ambitious town planners who arguably went too far in an attempt to engineer social change.

For her part, Ruth was still vaguely starstruck; after all, her earliest memories had been of the carnival life of make-believe. Hazy though those memories may have been, in retrospect they must have seemed more vivid due to their straitened circumstances when it was all over. She referred to herself as "an eager, imaginative kid." From childhood she went her own way with her own ideas; for instance, she never took to wearing shoes. Curiously, in later life shoes became her one luxury, and she had so many pairs she gave Imelda Marcos a run for her money. Ruth resented the life of poverty after the early days on the beach were just a memory. Life in the city was a constant struggle. It was a tough neighborhood. "You had to be on your toes every minute," she once remarked. "You couldn't let them see you were scared otherwise they would torment the life out of you." A natural tomboy, she gave as good as she got from the toughies of the locale and always stuck up for herself; she even hit the boys when they started. Despite all her early privations, Ruth

1. *The Carnival on the Beach*

The corner of Spring and Chambers streets in the West End of Boston where the Romans lived in the early twentieth century (courtesy Boston Pictorial Archive, Boston Public Library).

always insisted that her childhood was essentially happy. Everyone was in the same boat—they were all equally poor. She and her sisters made the most of what they had and learned to find pleasure in the simple things: "We played tennis and swam in the Charles River," she recalled. "We didn't miss out on anything, and we didn't always pay for it either."[8]

Ruth's experience of school was overwhelmingly negative. She went to the William Blackstone School but hated it and had little interest in her lessons. Her time was made worse because early on the authorities had decided she was undernourished and needed to be built up. Hence, they gave her all manner of special vitamin supplements, which she refused to take. She would put them in her handkerchief and dispose of them later. To make matters worse, her mother also thought she was anemic or sickening for something and insisted on her eating platefuls of spinach, broccoli, raw liver and her own homemade concoctions to strengthen her, which put her off those foods for life. There were several incidents that stood out sharply to her from her schooldays. For instance, when she was ten, she was hit on the hand 30 times by a teacher because she told a fib. Her hand became so badly swollen that her mother went to the school to complain.

As a child Ruth sometimes showed a tendency to overdramatize,

9

and even small incidents assumed major importance. However, when she was 12, she was, according to herself, truly sick. She developed a high temperature and fever and could not move her legs. The family medic, Dr. Charles Gardner, was puzzled by her symptoms and could only surmise it was a virus of some kind but was at a loss as to how to treat it. She drifted in and out of consciousness for some weeks but found the recurring presence of the doctor a great comfort. In her delirium she thought she had heard him say that she was well on the road to recovery and would be able to walk again. Eventually the fever broke and gradually she felt the power returning to her legs. She forced herself to move, spurred on by the doctor. Many years later, she met him at a family get-together and discovered that what he had really said was, "She's a very sick girl. She'll never walk again. Only a miracle can save her."[9]

At times she was boisterous and high-spirited and once remarked, "The neighbors hated me. I had a voice like an air-raid siren and when I ran up and down the stairs of the tenement in which we lived I shivered the timbers. I was a bad little girl." Food was scarce for the family, but Suky always insisted that any guests would find a hospitable table waiting. Her mantra was, "When you come to the Romans' house, you *eat*." This was something that stayed with Ruth, and she was always a generous hostess.[10]

Apart from the passing yen to be a ballet dancer, the one thing she always enjoyed was acting, and from her earliest years she loved to perform and be the center of attention. After school finished for the day, she seldom went straight home because there was nobody there, as her mother was always working. Instead, she became a regular at the Elizabeth Peabody Settlement House where she got involved in a project that put on one-act plays. From the age of eight or nine, she appeared in playlets as pixies and elves in *Bridget and the Fairies* for her first captive audience of the other children and their parents. It was not possible for her to play the lead because that was usually the preserve of the blonde. The Settlement House was a lifesaver to her as it was for many others. In an area where most parents worked long hours, children might have gone home to empty houses but instead could get involved in all kinds of practical activities. There was a kindergarten, a library and sports facilities, besides all the other amenities. The social and cultural center had first been established in 1896 and was a magnet for the children of the West End, providing a lifeline to culture. Leonard Nimoy was just a few years younger than Ruth and like her spent his formative years in the West End. Growing up, he never knew her, but he too was thankful for the Settlement House where he first unwittingly discovered his vocation. He recalled: "To put it simply, the Elizabeth Peabody House was a blessing. Programs were offered in sports, theater and science as well as classes of all kinds to help immigrants find their way in the American culture. My brother was active in the science lab and became an MIT graduate and a chemical engineer. I was drawn to the theater program and it set me on a path which became my life's work."[11]

Ruth was always forthright and called a spade a spade. Her mother was immensely practical and eschewed all sentimentality. She never married again. Suky was not educated and never learned to speak English properly but had a native wisdom and instilled self-belief into her daughters. Ruth learned the most from her attitude; as she reflected, "She taught me to live, to accept pain without complaining, and to never, never give up."[12] Her upbringing instilled resilience into her character. After the loss of her father, there were no other influences in Ruth's early life, only her mother, who was a dominating presence and also ambitious for her daughters. Budd Moss once described Suky as being "a typical showbiz mother."[13] Of Ruth's two sisters, Ana also had early dreams of stardom but would appear to have lost interest over time. The other sister, Eva, later became a saleswoman for Jordan Marsh, a prestigious department store in Boston.

Ruth's attitude to education did not improve even when she went to the Girls' High School in the city. There she would continue to skip classes and spend her time at the movie theater instead. In the darkened auditorium she would dream of one day being up there on the big screen. Her favorite star was Bette Davis, and she would often sit through five or six shows at one go. Afterwards, she would imitate her celluloid heroines on the way home. One time after she had seen *Spitfire*, she walked down the street mimicking Katharine Hepburn and was in her element when someone recognized who she was trying to be. She left school before her time, and of her graduation she remarked jocularly, "I just got passing grades. The teachers passed me along just to get rid of me."[14] Thus, there were gaps in her education which she later felt.

Ruth's desire to act took root, and by the time she was 13, she was keen to garner more leading roles. Her ambition led her to try that much harder even from an early age. For instance, she was far too young for the part of Lollie she wanted in *Excursion*, which called for a girl of 18, but she was big for her age and not lacking in confidence. The director Robert Delaney admired her keenness and gave her a script which she studied closely. After that encouragement, she worked, in her own words, "like a Trojan." There was something about the role that spoke to her. All the hard work paid off, and she got excellent notices. She gave her own typically honest assessment of that early performance: "It wasn't so much that I was a good actress then, because I wasn't. But Lollie was me. Her anger and loneliness were things I knew too well. That's why those lines rang true when I read them."[15] The positive response she received gave her the impetus to think she could make a go of acting, and she stayed with the group for further plays, including *The Vinegar Tree* and *Milestone.* She also played Clarissa in *Disraeli.* She later said that Delaney did more than anyone to help her in her career. In her thirst to see the best theater she once walked miles across town to see her first big three-act play, *The Philadelphia Story,* starring Katharine Hepburn and Van Heflin, which left an indelible impression on her. Ruth soon tried to gain experience where she could on the straw-hat circuit and appeared at Keene, New Hampshire, which at that time was run by Freeman Hammond. She regularly played in summer theater.

Although she always maintained that she hated school and played truant most of the time, she did show promise in high school in art and sport. She did well in tennis and even won some amateur singles matches at Forest Hills. In art she once won a painting competition and was offered an art scholarship but turned it down because her heart was in acting. From the first she was determined to be the best actress she could possibly be and never wavered from that aim. In due course, her stage work caught the attention of scouts from the Bishop Lee Theater School, and she was offered a three-year scholarship, which she readily accepted. The school had been established in 1935 by Mrs. Emily Perry Bishop, who had long experience in theater and ran several groups, including the Nell Gwynn Players based at Malden Bridge, New York. The building was situated on Mount Vernon Street in Boston. Insofar as acting could be taught, they did it by means of charts and showed a technique for expressing a range of emotions through gesture and posture, identifying three aspects: the physical, the mental and the emotional.[16] Students attended workshops and also took part in local theater tours. She worked hard to try to eliminate her Boston accent, something which she found difficult to do but persisted in doing. At that point, Ruth keenly felt her lack of funds and social connections. Most of the other girls at the school were from far more affluent backgrounds. They wore cashmere sweaters, and none of their mothers worked. "Here I was truly the ugly duckling in a group of swans," she reflected. Nevertheless, she did not stick fast and made the most of her limited wardrobe, finding new ways to reinvent her clothes to make it seem that she had plenty to wear and was not short of money. Years later, she discovered that the others were somewhat in awe of her confidence and air of sophistication. "Now they tell me," she commented wryly.[17]

Buffeted on Broadway

"For weeks and months, I haunted agents' offices, rushed to any theater at the slightest hint of a vacancy.... But the place beat me and I was forced to take up a variety of jobs."
—Ruth interviewed by Dick Richards, London, 1955[1]

After passing through the Bishop Lee Theater School, Ruth eloped and married in Nashua, New Hampshire, on May 16, 1939, when she was still 16. By the time she was 17, the marriage was all but over, and she had moved to New York. There she hoped to get a chance on Broadway on the road to fame and fortune. The reality was rather different, and her time in the city was a sobering experience. Hers was a hard-won education during which time she became more determined than ever to break into the movies.

Her husband, Jack Flaxman, was a 21-year-old assistant at an art gallery on Beacon Hill in the better part of Boston.[2] They set up home together in the city. However, married life was not what she thought it would be, and they lived together for only about six months before they split up. She seldom spoke of it afterwards but once said that it was "inevitably doomed to failure." She continued, "He was a dear, but it just couldn't work out. I was far too young."[3] In another interview she dismissed her first marriage as being just "one of those adolescent things that didn't pan out" and preferred to draw a veil over it. The marriage was officially dissolved two years later in 1941. Flaxman later used the professional name Jack Mann, and at one time he ran an art gallery on La Cienega Boulevard in Hawthorne, California.[4] It was reported that at one time he lived in the same house in Hollywood where she had once lived, but they did not stay in touch.[5]

If nothing else, her marriage got her away from the family home,

14

and when it ended, she decided to go to New York. Her ambition was to carve out a career on Broadway and get a shot at the film business. Her chance in films came along sooner than she imagined, and she was offered a screen test by Sam Goldwyn at the New York City studios when she was still 16. Her mother accompanied her to the studio but did not stay for the actual test. Ruth was so excited at the prospect of doing her first test, but, unfortunately, it did not go to plan. She remembered: "He [Goldwyn] left town but told his assistant to use only a wind machine on me and no make-up. I ended up with a big wig and Grand Canyon mouth. The test was terrible."[6] Needless to say, nothing came of it.

All the other girls from Bishop Lee had followed the same well-worn path as her to Broadway, but she had much less success. When she first announced to her mother her intentions, her mother asked her if she was ready for Broadway. Ruth thought she was, but, as she later reflected, it seemed that Broadway was not ready for her. No matter how often she bombarded agents' offices and tried to get a part—any part—in a production, she rarely got as far as a backstage interview, let alone a role in a play. She was so spectacularly unsuccessful that she even failed to land the part of a robot in a version of Karel Capek's *R.U.R.* There were the occasional bits, and she once had a walk-on role in the comedy

THE GAY WHITE WAY, N. Y. . . . Broadway and Seventh Avenue meet in a blaze of light.

The tantalizing lights of Broadway which did not shine for Ruth during her time in New York.

Junior Miss at the Lyceum. Sometimes she popped up in crowd scenes and another time landed a cameo in a flop that barely made it to the end of its first week. Once when she was an understudy in a promising play, she thought her chance to shine had come at last. She was word-perfect and full of confidence but found no opportunity to show what she could do. "I was magnificent," she joked. "They never forgot me. In fact, they never even saw me."[7]

It soon dawned on her that Broadway was not the road to riches, and she would need to find other means of earning a living. Hence, she did all kinds of work, including selling candies in a theater lobby and being a soda jerk, a movie theater usherette and a waitress. She found working as a waitress tiring and frequently demoralizing. One time a haughty customer harangued her in front of everyone and itemized all her shortcomings and why she had not earned her tip. Not for the first or last time, Ruth ran from the room in floods of tears.

She modeled dresses for buyers at wholesale houses on Seventh Avenue and worked as a photographer at the Mayfair and Latin Quarter. There followed long spells working as a cigarette girl and a hatcheck girl at such swanky nightspots as the Versailles and Copacabana night clubs. Despite the allure of their names, there was nothing glamorous for those working there. She recalled, "The jobs were hard on the feet and the long hours and smoky atmosphere were such that I decided there and then, if ever I could get out, I wouldn't fret if I never saw another night club."[8] Nor did she have any illusions that a visiting talent scout would suddenly notice her and whisk her off to fame and glory. "Who takes time to look at the dame who sells him a pack of cigarettes," she remarked ruefully. Besides, she did not see herself as a beauty or even good-looking at that age. "I was funny-looking in a way," she maintained. "I had a mature body and a sort of baby-fat face and they just didn't look as if they belonged together. I never dreamed of making the Copa chorus. I thought they were the most beautiful in the world."[9] Her Broadway career stubbornly failed to take off, but she had lots of modeling work and made $5 an hour posing for what she called "gruesome" crime magazine stills. In addition, she modeled for advertising layouts.[10]

Her life became a constant succession of tramping up and down Broadway, "sandwiches and malts at Walgreen's drug store, [and] tracking down rumors about possible theatrical jobs that she heard around the Cue Club."[11] Often, she would spend time with other young actors down on their luck. They would all gravitate to the same places to share their disappointments over coffee. It was there that she first got to know Steve Cochran at which time they used to borrow lunch money from each other. He recollected, "There were a lot of times when Ruth and I would sit at a lunch counter trying to figure out where we could land any kind of job in the theater. We belonged to the same crowd of acting hopefuls who found the going tough, with not much chance of making the grade in New York."[12] He knew her when she was just starting out and once commented: "At the beginning of her career Ruth was always on the defensive. Her success didn't come easily. There were many disappointments and disillusionments along the way."[13] She got used to walking long distances for work, and years later when she was filming *Tomorrow Is Another Day*, it was reported that she walked about eight miles during rehearsals and between takes, as recorded by a studio car. When asked about it, she commented laconically, "That's nothing, I once walked seventeen miles in New York in one day looking for a job."[14]

At one time she shared a room with a girl in a boarding house on Park Avenue. Her flatmate came from a good background and was always generous to Ruth. The building next door was so close that their window was just a couple of inches away, and all they could see was a brick wall. That was effectively a metaphor for her situation. But they did not stick fast and used to write messages on it, such as "Nobody Called," which was the usual news of the day. Throughout everything she always maintained her sense of humor. Despite all her knockbacks she was never discouraged but had unshaken self-belief and just beavered away. She continually tried to find stage work where she could and for several seasons played in summer stock with various companies such as the New England Repertory Players. At the Joy Street Barn Theater, she began to receive decent notices for such plays as *The Imaginary Invalid*, of which one reviewer wrote admiringly, "Ruth Roman lends beauty and humor to the role of Toinette, pert scheming little maid."[15] Another critic declared her "attractive and forthright" as Bunty in Noel Coward's *The Vortex*.[16] She spent the summer of 1942 at the Lake Walhom Playhouse, Fitchburg, Massachusetts, where she got the chance to essay a variety of roles in several plays, including *The Gay Divorcee*, *The Bishop Misbehaves* and a version of Cole Porter's musical *Anything Goes*.[17]

She went on occasional dates, but, after her disastrous early marriage, she was not keen to take the plunge into matrimony again so soon, although she was proposed to by a handsome farmer who was visiting from the Midwest. She really liked him and seriously considered it, but then one night they went to a cocktail party, and she saw that his charm was just a veneer. His whole personality changed after a few drinks, and he became argumentative and controlling. "It was a tough decision to walk out on that love," she remembered, "but I knew it wouldn't work."[18]

All the while she kept auditioning for film roles and eventually got her first big chance as an extra in *Stage Door Canteen* (1943) for $12.50 a day. Coincidentally, she debuted with Steve Cochran. The movie was an all-star affair based on the famous canteen where stars of Broadway entertained returning wounded troops. The idea was taken up by Hollywood, where film stars danced with servicemen, and led to a sequel, *Hollywood Canteen* (1944). Many of the big names of the theater world appeared, including Tallulah Bankhead, Katharine Hepburn, Alfred Lunt and Lynn Fontanne. Ruth's scenes were shot in the studio on 48th Street and 6th Street in Manhattan. She was lost somewhere among the hordes of girls in the background, but at least it was a start in an august company. However, it was not her acting skill nor even her looks that had first caught the casting director's attention. It was something far more prosaic, although nonetheless vital, for anyone contemplating a successful career in acting. Casting director Leonard Harper recalled: "I felt right away that here was a girl who would show up on time in the morning with her lines learned and no nonsense."[19] That observation was accurate on all counts. Punctuality was one of her great attributes and something she expected in others.

Despite all her problems in the Big Apple, she certainly learned a lot about life and in retrospect believed it helped her a lot in the long run; "I personally think that a girl planning to come to Hollywood would do well to go to New York City for a while first," she once reflected. "Living there gives you an air of sophistication. I'm glad I lived there for three years before I came to Hollywood."[20] Her education was in the school of hard knocks and contributed to that air of jaded sophistication which she always seemed to have and which made her a natural for those kind of roles in films. She reckoned that her time there had netted her a total income of $1,500 and that she lived on an average of about $9 a week. That sounds pretty healthy all things considered. Her years in New York were difficult to say the least. She learned a lot and lost many of her illusions but not, crucially, her sense of humor or her desire to make it in Hollywood.

In between times she continued to pursue her stage ambitions, often at night. It was while appearing in a summer stock production of *Yes, My Darling Daughter* that she was noticed by one of Producer David O. Selznick's scouts. He tantalized her with the promise of a plum role in a big film he was planning, *Little Women*. With this prospect in mind, she decided to head to Hollywood, something she had planned for some time. With the $200 she managed to scrape together, she bought a ticket west to fulfill her dreams.[21]

❖❖ 3 ❖❖

Hope Deferred
in Hollywood

"Hope deferred maketh the heart sick: but when
the desire cometh, it is a tree of life."
                                    —Proverbs 13:12

"You've got to go out and fight for it. You batter
down doors at agencies. You scramble for tests.
You put your whole heart and soul into it until you
get your chance."
              —Ruth interviewed by Jack Quigg, 1951[1]

In 1943 at the age of 20, Ruth went to Hollywood with about $100 and a lot of hope. She gave herself ten years to crack the movies, and once she found a good place to live with a group of like-minded girls her own age, she began to get bit parts and advance inch by inch. It was a long, hard slog, and she had to face many disappointments en route to her goal, which took over six of those ten years.

Of the $200 she had saved up in New York, she spent $96 on a ticket to Los Angeles and $4 on food. "It was a day coach all the way," she recalled, "and I arrived here with a broken back, a three-piece suit from Klein's, and $100."[2] When she first came to the town, she knew no one and stayed in a small hotel above a drugstore. Like many another star-struck actress her first visit was to the forecourt of Grauman's Chinese Theatre on Hollywood Boulevard to try her own feet in the footprints of the stars. It so happened that Steve Cochran was there at the same time and saw her there doing just that. He was down on his luck, and, although he had a chance for a play in San Francisco, he was not able to go because he was broke. She had little money herself but loaned him some so he could get to San Francisco. Steve never forgot the simple

20

act of kindness: "That was the turning point in my life," he reflected. "I've been working ever since."[3]

Ruth did the round of agents' offices and lobbied for screen tests. Although she had a lot of tests, nothing came of them for a while. To begin with she was not much better off than she had been in New York and found work as a shop clerk on a perfume counter in a department store. She walked everywhere to save on bus fare but was used to walking long distances and enjoyed it. In time she forked out for a secondhand car, which was a bit of a jalopy that she kept going somehow despite the fact it threatened to break down at any moment. As she recollected, "For a couple of years here I had to find twenty different ways to start it, because it had the world's most feeble battery. I could coax it along with practically no petrol too, because I had to."[4]

It did not take her too long to find better accommodation than her one room above a drugstore. One day she was invited out for a game of tennis at an old mansion near the Sunset Strip, which had once been the home of the silent star Wallace Reid. The place was run by Marie Cote as a boarding house for young screen hopefuls. It was a spacious house with big, airy rooms and a large garden including tennis courts and a swimming pool. At first, she thought it was way beyond her means to stay there, but Cote assured her she could afford it, and she fell in love with the place, so much so that she lived there for almost six years. For the most part it cost $7 a week. By the time she left, the rent had increased to $125 a month. Ruth described Cote as "bright eyed and kind" and said that although she was not much older than most of the girls there, she acted like a mother hen to them, helping and advising, when asked,

An early publicity photograph of Ruth when she was striving to make her name in Hollywood.

but crucially letting them make their own mistakes along the way. She took an interest in all they were doing, even after they left. The girls were all finding their way in life, and some inevitably decided they did not want to stay in the movie business. Many found the life too difficult to contend with or the demands—and the disappointments—too great. Ruth brought many of the girls there, including Kristine Miller, Karen Gaylord, Eleana Sheridan, Beverly Haney and Deannie Best. Other later famous names passed through the house, including Linda Darnell. It was apparently Ruth who nicknamed the place the "House of the Seven Garbos." She even wrote an account of their many adventures there in a short story. Ruth remarked, "Marie Cote became my warmest friend and was the source of much good advice. We would go out shopping together—or for a walk—when she would very diplomatically bring some of her good common sense to bear—and I listened."[5] She kept in touch with Cote long after she left the house and for years afterwards would call her on the phone most weeks to have a good natter and keep her informed of the latest happenings. From their first meeting, Cote felt there was something special about Ruth that would see her get somewhere. That inner drive and determination were obvious. Even after she became famous, Cote still extolled her virtues and encouraged her to keep trying harder. She was never convinced that Ruth had ever fulfilled her full potential. Of all the girls who lived there, Janet Stewart was perhaps Ruth's closest friend, and the two remained close in later life. For a long time, they shared a room. Stewart had small roles in several films but never reached the big time. "She is such a wonderful person and has helped me a lot," Stewart recalled.[6] Stewart also remarked that Ruth was more than a little restless. She could not just sit quietly on the beach but insisted on walking around, dancing or reciting Shakespeare. It was a creative time for her; she indulged in her love of sketching in oils and even wrote two short stories while living there. She remarked, "How I ever got those two stories written in that madhouse with six other eager young actresses screaming and chattering most of the time I'll never know. But we had fun. We shared advice, experiences and stockings, and we really worked hard at our studios much of the time."[7] She was not domestically inclined and readily admitted that she never learned to cook, but at that time Marie Cote used to let her loose on the kitchen once a week on Saturday when she would rustle up her favorite specialty dish of thinly cut fried potatoes. The other girls were struck by Ruth's single-mindedness, which made her something of an outsider in the group. Doris Lilly had strong recollections of Ruth during her time in the house: "She rarely went out on dates, but studied endlessly, and as the Divine Sarah of the group, she used to regale us with scenes enacted from the great tragedies," she recalled. "Ruthie's favorite attire was a pair of worn dungarees and ballet slippers, a sweat shirt and no makeup.... As we came home after a date at night, we would gather at the kitchen table to chat and drink cups of coffee. Ruthie would always join us, in her usual casual attire, and give us all a lift with her bright personality."[8] Ruth loved living at the house and remarked, "One thing, we had no boy trouble there. We self-regulated our place like a well-managed college sorority, and all in all it was one of the most enjoyable experiences of my life."[9] She was kind to the other girls and helped them out when she could. For example, she introduced Linda Christian to the casting director of RKO, which effectively got her a real start in her career.[10] Ruth was always generous whenever she had money, returning the favor to those who had helped her when she was broke.

She kept trying for screen tests. Eventually one of them led to a bit part as a WAF in *Ladies Courageous* (1944), sometimes known under the title *Women with Wings* starring Loretta Young. Roman was hardly noticeable as one of the girl pilots in the background, but she was given one line to say for her four days' work. Even that small victory had been hard to come by. "To be precise, I was interviewed for sixty-three roles before I landed my first one," she once declared. "Hollywood saw *me* and swooned?"[11] Most of the tests led to nothing, and she frequently drifted back to modeling work for beachwear and skiwear, as well as more of those "gruesome crime stills" she so hated doing. Still, it was partially through that line of work that she was noticed when she made the cover of the *National Police Gazette* for October 1944. To take the gilt off the gingerbread, they got her name wrong and billed her as Ruth Roland, having confused her with a half-forgotten silent screen star.

Radio host Art Linkletter has often been credited with Ruth's actual discovery. It was through his radio show *People Are Funny* in 1944 that she got one of her earliest breakthroughs. At the time she was still working at a perfume counter in a store. When she was first approached while working, she was convinced it was all a gag; however, she was soon reassured that it was not. She featured on the show as part of the lineup with Louella Parsons and the character actor Walter

Slezak. In one program she even sang a song, "Your Dime is My Dime," with Rudy Vallee. The upshot of her radio fame was that she was given the chance to do a screen test for the director Edward Dmytryk, who was casting his latest film *Cornered* (1945) starring Dick Powell. When she did the test, Dmytryk reportedly "wasn't sure" about her, and the part later went to a French actress, Micheline Cheirel. However, the exposure landed Roman a contract with David O. Selznick's Vanguard Films company. Selznick had first promised her the chance of a plum role in *Little Women*, but those plans had long since stalled, and no more was heard about that project for a while. In the event it would be several years before the film was made, by which time Roman was no longer in contention. It was a deeply frustrating time for her. She drew a salary of $75 a week, but Selznick gave her nothing to do. She recalled, "I chewed my fingernails for a solid year without even seeing a camera, let alone acting in front of one."[12] The consensus was that she needed more stage training, dancing lessons, instruction in diction, elocution and deportment, etc. However, it would have to be at her own expense because the studio was unwilling to pay for any of it. As a sop, Selznick gave her a few parts in plays at the Belasco including the three-act drama *All Women Are....* She was touted as a possible lead in the wartime weepie *Since You Went Away* (1944). It was a prestigious production with a big cast, and a lead role could have made her name overnight. Unfortunately for her, after Selznick met Jennifer Jones, the role was handed to her instead. Roman was given the consolation prize of a bit in the same film. She played one of the characters seen in the famous railroad station scene as the camera pans around and catches glimpses into the lives of all those coming and going on their journeys. Ruth got one line to say; as she walked along, she turned to her friend and declared, "Agnes, look, on that dame. Nylons!" That highpoint was followed by a minuscule turn as a background dancer in the Roy Rogers western *Song of Nevada* (1944) at Republic. For the same studio she played a checkroom girl in the espionage adventure *Storm Over Lisbon*. She featured in a scene in which she tried on one of the fur coats for size and liked the feel of it. Despite her lowly status she was not overawed, and on the set, she even managed to corner studio boss Herbert Yates to ask him to look at a script she had written. The manuscript was *The Whip Song*, and although Yates was noncommittal to begin with, he actually bought the idea from her for $100. After several alterations, it later became the basis of the Zorro story, *Zorro's Black Whip* (1944). The protagonist, a black-leather-clad female Zorro fond of cracking a whip, was one she might have envisioned playing herself.[13]

Her next film role was the B-western *Harmony Trail,* sometimes known as *White Stallion,* that gave her near-top billing as the daughter of a quack doctor. She had little to do but looked beautiful and at ease, and, as part of the medicine show, she showcased her dancing skills. A highlight was when Eddie Dean sang to her his own composition, "On the Banks of the Sunny San Juan," while standing by a tree. Among the cast was Max Terhune and his dummy Elmer, and it was something of a novelty to see a ventriloquist on horseback. Hardly a classic, it was amiable enough, and at least she was in a leading role. However, her efforts proved largely in vain because the film was not given a general release. It was shown on CBS television as early as 1948, but not that many people had a TV set in those days. A few years later it was reissued, by which time she was already well known. Other mostly bit parts ensued, including one as a girl in a nightclub who gets to kiss George Brent in *The Affairs of Susan* (1945). That was followed up with a cameo as a "glamor girl" in the Joan Davis-Leon Errol comedy *She Gets Her Man.* At least she had a couple of lines in that picture and may have been noticed when she breezed into a swanky nightspot dressed to the nines, her entrance inducing a wisecrack from Errol.

Her first big break—or so it seemed to her at the time—was the lead in a serial, *Lothel—the Jungle Queen* for Universal. Those formulaic Saturday afternoon serials had remarkable staying power, despite the cliff-hanging formula being long in the tooth. She beat Yvonne De Carlo to the role, but even that was a pyrrhic victory, and she was disappointed to discover later that De Carlo landed the lead in *Salome When She Danced* (1945) instead of her. *Lothel—the Jungle Queen* was concerned with espionage intrigues in Africa, but, although some of the plots were rather convoluted, it was a widely popular entertainment. Lothel herself, Queen of the Gongghili, was a rather ethereal and mysterious figure in her flowing white robes. She appeared out of nowhere and disappeared just as quickly as if by some strange magic. Her striking appearance made her character a memorable one to devotees of the series. As a leading authority on the serial genre noted, "The lovely vision of her beauty in that chapter film still haunts many a remembering fan."[14] For her part, Roman had no illusions about herself or the glamor of life behind the scenes while making the series. As she later recalled, "They had me in a lava pit, they shot me six times, and then they let me get caught in an avalanche. This dame could never die. But I died. I was awful."[15] Still the serial gave her a lot of exposure and may have helped more than anything else in her push for stardom. In more practical terms it was 13 episodes, and that assignment lasted her for about four months. Alas, when it finished, she was out of work again for a spell.

Her lack of Broadway success was likely a hindrance to the advancement of her career, but she deserves credit for being honest about it and not fabricating a ream of imagined triumphs as others had done before her. Friends contended that she always had an unshakable inner self-belief and a determination to succeed from the beginning. That must have carried her through all the many setbacks she encountered. Above all, it was her tremendous and unflagging drive which impressed people. She had an innate restlessness, a desire to prove herself. Her own assessment was that she was just stubborn. Others saw her

One of Roman's first breaks was the title role in a popular and fondly recalled serial *Jungle Queen* (1945) for Universal. Left to right: Roman, Edward Norris, Eddie Quillan.

differently: "She was like a wild colt down from pasture," recalled Marie Cote. "Wouldn't stop trying for a minute. Even when she was just reading plays around the house with the other kids, she acted as though it were the most important thing in her life."[16] After her inspiring lead role in the serial, Ruth was relegated to the back row of the chorus once more in the weak Broadway spin-off comedy *See My Lawyer* in which she was hardly noticeable or overtaxed as a dancing mud girl. There was a small role in the lavish romantic war comedy drama *You Came Along* (1945) at Paramount for John Farrow. It was the first of three tiny parts she would have in his films. At least on that occasion she played a named character, albeit still uncredited. The stars were Robert Cummings and Lizabeth Scott, and the film marked the latter's debut. It did decent business at the box office, and Scott drew much attention. In between features Roman appeared in short WAC training films. One such was *Time to Kill* (1945), a navy short about the value of using the educational services available to servicemen courtesy of the Armed Forces Institute. It was particularly geared to preparing men for the challenges to come in the postwar world. Several future stars appeared, including George Reeves and Betty White. Roman played the girlfriend of DeForest Kelley, making his screen debut. They shared a well-judged scene in a café in which she was at her most winsome and sympathetic. Only 22 minutes of the film are known to survive intact, and, although the quality is lacking, that portion can be viewed at the Internet Archive.[17]

Working for Selznick was frustrating, and apart from a few odd assignments that were supposed to keep her on the payroll, she was chiefly employed to boost other films she was not actually in, such as *Duel in the Sun*, which she was required to advertise on the T-shirt she wore around the studio like a human signboard. She was bored and frustrated. He kept her idle so long that she could stand it no more. She finally confronted him in his office and asked him point blank to be released from her contract. At first, he just laughed, but she kept badgering him, and eventually he acquiesced.

There were several roles she coveted but failed to get. For instance, she tried hard for a part in *Spellbound* (1945), but Hitchcock told her bluntly that she was the wrong type and cast Rhonda Fleming instead. She thought of every angle to try to be noticed. At times she even wished she were blonde but then later reflected, "As time passed, I was glad I wasn't blonde because that automatically put you in a precarious boat."[18] She wondered why everyone else seemed to be getting ahead while she was still languishing in bit parts after years of trying. She began to think there was something wrong with her whole mindset and even sought psychiatric help at one stage. In time she came to understand things better and particularly her own character. She once remarked: "I realized one day a long time ago that the toughest obstacle to overcome was me. I could take care of the outside things. It was the inside I had to control. If I can beat myself, I decided, I can beat anything."[19]

All the while she constantly tested for roles, but that one big breakthrough always eluded her. Somehow, she was just not able to get past first base; perhaps she tried too hard. She was frank about her distinct lack of success: "My first screen-tests were graded stinko," she once remarked. "Two studios dropped contracts with me. My agents dropped me. Kind souls advised me to go home and raise a family. I tested for *Crossfire* (1946) and *The Killers*; Gloria Grahame and Ava Gardner got the parts."[20] In the parts she did manage to snare she was usually somewhere in the background making up the numbers. For example, she was lost in the crowd as a chorine in the nightclub scenes in the lively Technicolor drama *Incendiary Blonde* starring Betty Hutton. There was a cameo as a girl in a negligee on a train in *Without Reservations* (1946), a misfiring comedy built around the unlikely and unsuccessful pairing of John Wayne and Claudette Colbert. Ruth also appeared in yet another crowded background scene in the classic *Gilda*. She loved the glamor, the costumes and the consummate style of the movie and was happy to be even a minor part of it. She called it "the last of the real sexy pictures" and said it was the kind that she hoped one day to star in herself.[21]

Her disappointments were not confined to her screen career. In August 1946, she was billed as the star of a play *Dear Ruth* at the Laguna Playhouse under the aegis of Mel Ferrer. However, two days before opening Ferrer replaced her with Natalie Schafer. It was another slap in the face for her among many.[22] To make matters worse, Ruth's then boyfriend, Bill Walsh, had driven thousands of miles to see her first night and was less than pleased with Ferrer when he discovered what had happened.

After a run of meager roles, it seemed her luck was changing at last when it was announced that she beat 200 lovelies to appear as a harem girl in the Marx Bros. comedy *A Night in Casablanca*, their first movie for five years. Moreover, the brothers had given her their personal seal of approval. It was a showy part that gave her some scenes in a tent as a foil for the immortal Groucho, and she must have entertained hopes that it would be her longed-for entrée into the big time. That was the heyday of the sarong movie, and her immediate ambitions strayed no further than the prospect of filling some of the roles Dorothy Lamour and Yvonne De Carlo discarded. Alas, after so much buildup, including lots of press attention, her entire contribution to *A Night in Casablanca* ended up on the cutting room floor. It was typical of Hollywood that they rubbed her nose in it. Her image was used extensively in all publicity, despite the fact that she was not even in it. The studio went to town with the ballyhoo and installed a massive 50-foot-high cutout of Ruth lounging in harem mode on the roof of a Broadway theater. All that, without her seeing a penny from it and not even being in the film. Crestfallen, she went back to more bit part work, including a tiny one in *The Web* (1947) at Universal.[23] It must have appeared to her at that point that she was continually taking one step forward and two back, thwarted in her every attempt to be noticed. She tested for *The Bachelor and the Bobby Soxer* opposite Cary Grant, and, although she was not successful in securing the role, she nonetheless impressed Paramount bosses so much with her test that they awarded her a contract on the strength of it. Things were looking up for her because other studios also expressed an interest in her around the same time. However, she went for the Paramount offer as seemingly the most promising. It did not turn out to be quite the boon it first appeared. Paramount promised much but in practice gave her practically nothing. She was added to the cast of *Night Has a Thousand Eyes* (1948), but one had to search hard to spot her, and some sources do not acknowledge her appearance in the film. She was definitely there, however, in what she called a "blinking" role (blink and you miss her) as a secretary in the prosecutor's outer office on the telephone while simultaneously dealing with an irate couple as the camera pans along. She reckoned her total screen time was all of 15 seconds.[24] A promising lead role in *The Big Clock* (1948) beckoned, and she thought this was her big chance in a prestige picture opposite two big stars: Charles Laughton and Ray Milland. The film was directed by John Farrow. However, partway through production, Farrow's wife, Maureen O'Sullivan, suddenly decided she wanted to return to the screen after several years away. She was required by the studio to undergo a screen test, but since her husband was the director that was surely only a mere formality. So it proved, and O'Sullivan was given the lead instead of Ruth, who was once again demoted to the ranks. After such an inflated buildup, a fleeting appearance as a secretary in a boardroom scene was all she had to show for her time, thereby ending her largely fruitless Paramount dalliance. "That lasted a year and a half," she reflected ruefully, "a long wait for a role that never materialized."[25] On the plus side, *The Big Clock* turned out to be her last uncredited role.

The continual holding out of big roles just to snatch them away again was a particularly cruel trick to play on anyone, especially a young actress trying to make her way, but Hollywood was hardly a sentimental place. It took a certain steel in the makeup to be able to take all the knockdowns. Building up someone's hopes just to continually dash them would surely have an effect on anyone's psyche, no matter how tough they appeared to be. Ruth had a similar experience on *Good Sam* to that she had working on *The Big Clock*. Once more she was promised a prominent role but later was pushed down the batting order, purely because her husky voice was deemed too similar to that of the star, Ann Sheridan. Ruth appeared briefly as a co-worker at the department store where do-gooder Gary Cooper works. The movie was an overlong and

Left to right: Gary Cooper, Joan Lorring and Roman in a scene from the so-so comedy *Good Sam* (1948).

weak homage to Frank Capra that largely wasted the talents of a fine cast. There was one good scene on a bus, but for the most part the comedy failed to spark. It was a notable role for Roman only insofar as she was credited and got to work for the first time with Cooper, to whom she had sent her one and only fan letter as a girl. The two shared only a short scene together in which, if anything, she seemed slightly nervous. Joan Lorring, who played the singer in the same scene, ended up with the role that Roman was first assigned. At least her time spent behind a perfume counter finally came in useful after all. Other movie prospects came and went. She tested for *Outpost in Morocco* with George Raft but lost out to Marie Windsor in what was a poor picture but which nevertheless got Windsor noticed.[26] Roman might have starred in the comedy *Luck of the Irish* that would have teamed her with Tyrone Power. It was her dream to star with Power, but the part went to Anne Baxter instead.[27]

She grew so tired of being fobbed off that she started to make

Belle Starr's Daughter (1948) was her first big starring role in a decent western for 20th Century–Fox. A still from the film showing Roman with George Montgomery.

herself known. Her time at Paramount was especially dispiriting, and she had once barged into the front office and made certain that she was noticed. Hedda Hopper was there at the time and recalled the occasion. Not that it did any good because nothing came of it. Ruth's action was not prompted by arrogance or showmanship but sheer frustration. It seemed that everyone else was advancing, and she was not, but no matter what she did she still had to wait her turn for stardom. A number of projects were suggested, but many fell by the wayside, such as a dramatic role in *If This Be My Harvest*, which it would appear was never made.[28] In time she became inured to being let down. Of those years she later remarked, "Every time I got a role, I touched wood and thought: 'This is it!' But of course, it wasn't—and it seemed to me that trying to become an actress needed ten percent talent and ninety percent grim, enduring patience."[29] Undaunted, she kept auditioning, plugging away and hoping for the best. Among others she tested for *That Wonderful Urge* (1948) but lost out to Jayne Meadows. She was also in the running for the lead with Bob Hope in the hit comedy *The Paleface* (1948) and the Alan Ladd western *Whispering Smith* but failed to land either role. Whenever she was unsuccessful, she rationalized it by convincing herself that the part was just not suited to her or the time was not yet right or something better would come along soon. At 20th Century–Fox she tried for *When My Baby Smiles at Me* (1948). "I made what I thought was the best test of my life, a Technicolor scene," she remarked. "After seeing it, I was sure I was in it. I wasn't. The contract was handed to Jean Wallace."[30] Although she missed out on that, Fox offered her the starring role in *Belle Starr's Daughter*. As the title suggested, it was a follow-up to the successful *Belle Starr* made a couple of years before that which had helped make a star of Gene Tierney. Of course, neither film bore much relation to the real person. The working title was *Rose of Cimarron*, and the screenplay was written by the dependable W.R. Burnett, who first made his name and that of Edward G. Robinson with *Little Caesar* (1931). Burnett was sometimes known as the "Star Maker" having been credited with giving early career boosts to, among others, Humphrey Bogart in *High Sierra* and Alan Ladd in *This Gun for Hire*. In some ways he could be said to have done the same for Roman in *Belle Starr's Daughter* because the film was her first big starring role and marked a definite turning point in her fortunes. Featured among the supporting cast were several screen stalwarts, including Wallace Ford and Charles Kemper. Much of the filming took place at the Iverson Ranch in Chatsworth and also at Bridgeport, both in California. A jolly and colorful western, it rattled along at a decent pace thanks to the no-nonsense direction of Lesley Selander, who directed over 100 westerns in his 30-year career. Roman did well as the spirited heroine, which gave her more opportunities to be feisty than the conventional female roles. The film did good business at the box office and provided her with lots of publicity. It also brought her to the attention of influential Hollywood personages. Dore Schary, for one, was impressed and offered her a role in *The Window* (1949). At last, she had turned a corner, although at the time it did not feel like it to her. Ironically, just as she started to make an impression in Hollywood, she began to receive offers from Broadway and turned down at least three because she had by then decided to concentrate solely on her screen career.

She continued to play in stock, and in January 1949 at Tucson, Arizona, she finally got a chance to appear in a version of *Dear Ruth* that she had missed out on three years earlier; this time she starred opposite William Lundigan.[31] She won some good notices for her performance. After so many false dawns, all her years of striving and heartache were about to pay off. The year of 1949 proved to be a pivotal one for her when the films she had made in the previous few months were finally released and began to catch the public's attention. After six and a half years of trying, it finally seemed as though her dreams were about to come true. Considering all she had gone through, she was wary but felt vindicated. As she commented at the time, "My career—when it was nonexistent to the human eye and now—is like a chess game to me.... I always felt I couldn't lose forever. Anybody can figure out that if you keep trying one day you'll win."[32]

◆◆ **4** ◆◆

Warner Bros.
Contract Star

"Even when one person in authority after another
told me I wasn't beautiful enough or sufficiently
talented to make the grade, I didn't let them dis-
courage me. I was determined to prove that they
were wrong."
— Ruth interviewed by Lydia Lane,
Albany, New York, 1953[1]

After almost seven years of trying, Ruth had a breakthrough in
1949 when she appeared in some interesting roles in a run of excellent
films. She received fine notices and began to garner a lot of attention.
As a result of her performance in *Champion*, she was awarded a Warner Bros. contract for seven years and in January 1950 was officially ele-
vated to star status.

She had an unusual role in *The Window* (1949) as Jean Kellerson,
married to Paul Stewart at his most sinister, in the tale of a boy (Bobby
Driscoll) who is convinced he has witnessed a murder in the Kellersons'
apartment but is not believed. Director Ted Tetzlaff was a former cinematographer who switched to directing a couple of years earlier. He
had also been at the helm for other noir-inspired titles including *Riffraff*
(1947) and *A Dangerous Profession* (1949). However, *The Window* was
arguably his greatest cinematic achievement and holds up well today as a
fine example of intelligent and economic filmmaking. Tetzlaff's impressive cinematographic skill was telling in several key scenes within the
claustrophobic urban scene, particularly those involving the fire escape
and the murder viewed through the slats in the blinds. Everything was
essentially seen from the point of view of the boy. Surprisingly, RKO
studio boss Howard Hughes had no faith in the picture or its young

star, and it was held back from release for almost a year. When it was released to wide acclaim, Driscoll won a special juvenile Oscar. In addition to several other accolades, it was nominated as the Best Film from Any Source at the BAFTA awards. Richard Winnington ably encapsulated its strong and lasting appeal when he wrote that it was "logical, well-shaped, cohesive, admirably-acted beautifully-photographed and cut to a nicety."[2] The story was based on yet another Cornell Woolrich novella *The Boy Cried Murder* excellently adapted for the screen by Mel Dinelli, who had done such a fine job on *The Spiral Staircase* (1946). Another important element was the tense score by Roy Webb. Filming took place at the newly constructed RKO-Pathé Studios in Harlem, New York City, and in abandoned tenements on 105th and 116th streets. The action was supposed to occur during a heatwave, but it was actually filmed on location in Manhattan in the middle of a bitterly cold winter. Roman struck up a friendship with Barbara Kelly, and they often went out on shopping trips around the city together. It was a strong but unsympathetic role for Ruth, which rendered it an arresting one that audiences remembered. Jean Kellerson was a subverted image of the traditional woman on screen at that time. Normally, where children were concerned, women in films were sympathetic and reassuring characters. Even in noir movies, although they might prove fatal to the male of the species, they were often kind to children. It was disconcerting to see a threatening woman in a seemingly innocuous domestic environment, which itself becomes a place of peril for the boy. Even such everyday household objects as a pair of scissors turn into a lethal weapon in her hands. The boy's sense of security inside his own home is lost, and he becomes the prisoner of it, constantly threatened by the Kellersons. No longer a protector, she appears more disturbing by the fact of being a woman, devoid of the expected qualities of her sex. Robert Herring, a critic of the *London Mercury*, described her as "a startlingly unvarnished villainess."[3] When Ruth first watched a rough cut of the film without music, she was reduced to tears when she saw herself, convinced that her career was over before it had begun. Needless to say, she was mistaken, but she was often her own harshest critic and eventually realized that she was not always the best judge of which roles suited her. Some years later she remarked, "I know I've frequently been wrong about myself. I've learned how to take confidence in the judgement of others who are more qualified, to go ahead and act my chosen part to the best of my ability, even if I think I'm wrongly cast."[4]

Ruth Roman

Roman as Jean Kellerson, with her husband and partner-in-crime (Paul Stewart) in *The Window*.

Her role in *The Window* caught her a lot of attention, and on the strength of it, George Glass persuaded his partner, producer Stanley Kramer, to cast her in *Champion*. To prove that nothing was ever entirely wasted in Hollywood, Glass had remembered her from the time when he worked as a press agent on *A Night in Casablanca*. Believing she was auditioning for the showy part of Grace Diamond, she poured herself into the tightest black dress imaginable and gave it all she had. Kramer told her that he was thinking of her for the other role as Douglas's put-upon wife. She said that she would have preferred the glamorous part that was played by Marilyn Maxwell but nonetheless relished the opportunity to work with Stanley Kramer and the up-and-coming Douglas. A true classic, *Champion* is widely considered one of the finest boxing films of all time and gave Douglas a defining role of his career as Midge Kelly. He turned down an offer of $50,000 for *The Great Sinner* in order to make *Champion* for $15,000, and it proved to be one of the best decisions he made. The supporting cast was perfect, with especially telling contributions from Arthur Kennedy as Midge's crippled brother, Paul Stewart as his world-weary manager, and Roman. Despite her initial disappointment at what she saw as a lesser part, she brought great sensitivity to a difficult role in which she conveyed the conflicts and underlying sadness of her character. The critic of the *Hollywood Reporter* wrote that she was "hauntingly lovely."[5] She loved working on that film, which she said was her most rewarding experience to date because it gave her the feeling that she was finally getting somewhere at last. As she recalled: "My happiest 26 days in the movies were spent making the picture *Champion*. For, though you hear a great deal about teamwork in Hollywood, you almost never see as much of it as we did while shooting this film. Whenever there was a question about a scene, we'd hold a group conference, complete with producer, director and cast, to thrash the matter out. Each suggestion was not only considered but also thoroughly discussed. All this was immensely helpful to me in playing the role of Emma, for I was very young in pictures then, and this was quite a different type of role from the few I'd played."[6]

Champion was considered a low-budget venture. It cost an estimated $500,000, which to the man or woman in the street sounded like a lot of money but did not amount to a hill of beans considering all the

A shotgun wedding to remember in *Champion* (1949), considered one of the finest boxing films. Left to right: Harry Shannon, Kirk Douglas, Ruth Roman and Arthur Kennedy.

production costs. One area in which the studio saved money was apparently in the costume department. The story did not require extravagant costumes, particularly for her character as the unfortunate waitress. Ruth later revealed that the studio let her buy her entire wardrobe from the picture for $100.[7] Those clothes were designed by Adele Parmenter, a little-known name in Hollywood fashion circles who nonetheless worked on some major films, including *Red River* and *Wagon Master*. Her path later crossed with Roman again when she designed the far-more-stylish costumes for the Cold War thriller *Five Steps to Danger*. *Champion* was a big box office hit and was nominated for five Academy Awards, including Best Actor for Douglas and Best Supporting Actor for Kennedy. However, the only winner was the film editor. As a reward of a kind for her good work in the film, Roman was nominated as Most Promising Newcomer at the Golden Globe Awards of 1950. (Mercedes McCambridge won for *All the King's Men*.) Almost immediately, director Mark Robson hoped to reunite most of the cast of *Champion* in a football-themed story, but that did not come to pass.[8]

Her breakthrough performance opened a lot of doors, and in April 1949 she was awarded her Warner Bros. contract. It was a term contract for seven years with options, which meant that she was bound to the studio but that they could let her go anytime they wanted. There was great rejoicing at the "House of the Seven Garbos." As Roman observed, "Marie could not have been happier for her own child."[9] A burst of timely publicity did wonders for her prospects too, and her name was to the fore when some good films were being cast. She was suggested for the leading female role in *White Heat* (1949), but that was later assigned to Virginia Mayo, with whom she often vied for parts despite their different qualities.[10] Kramer wanted to pair Roman and Douglas again when he was planning his classic *High Noon* (1952), which would have been interesting.[11] According to some reports, she harbored an unrequited longing for Kramer, who at least one obituary writer called the real love of her life. She kept up a lively correspondence with him over the years. Once when her name was mentioned for a role in the virtually all-male *My Six Convicts*, Ruth playfully wrote to ask him, "Which one of the convicts do I play—and should I start shaving now?"[12] After seeing her in *Champion*, John Garfield wanted her to star opposite him in *The Breaking Point* (1950), but Phyllis Thaxter prevailed.[13] Roman once did a test opposite Garfield but failed to get the role. It was unclear if the test was for *The Breaking Point* or for an earlier film. Ruth commented,

"It would have been a wonderful break for me, but I knew I wasn't right for the part."[14]

A good chance came her way in *Beyond the Forest* (1949), directed by King Vidor with a stellar cast headed by Bette Davis. It was Davis's final Warner film, a genuine potboiler with a memorable townscape forming a backdrop of the stifling small-town life from which her character longs to escape. The sense of frustration mirrored Davis's much-publicized tussle to break free of Warner Bros. and gave her the immortal line, "What a dump!" One of the bylines to advertise the film was, "No one's as good as Bette Davis when she's bad!" Roman was still in awe of her early idol. To begin with, she felt intimidated by Davis, particularly in an early scene at the railroad station where her character was the object of the intense jealousy of the Davis character. Roman felt the jealousy was for real but was probably reflecting her own insecurity.[15] Nonetheless, in several interviews, Roman said she loved working

Roman featured in King Vidor's *Beyond the Forest* (1949), which was Bette Davis's final film for Warner Bros. Lobby card showing Minor Watson and Roman.

with her, and at the time it was reported that Davis had not only supported her in several scenes but had been extremely helpful. Joseph Cotten remarked on Roman's restlessness on set and contrasted it with her
calm demeanor when actually shooting a scene.[16] On screen she came
across as completely relaxed in the role and equal to all that was needed.
Her nerves were understandable in such a cast. She was highly strung
and keen to do well, but her tenseness tended to emanate to others and
make them nervous too. In time she combated that to some degree and
worked off that excess energy on set in other activities such as whittling. In one particular sequence she did not feel comfortable playing
the scene as the director wanted. On that occasion, Davis leaped to her
defense, perhaps thinking of her own struggles as a young actress at
the start of her career; "She was great. I kept blowing my lines in one
scene with her because they were so awful to try to say. I finally told
the director that and Bette immediately came to my aid."[17] In response,
Davis declared, "She's right. She's too honest to do anything phony. If
you want someone to play the scene that way, get some little whipper-
snapper for it; not this girl."[18] In an interview some years later, Ruth was
full of praise for the way Davis helped her, and always remembered her
advice: "'Ruthie,' said Bette to her after the scene, 'You learned a valuable lesson today. Never be afraid to fight for what you know is right.'"[19]
That was an experience Ruth did not forget. Once again, when she saw
a preview of the film, she confessed in a letter to a friend, "I wasn't too
happy with my part in it."[20] She was intensely self-critical and seldom
felt content with any of her performances on screen. There were a great
many tensions behind the scenes during the making of *Beyond the Forest*, not least because Davis loathed her role and thought she was too
old for it. The main problem for Vidor and his writers were the restric-
tions of the Hays Production Code, by which they felt hemmed in on
all sides. The overriding sense of desperation in the movie was not just
reflected in the characters but was derived from the substance of the
original novel by Stuart Engstrand on which it was based. Engstrand
was described as "hypersensitive" and continually tortured by guilt over
his sexuality as well as a failed marriage. He committed suicide by walking into the MacArthur Park Lake at the age of 51.[21] The striking music
of the inimitable Max Steiner heightened the drama and underscored
the sense of tragic desperation personified in the Davis character.

Roman was lined up for a lead role in the musical *Painting the
Clouds with Sunshine*, which was originally planned for Doris Day, but

Virginia Mayo was later cast, and Roman did not appear in it.[22] Her next was in a similar vein, a good part in *Always Leave Them Laughing* (1949) for director Roy Del Ruth, which also starred Mayo. Essentially a vehicle for Milton Berle, it was one that fans of the ebullient comic would savor. The story followed the trials and tribulations of an unscrupulous comic over his career, which shadowed the changing fortunes of vaudeville itself. It was a bittersweet tale full of knowing humor about the fickle world of the variety stage and committed some of the old classic sketches to celluloid for all time. Bert Lahr was a standout among the supporting cast, and his ten minutes of screen time counted for much. Berle may not be everyone's cup of tea and can be wearing after a while. He was a busy actor, and it was easy to see why he was dubbed "Public Energy No. 1." The character he played was brash and unappealing, a man who purloins another comedian's material and his wife, as reflected in the original title, *The Thief of Broadway*. The story was cowritten by the satirist Max Shulman, and the script and jokes kept things moving along. Beneath the humor there were glimpses of the harsh reality of a comic's life, full of insecurities. Roman gave an astute performance as the love interest/confidante. On paper it seemed a thankless role, but she made it live with all the doubt and uncertainty of constantly being the "other woman," who is largely taken for granted and harbors no illusions about her lot. She personally got along well with Berle and his mother, who often visited the set during filming. Ruth recalled that she learned several dance steps from him for the song and dance routines they were required to perform. On several of the musical numbers, including "You

Publicity still of Ruth with Milton Berle in *Always Leave Them Laughing* (1949), a telling but often underappreciated film about comedians and the nature of comedy.

41

Do Something to Me" and "Tea for Two," she was instructed by LeRoy Prinz, whose choreography was especially suited to presenting the stage show as it was, and in some cases, he treated the camera as though it was a member of the audience. While Roman loved to dance and was a good dancer, she had no singing voice to speak of. Her voice was dubbed by Trudy Erwin. All the actors worked hard on the film, which involved many long rehearsals. The movie did excellent business at the box office and was one of the highest-grossing films for Warner Bros. in 1950. Moreover, it provided an interesting insight into the backstage world of the Broadway stage as it had been and was almost like a snapshot of the waning days of vaudeville. Among the support there were several veteran acts who brought a true flavor of the old days, including Wally Vernon, O'Donnell & Blair and a group of acrobats, The Moroccans. It was one of the few screen appearances by Charles O'Donnell & Jack Blair, who had a popular knockabout stage act that was captured for posterity in a couple of shorts almost 20 years earlier. One marvels at their physical comedy and how they managed to avoid serious injury over the years. Director Del Ruth enjoyed a varied career and was nominated for several awards. He was well equipped to handle *Always Leave Them Laughing* and certainly knew his subject; after all, he began his working life writing for Mack Sennett. The film has often been underappreciated, but Martin Scorsese for one recognized its merits. He admired Berle for taking on the essentially autobiographical role of a dislikable comic. Scorsese wrote, "I find comedians fascinating; there's so much pain and fear that goes into the trade, and this is one of the most honest films about comedians."[23]

After six eventful years, Ruth reluctantly left the so-called "House of the Seven Garbos" and moved to a house in Coldwater Canyon that had once been rented by Olivia de Havilland. It was a wrench for Ruth, who was understandably reluctant to give up her big, sunny room with three meals a day and maid service. Above all, she never forgot her friends or the place that had been the closest thing to a real home for her. Afterwards she readily admitted to feeling lonely at first in her new place, despite the constant companionship of her dog Shawn and a Siamese cat. Most of all she seemed to miss Marie Cote and once commented, "Marie was born with a capacity for making others happy. She put everything she had into making us feel like one big family—it certainly kept any semblance of homesickness down to nil."[24] She maintained all her links with the old place and the girls she had known there.

4. Warner Bros. Contract Star

When a young Leonard Nimoy first arrived in Hollywood, he did not know anyone in town and was urged to contact Ruth, a fellow Boston West Ender. Although they had never known each other previously, Ruth met him and took him over to her old rooming house, where she introduced him to Marie Cote. Nimoy stayed there, and, through living there, he soon made friends and got to know a lot of people in the business.[25] Before too long, Ruth moved on once again, to a house in the San Fernando Valley. She soon set about improving her new place, which she gave her own stamp with a bit of help from her steady date Bill Walsh. It was easy to spot which one was hers because it was painted barn red. She enjoyed decorating it to her own designs and was pleased as punch whenever anyone praised her interior design skills. One of her favorite pastimes was trying to find bargains in the local antique shops and at fairs. In her new home, with her newfound fame, she was immortalized in oils by the artist William Ross Shattuck, who was then married to the publicist Margaret Ettinger. Shattuck (1895–1962) was born in North Dakota and studied at the Chicago Academy of Fine Arts and the PAFA. He served in both world wars. In 1929 he moved from New York to Laguna Beach and worked as art director at MGM in the 1930s. His portrait of Ruth depicts her in a white dress sitting at a table and has a rather melancholy look, which is perhaps enhanced by the blue décor behind her, with the lamp and an ornate coffeepot prominent. Her dog Shawn can be seen in the background. The most striking thing about the portrait is her sad eyes, which in a time-honored way one can imagine would follow one around the room.[26]

Ruth was flying high at that time. Life was full of possibilities, and her name came up when several big productions were being cast. She was among those seriously considered by Cecil B. DeMille for the biblical bad girl in *Samson and Delilah* (1949). The great director even had a picture of her in costume on the wall of his office for months as his ideal for the role. She did several screen tests with Bill Hopper that used the script of the 1935 version. The actor Henry Wilcoxon recalled that DeMille was impressed with her, especially the way she had captured both aspects of the character as he had envisioned it in his mind's eye.[27] However, DeMille always spent a great deal of time carefully casting his films, especially the women, and after much deliberation, he opted instead for the well-established star Hedy Lamarr. He later considered Roman along with numerous others for the small role of Sephora, the wife of Moses, in *The Ten Commandments*, but Yvonne De Carlo got the nod instead.

Warner Bros. had their own plans for Roman and lined up *The Two Worlds of Johnny Truro* as a vehicle for her. The film was originally intended for Bette Davis, who had dropped out of the project. It was one of a number of Davis's cast-off roles that came her way and was all part of the grand design on behalf of the studio to push her into the mold of Davis's chief replacement. Carleton Carpenter recalled that he would have co-starred with Roman in *Johnny Truro*, but Warner Bros. shelved the idea.[28] She was considered for at least two notable entries in the Red Scare wave of films. *Walk a Crooked Mile* (1948) would have teamed her once again with Kirk Douglas, but Louise Allbritton and Dennis O'Keefe were assigned those roles. Roman was the first name on the team sheet for a leading part in *I Was a Communist for the F.B.I.* (1950), but she declined the offer. *The Daily Worker* for one applauded her decision as "to her credit." Their assessment of the film was that it was "a travesty of Americanism."[29] Dorothy Hart was her substitute. George Stevens was tempted to cast Roman as the unfortunate victim in *A Place in the Sun* (1951), but the role went to Shelley Winters.[30] Roman had yet another opportunity to co-star with Douglas in the Raoul Walsh western *The Travelers*, but she lost out once more to Virginia Mayo in the film which was retitled *Along the Great Divide.*[31]

Instead, she was put into the western *Barricade* which starred Dane Clark as an ex-con who winds up working for ruthless mine owner Raymond Massey. The movie had a familiar plot, which was partially lifted from *The Sea Wolf.* Nonetheless, it was efficiently made and intriguing in its own way. Technicolor lifted the enterprise and definitely added to its visual appeal. There were good performances from the leading

Publicity still of Roman with Dane Clark from *Barricade* (1950), one of several westerns she made at Warner Bros., much to her chagrin.

players, and especially noticeable in the supporting cast was Morgan Farley as a ruined judge. Clark and Roman made an attractive screen couple, and she showed plenty of spirit in the opening scenes when she escaped the clutches of the local sheriff and hijacked the stagecoach. Despite her good showing, she heartily disliked the film, not only because she lost her voice when she had to scream so often in the dusty desert atmosphere of the location shooting at Santa Clarita. She was not overenamored of westerns generally, and the prospect of more such roles made her wish to be released at once from her contract. Unsurprisingly, her bosses would not hear of such a thing and insisted she keep working. While they may have wanted her to take Bette Davis's place in a manner of speaking, they were not about to tolerate any Davis-like rebelliousness from a mere starlet. Roman had many more disappointments to come at Warner Bros. For instance, she had set her heart on the lead opposite Alan Ladd in *The Iron Mistress* (1952), and when it was handed to Virginia Mayo, it was widely reported that Roman once more demanded her immediate release. Needless to say, she failed to get it. Instead, her bosses had more of the same lined up in store for her, including *The Candy Kid Levels,* a proposed teaming with John Wayne which, perhaps fortunately from her perspective, never actually transpired.[32] Despite her dislike of westerns, they were popular, and she noticed that the more she made the more her mailbag swelled; indeed, much of her fan mail came from western fans. She stayed out west for *Colt .45,* a typically lively color feature starring the dependable Randolph Scott as a gun salesman who loses a set of newly minted pistols to frenzied killer Zachary Scott. There was an inordinate amount of shooting in this clichéd but surprisingly popular adventure. Roman had a prominent role as the wife of Lloyd Bridges, a weak character and henchman of Zachary. She was once more practically the sole female in evidence, who again showed plenty of gumption. In addition, she was able to display her newly acquired riding skills, which had been provided courtesy of Warner Bros. The pistols seen in the film were genuine antique models from 1848. They were loaded with black powder and used hand-crimped bullets. In the scene in the stagecoach, as Scott fired the guns continuously, the cramped quarters of the carriage were filled with acrid, black smoke, and a burning powder discharge resulted in Roman receiving burns to her neck which had to be treated.[33] The romance between Scott and Roman came a poor second to that between Scott and his firearm. Indeed, the film was aptly titled because it was

essentially a paean to a gun. Edwin L. Marin was an efficient director across different genres who latterly favored westerns and was also
remembered for the *Maisie* series starring Ann Sothern.

For Ruth, one western seemed to lead to another, and she was pro-
pelled into *Dallas,* a decent offering in which she co-starred with Gary
Cooper, the second of three films she made with him. They worked well
together, but the exigencies of the plot meant that they did not share a
great deal of screen time because the focus was almost entirely on Cooper. There was good support from Raymond Massey and Steve Cochran
as unlikely brothers and Will Wright as an ambivalent judge. The only
other woman involved was Barbara Payton, who was given just a few
lines. Despite her small input, Payton was the center of attention for
most of the men working on the picture, including Cooper. As the
ostensible star of the show, this attention apparently irked Roman, at
least according to friends of Payton, something which was confirmed
by Milo Anderson, who claimed that there was no love lost between
the two actresses.[34] Director Stuart Heisler began his career as an editor and was at the helm for some interesting features, including the
excellent *Storm Warning* (1951). He made only a few westerns, of which
Dallas was one of his most popular. A more even distribution of the
workload would have made this film more rewarding. It was eminently
watchable, undemanding fare, and the soft color was pleasing to the eye.
Roman tentatively learned some Spanish for the occasion. She made a
convincing senorita with her sultry, dark looks, and the appealing costumes of Marjorie Best accentuated her figure. Long-standing screen
hero Cooper let it be known that he relished one part of acting above all:
kissing his leading ladies. Over the years he had plenty of practice with
most of the foremost actresses of the previous 20 years. He rated Roman
one of the best and described her style as "rhythmic ... like a dance."[35]
The difference in height caused a few problems, and in order for the
six-foot-three Cooper to kiss the five-foot-four Roman she had to wear
lifts. The studio planned to team them again in *Distant Drums,* but Mari
Aldon was given the part. Cooper and Roman had also been mooted to
star in *Bright Leaf* in which she came in again as a replacement for Bette
Davis, who had first been designated the role. In the event, Patricia Neal
was cast.[36] However, Roman co-starred in a radio adaptation of the story
with Gregory Peck around the same time.

At one time she was in the frame for a choice role in *Serenade* based
on James M. Cain's 1937 potboiler. A feature film version had been

A German poster for *Dallas* (1950), the second of three films Roman made with Gary Cooper.

planned since at least 1943. By 1950, Roman was a front-runner and even did a test in which she wore a special wig that belonged to Bette Davis which she thought might bring her luck. Alas, it was not so lucky for her because it was another six years before the film was finally made, by which time she had fallen out of the reckoning, and instead Joan Fontaine and the Spanish singer Sara Montiel took the leading parts.[37] Jack Warner clearly thought highly of Roman and put her forward to be tested for the role of Stella Kowalski in the screen version of Tennessee

Williams's *A Streetcar Named Desire* (1951). Director Elia Kazan agreed to test her, and in his exchange of letters on the subject, Warner wrote of her, "This girl has developed not only into a good actress but a good draw at the box office."[38] Despite his glowing endorsement, she was not successful, and Kim Hunter recreated the role she had first played on Broadway. Kazan considered Roman too sexy for the part, which made her laugh because some years earlier she was rejected for a part because she was thought not sexy enough.

She had a good co-starring role with Patricia Neal and Eleanor Parker in *Three Secrets* (1950), a well-made drama directed by Robert Wise. The story revolved around the fate of a missing plane that was carrying a young boy and trying to discover which one of the three was the mother. From the outset, Wise stressed that the three actresses' roles were all equally important, and indeed the finished film stayed true to that. They were a similar age and three of the most promising

Three Secrets (1950) gave Roman a good dramatic role alongside two of her great contemporaries. Left to right: Eleanor Parker, Patricia Neal and Ruth Roman.

upcoming stars at that time. There was no clash of egos as some reports tried to suggest or that the press willed to happen, and the fair division of labor that Wise insisted on helped no end in that regard. They were all total professionals and were evenly matched. Personally, they got along well and respected each other's talent. "We just like each other," commented Eleanor Parker. "Pat Neal and Ruthie Roman are two swell girls."[39] Although sometimes unfairly dismissed as a formula women's picture, it was interesting to see three leading actresses at an early stage of their careers and their different approaches to their roles. Wise said he realized it was close to soap opera but also spoke of how "intrigued" he was to be working with the leads.[40] Roman played an actress, and of the three tales hers was by far the most sensational, but her conviction kept it within bounds. There was sensitive interplay of understanding between them all that also made the whole thing work seamlessly. The story was partially inspired by the real-life Kathy Fiscus case in which a child had fallen down a well. The fate of the child captured the rapt attention of local television networks for several days. She was later found dead. Filming took place near Mount Waterman in Angeles National Forest outside Los Angeles and also at Lone Pine, California. Ten members of the Sierra Club were seen in the film being interviewed by Bill Welsh who covered the original Fiscus case. Wise captured the fraught feeling of helplessness among everyone while waiting desperately for news in several scenes where little was actually happening. The film was one of two in which she appeared that did well for Warner Bros. at the box office in 1950, the other was *Colt .45*.[41] She greatly enjoyed working on *Three Secrets* and later recalled it as one of her personal favorites.[42]

In the space of a year, she had made over half a dozen films with hardly a break in between, but it was all grist to the mill. "I like work," she contended. "I am restless when I am idle and the more pictures the better. The only thing I really enjoy is acting."[43] In recognition, in January 1950 she was officially given star status by Warner Bros. When she sat down to lunch at the studio commissary one day, all the writers to a man rose to her and applauded. Writers rarely rose for anyone, and, at first, she thought they were having a joke at her expense but then realized that it was true. Stardom was something she had wanted for so long and was much deserved after all her hard work, but, when it came, it almost caught her unawares. On past experience, something told her she ought to enjoy it while it lasted.

❖❖ 5 ❖❖

Strangers on a Train

"Acting is my life. The profession can break my heart. In fact, it already has several times, but I love it."
　　　　　　　　　　—Ruth interviewed, 1949[1]

As a full-blown star, Roman continued her successful run at Warner Bros., where she was kept constantly busy and appeared in ten pictures in a row in little more than a 15-month period. She worked for many leading directors, including Alfred Hitchcock. Although her experience on *Strangers on a Train* was not what she hoped it would be, she was forever grateful to have been part of a true classic by the acknowledged master at his peak.

Her run of good roles in some interesting films continued with King Vidor's *Lightning Strikes Twice* (1951). Initially Virginia Mayo was set to star, but Warner Bros. had a prior claim to her services to appear opposite Gregory Peck in *Captain Horatio Hornblower* (1951). Hence, Roman came into the frame, and it marked her first starring role. The rather unlikely lead was the British actor Richard Todd, who was then at the height of his stateside fame on the back of his appearance as the surly soldier in a surprising hit, *The Hasty Heart*. He had followed that up with a leading role in Hitchcock's *Stage Fright* (1950). The casting of Todd in *Lightning Strikes Twice* was a bold move in some ways. He seemed out of place; his clipped English tones and upright bearing were strangely at odds with the nature of the mysterious character he was playing. Although he was adept at military roles, the part required someone with far stronger emotional, and above all romantic, impact. Nor was it sufficiently explained why an Englishman was in the middle of Texas. Indeed, also in the cast was Zachary Scott, and the scenes Roman shared with him worked better and had far greater

50

Roman had her first big starring role for Warner Bros. in King Vidor's *Lightning Strikes Twice* **(1950). With Mercedes McCambridge (right).**

naturalness than those between her and Todd. An expert supporting cast was assembled, with telling contributions from Mercedes McCambridge, Frank Conroy and Kathryn Givney in particular. At the time, Roman described making the film as a grueling assignment. Cast and crew spent almost two months on location, much of it at Victorville, California, for the perfectionist veteran King Vidor. The scenes at the Nolan place were filmed at Vidor's own ranch at Paso Robles, where Todd learned how to ride western style, and Roman was presented with a pair of golden spurs. The two actors were involved in an accident when the bus in which they were traveling to a location shoot was hit by a car. They were badly shaken but not seriously hurt.[2] Vidor had long been an admirer of Ruth's, and this was their second film together. He had enjoyed an illustrious career beginning in 1913 and had numerous highlights, including *The Crowd* (1928), *The Champ* (1931), *Northwest Passage* (1940) and *Duel in the Sun* (1946). Late in life he was given an Honorary Academy Award for lifetime achievement. On the set of *Lightning Strikes Twice* he tried several neat tricks to encourage the perfect reaction in Roman; for instance, he once put alum in her coffee when she was not looking to get the desired facial expression on camera. He also scared her out of her wits with a tarantula in a bedroom scene while she was flitting about in her negligee. The scene made her feel self-conscious, and she remarked, "I feel silly as all get-out standing here in front of a crew of one hundred men with my pink slip showing all over." Vidor told her to forget how she looked and concentrate on her dialogue.[3] The screenplay was based on the 1940 novel *A Man Without Friends* by Margaret Echard, the rights to which Warner Bros. had held since 1945. Although completed in the early part of 1950, the film was held back by the studio and not released until almost a year later in March 1951 for some unspecified reason. *Lightning Strikes Twice* performed well at the box office, both domestically and internationally. It was Vidor's final assignment at the studio, but he later declared himself unhappy with the way it turned out. Many critics dismissed the story as melodramatic and improbable, but *The Times* of London for one was moved to praise Roman as "refreshingly normal."[4] In many ways the female characters were the strongest, and the dynamic between Roman and McCambridge was a striking one, accentuated by their masculine attire in the inventive costumes by Leah Rhodes. Author Patricia White offered a fascinating interpretation of the film and particularly this "mirroring of dress" in her interesting study *Uninvited.*[5] Roman and Todd were young stars in the ascendancy at that time, and a follow-up teaming was announced by the studio, eager to cash in on their joint wave of popularity. The proposed project was *A Force of Arms*, (1951) but, in the event, the arguably more successful teaming of William Holden and Nancy Olson were given the roles.[6] Personally, she got along especially well with Todd and with McCambridge. The three became good friends, and he invited both actresses to visit him and his wife in England. He greatly enjoyed his time working on his first big Hollywood film, despite his wife's illness partway through filming, as he recounted in his memoirs.[7] The end of shooting coincided with Zachary Scott's birthday, and the whole cast and crew enjoyed a dinner at the Apple Valley Inn to celebrate. The film has gained some reputation over the intervening years, and, in 2020 at the 70th Berlin Film Festival, it was shown as part of a retrospective tribute to Vidor, along with several others, including *Beyond the Forest.*[8]

Shortly after the release of *Lightning Strikes Twice*, Ruth celebrated her elevation to star status by having a swimming pool installed at her home, that abiding symbol of Hollywood success. Her income shot up during 1951, and she was 12th on the list of top-earning actresses for the year, having garnered almost $6,000,000 for three films.[9] She was also involved indirectly in a court action in which her current agent was sued by her previous agent. In court, her first agent spoke of her early years of extreme poverty, which she had left far behind.[10]

After a string of good, prominent parts, Ruth realized she had finally arrived when she appeared in *Starlift* as herself, taking her place alongside Warner's big guns, including James Cagney. Moreover, she had personally inspired both the film and the original scheme. The idea was based on Operation Starlift, a joint enterprise between the Special Services Officers and the Hollywood Coordinating Committee, in which stars got together to entertain wounded soldiers returning from the front. The scheme had been initiated by Roman's personal visits to airbases to entertain the troops, particularly at the Travis Air Force Base in Fairfield, California, which she had been doing for well over a year. She took part in shows before the men set off for Korea and when they came back, not only there but at other camps across the country. She also visited hospitals regularly and met wounded soldiers. These visits inspired her to contact many of her friends in Hollywood privately to try and persuade them to do the same. The work had great value; it was terrific for morale and was always greatly appreciated by the servicemen themselves. A Burma veteran, Charles Thompson, remembered she visited the camp where he was stationed as part of a USO troupe along with Pat O'Brien and Jinx Falkenburg. Thompson recalled, "The officers set up a special dinner for them, but the visitors declined and ate with us. I never forgot that."[11] Roman remained popular ever after with servicemen and, among other accolades, was voted the White Clover Girl for 1951 by the AMVETS organization.[12] She was also chosen by the American Legion to start the fireworks at the annual Independence Day celebrations at Fort Worth in that same year.[13] Louella Parsons took up the idea of using the good work that Roman and the other stars did willingly, and the general idea was sketched out as a tribute to the men fighting in the war. Jack Warner got on board, and James Cagney produced the venture. The whole thing was given the full-blown Hollywood treatment. Unfortunately, it was not given much of a storyline, and most of the personnel involved seemed ill at ease, as though unsure what to do once they were told to act natural and be themselves. Doris Day recalled both the silliness of the film but how much fun she had working with Roman. There were some awkward scenes in which Day and Roman, adorned in mink coats, visited hospital wards, and Day began singing to the men, or down the phone to their sweethearts, while Roman attempted to give them a shave. Considering the patriotic nature of the endeavor and the wealth of talent at their disposal, it was disappointing that Warner Bros. could not come up with something more fitting as a tribute to the armed forces than *Starlift*. Although undoubtedly made with the best intentions, it did not do justice either to the armed forces or to itself. The tone throughout came across as condescending to its supposed target audience and the men risking their lives in a distant land. What might have been interesting when presented as a minor item on a *Pathé* newsreel was hardly strong enough to stretch out to a feature-length film. As one author pointed out, the film cost almost £1,000,000 to make, but the real-life Operation Starlift far away from all the ballyhoo was funded only to the tune of $5,000 by the studio and consequently was forced to close in November 1951 when it ran out of money. *Starlift* was dismissed by many critics as a calculated and cynical attempt to derive kudos for Warner Bros. while not being genuinely concerned about the men fighting in Korea.[14] Despite the outcome, all those involved meant well, and the idea itself had undoubted merit. Roman was justifiably proud about her own input for the cause. She spoke about her personal involvement in the project: "This picture, I know for sure, sprang from an actual wonderful adventure in my life. Some of its incidents are almost biographical, because they happened to me, and the remainder true to what people today are attempting to do for our servicemen in the manner they know best—entertainment."[15] The film achieved moderate success, and a follow-up was planned, with the provisional title of *Here Come the Girls*, with Roman again as the star. Perhaps thankfully, considering Hollywood's track record, that did not transpire.[16]

For a long time, Ruth was going steady with Bill Walsh, who seemed to be stuck on her. He was a leading cartoonist for Walt Disney who also used to write gags for Bob Hope. After Disney's death, he was part of the seven-man committee who ran the Disney company and one of the most important figures in the organization even though he was little known to the general public. Walsh was an orphan and began working for Disney writing *Mickey Mouse* strips in the early 1940s. He was later put in charge of television operations and made a big success with *The Mickey Mouse Club* in the mid–1950s. Although Disney was only ten

5. Strangers on a Train

WARNER BROS. present
DORIS **DAY** . GORDON MacRAE . VIRGINIA **MAYO** . GENE **NELSON** . RUTH **ROMAN**
with JANICE RULE . DICK WESSON . RON HAGERTHY . Guest Starring JAMES CAGNEY
STARLIFT CERT U . GARY COOPER . VIRGINIA GIBSON . PHIL HARRIS . FRANK LOVEJOY . LUCILLE NORMAN
LOUELLA PARSONS . RANDOLPH SCOTT . JANE WYMAN . PATRICE WYMORE
Produced by Robert Arthur . Directed by **ROY DEL RUTH** . JACK L. WARNER Executive Producer . A WARNER BROS PICTURE

Roman was proud that she inspired the real-life Hollywood Starlift campaign to entertain the troops at their bases during the Korean War; however, the finished all-star musical of *Starlift* (1951) was a generally disappointing tribute to the men involved. Above: Roman on stage with Doris Day, left foreground, who between them provided most of the high spots.

years older, Walsh looked upon him almost like a father figure. Walsh was a talented and witty man in his own right, but he never struck out on his own as he might have done, perhaps because of his great loyalty to the company and especially to the man himself. Bill and Ruth had known each other since about 1946, and he was always helping her out and buying her presents. He bought her the dog Shawn as a birthday present, of which she was inordinately fond. She reckoned it was a Kerry Blue, but it looked to most like a mongrel. Ruth even invested a substantial sum in an ice cream parlor business that he operated along with veteran character actor Will Wright. Bill and Ruth spent so much of their spare time together that they seemed to outsiders almost like a married couple already. There were even rumors that they had eloped to Mexico and wed in secret. As it turned out, they never married but remained on good terms. Ruth later said that they were "very close

55

friends" and described him as a highly influential figure who helped her to find her direction in life.[17] Walsh probably knew her as well as anyone, but even he admitted she was difficult to fathom. As he once remarked, "At times, she's a complete extrovert; then again she's something out of Dostoevski."[18] A few years later he married Nolie Fishman, a young actress and dancer who curiously enough bore a striking resemblance to Ruth. Bill and Nolie had two sons and a daughter, but the marriage eventually came asunder. Nolie admitted that she just could not compete with Disney, saying that Bill was effectively married to the Disney company which was his life. The divorce proved a particularly bitter blow to Walsh. He was devastated by it and, according to friends, never recovered.[19]

Ruth's name was also linked romantically with several Hollywood personalities, including the screenwriter Sy Bartlett. At one time she went out with Ronald Reagan and was the sudden center of press attention when she accompanied him to the premiere of *The Hasty Heart*. Personally, she admired Reagan a lot, who she described as "clean cut and full of information."[20] Generally, she was just as chatty on dates, and from him she found out all about the inner workings of the Screen Actors Guild, which she said was interesting. Their romance was considered serious at one time. She had casual dates with many of the usual suspects of the era, including Peter Lawford, John Agar, Stewart Granger and Steve Cochran, among others. Once her pet Siamese cat took an instant dislike to Lawford and jumped on his back, clawing him in the process. With some of her other dates, she was less than impressed: "All they do is take you out for an early dinner, yawn in your face, and whisk you home by 9 pm," she once complained. One promising young chap asked her to come and see his new house. "I figured we'd look at the inevitable etchings, then I'd go home," she commented, adding wryly, "We spent the whole afternoon whitewashing his picket fence."[21]

After her early entrée into radio on Art Linkletter's *People Are Funny* show, Roman's career in the sound medium was good but fairly brief. Among her highlights, she featured in several installments of *Lux Radio Theater*, the longest-running drama series of its kind. She reprised her screen role in a well-regarded version of "Strangers on a Train" with Ray Milland, which was later released on a CD compilation of Hitchcock radio adaptations. She took on the Anne Baxter role in an appealing version of *The Blue Gardenia* with Dana Andrews. In the same series, she finally fulfilled her long-held ambition to work with her idol Tyrone Power in "The Third Man." Producer Malcolm Boyd recalled that Roman, along with cinematographer James Wong Howe and other Hollywood personalities, once appeared on his show without a fee.[22] One of Roman's most interesting radio ventures was "A Star Is Born" opposite Frederic March for the *Screen Director's Guild* (1950). A selection of her radio work is available as a CD or download (see Discography).[23]

After all her cajoling of Alfred Hitchcock to try to persuade him to cast her in *Suspicion* several years before, Roman finally got her chance to work with the great director thanks largely to her studio boss, Jack Warner. Indeed, Warner's insistence that she was cast as Ann Morton in *Strangers on a Train* put the kibosh on things as far as Hitchcock was concerned and set him at loggerheads with the leading actress who had been foisted on him against his wishes. Hitchcock had as usual envisioned his favorite blonde, Grace Kelly, in the role. Consequently, according to Farley Granger, he made life hard for Roman during filming. Granger wrote, "Hitchcock's disinterest in Ruth Roman and the role she played led him to be outspokenly critical and harsh with her, as he had been with Edith Evanson on the set of *Rope*. He had to have one person in each film he could harass."[24] Anne Baxter suffered a similar experience during the making of *I Confess*.[25] Not only that, but he seldom missed a chance to criticize Roman in subsequent interviews, a view with which the vast majority of critics concur. In his famous conversations with him, Francois Truffaut identified her as "the only flaw" in the film.[26] Author Patricia Highsmith approved of the movie when she first saw it but years later changed her mind and said she believed that Granger could not possibly have fallen in love with Roman, who she referred to disparagingly as "that stone angel."[27] In truth it was a thankless role for any actress because, although she might have been the conventional lead on paper, the focus of the screenplay—and of Hitchcock's interest—was clearly elsewhere. The whole respectable eastern family was treated in the same arbitrary way, and Leo G. Carroll, for instance, had little to do. A university thesis might be constructed about Hitchcock's offhand treatment of brunettes in his films. In Ruth's case he considered her lacking in sex appeal and described her as "bristling."[28] To add to his problems, he did not want Granger either, who he felt was not strong enough; he wanted William Holden. Hitchcock further undermined Roman when he hired an English tutor for her so that her accent would be closer to that of his daughter Pat, who played her sister in the film. Despite all her apparent problems on set, she nonetheless looked back on the whole experience with great fondness. Years later in an interview she recalled; "I loved working with Hitchcock. He told me a joke after every scene. He once said to me, 'Ruthie, six months from now no one will ever remember we did this.'" She enjoyed working with Robert Walker who she said was "a very sweet guy."[29] She got along especially well with Pat Hitchcock and gave her a stamped silhouette portrait of the great actress Eleonora Duse as a farewell present. The item had great sentimental value to Roman, who considered it her personal good luck charm.[30] The tennis background to the film appealed to her greatly. If nothing else, she joked, at least she was able to improve her tennis form during shooting. In a tie-in with the movie, she was voted the Queen of National Tennis Week for June 23 to 30 sponsored by the Sporting Goods Dealer.[31]

Not all critics were of the same mind about casting and particularly Roman's contribution. Over the years there have been several dissenting

Robert Walker (left) with Roman in a telling scene from *Strangers on a Train*.

voices, a number of which have praised the casting of both leads. In an interesting discussion, one reviewer wrote glowingly in praise of Roman and went so far as to say that she was "even in one or two places quite masterly." The same reviewer called attention to the "perfect scene" where she interviewed Bruno's deluded mother.[32]

Hitchcock must surely be one of the most dissected directors ever. Every one of his films has been put under the microscope and investigated from seemingly every angle. *Strangers on a Train* has been discussed perhaps more than the others. Such analysis might be understandable but not always helpful. The performance of all the actors involved has also been a subject of earnest but perhaps unnecessary debate, judging by his own frequent disavowal of actors in general. Regardless of any individual input, it is a great film and one of the director's best. On balance, the actress has perhaps been overly criticized when in fact it is the part itself which was a thoroughly conventional one that called for a certain coldness, at least in Hitchcock's interpretation of the characters. The various cuts in her dialogue demanded by the censors may also not have helped her characterization; for instance, there was one specific speech which the Hays Office considered "appeared to condone wrong doing."[33] Raymond Chandler's witty script did not benefit from such interference. A case could be made that each actor was ideally cast and that Granger was perfectly suited to play the weak and vacillating Guy. In Roman's defense, a New England senator's daughter of that time would more than likely be aloof if not patrician in outlook. Her clothes accentuated this: the trimmed, neat appearance, fashionable but conservative, utilizing a simple elegance. Some commentators have remarked that even Grace Kelly could not have done much with the character as written. In any event, Roman was forever grateful of her chance to work with Hitchcock, whom she described as an inspiring director. Even if her own experience was not the supreme joy she imagined it might have been, she loved being a part of a film that is unlikely to be forgotten by devotees of the cinematic art.

❖❖ 6 ❖❖

Tomorrow
Is Another Day

"I'm impulsive. When I'm not working, I like to
arise at six, as usual, and drive out to the beach:
there I like to sit for hours dancing a gavotte. Or I
like to hike to the top of one of Hollywood's hills,
Shawn at my heels, and muse for hours at the misty
panorama stretched out below."
—Ruth interviewed for *Screenland*[1]

In December 1950, Ruth surprised many people when she married
radio station manager Mortimer Hall. She continued to work feverishly
and played in some good roles. Her career was put on hold when her
son was born in November 1952, after which her days as a Warner Bros.
contract star were numbered.

The day after filming of *Strangers on a Train* finished, she eloped
with Hall and they married in Las Vegas shortly before Christmas on
December 17, 1950. He was 26 and the general manager of radio station KLAC, which was owned by his mother Dorothy Schiff. There
was no time for more than a one-day honeymoon; it was a case of flying to Nevada on Friday, getting married at 5 a.m. Saturday, then flying back to report for duty on her next film the following Monday.
It was such a rushed affair that she did not even have a ring and had
to borrow one from her stand-in and best friend Grace Kenny.[2] Ruth
first met Mort when she was having dinner with friends at the swanky
club the 21 Club in New York. They seemed to hit it off from the first:
"He's the first wealthy man I've enjoyed being with who doesn't talk
about yachts," she once observed.[3] Theirs was a whirlwind romance,
and she said that as soon as she met him, she knew he was the man
she would marry. They dated for the following week. As she explained:

6. *Tomorrow Is Another Day*

"Then it was time for me to return to the coast. He escorted me to the airport and handed me my luggage checks plus a little box. In it was a superb diamond. Just as the plane was about to take off, he asked me to marry him and I said Yes."[4] Her marriage was a secret, and she told no one about it beforehand. It was reported that at least one prominent gossip columnist bawled her out over the phone on the set of her next picture because she had not been given an exclusive.

It was a second marriage for both of them because Hall had previously been married to Mary Ann Parker, who had died in 1945. Despite the disparities in their backgrounds and temperaments, Ruth and Mort shared a love of sports, especially swimming, badminton, and tennis. Shortly after their marriage they bought a new home at 436 Rockingham Avenue, Brentwood, which they set about renovating. The finished décor drew much praise for its taste that particularly reflected Mort's interest in art. They were never into the Hollywood party scene but often gave barbecues for a few friends. Most weekends they spent sailing together. Some acquaintances were quoted as saying that the marriage was a nonstarter. Avid press attention on their allegedly semi-constant bickering since their early days together hardly helped matters. Ruth was by then a minor star in the Hollywood firmament, but even minor stars were considered fair game for the gossip mill. Like any showbiz newlyweds, they received the merciless focus of a hungry press which almost seemed to be willing them to fail. "Why the ink was hardly dry on our marriage certificate before people were talking about our splitting up," she once remarked.[5] There was fervid speculation that their opposite social status would be the root cause of their undoing. For all the modernity of the postwar era, status was still deemed important at that time. Hall came from an affluent background, and his mother, Dorothy, was a prominent and influential businesswoman, the owner and publisher of the *New York Post.* She famously had a long-standing affair with F.D.R. and exercised a great deal of influence in New York. Ruth was suitably impressed by her new mother-in-law: "She's the handsomest woman I've ever seen," she declared. "I love her."[6] For her part, Mrs. Schiff reserved judgment on her son's bride. However, as if to emphasize that he had somehow "lost caste" by marrying a movie star, Mort's father, Richard B. Hall, was suddenly dropped from the social register after 50 years, with seemingly no explanation, and Mort soon followed. Every statement Ruth had previously made about matrimony was dredged up for scrutiny, and she was reminded that she had once uttered the probably throwaway remark, "I'll be the world's worst wife, but I'm willing to try." Leslie Snyder commented on Roman's similarity to Betty Hutton. Both were earthy but went for someone out of their milieu. Hall was a big name in his immediate New York circle but was hardly known in Hollywood, where he was sometimes dubbed Mr. Ruth Roman.[7] Just after the marriage they had a public set-to at an informal gathering at one of their friends' San Fernando home, where the guests included John Ireland, Andre De Toth and Joanne Dru. At that time, she was left in tears. There was a central dichotomy in their marriage from the first. Their interests failed to coincide sufficiently; his work and most of his life was based in New York, but she loved Hollywood and her burgeoning career too much to give it up so that if they were ever going to have a satisfactory family life, something would have to give.

For Ruth, work took up most of her time and attention in the first year of her marriage. Warner Bros. believed that actors should act, and she was kept busy for months on end. It was not until the summer of 1951 that they finally found time to embark on their delayed honeymoon. They went to Hawaii and stayed at the Royal Hawaiian Hotel, Honolulu. Even then they did not travel down together, but she went first and he came on later. Ruth made the five-day journey with an armful of books. She loved Hawaii and relished stepping off the studio treadmill for a spell. After two-and-a-half years' intensive work, she really felt she needed a break and returned invigorated: "I didn't know how badly I needed a change of scenery until we sailed from San Francisco," she remarked. She later enthused about her time away, "We drove out to Doris Duke's home; we rode in an admiral's barge to Pearl Harbor and we visited the Korean wounded. We also had bowls of orchids in our room every day and I wore sarongs and flowers in my hair. It was wonderful."[8] Mort was often lavish with his gifts; for instance, as a wedding present he bought her an imported car which cost $5,000, a princely sum at the time considering that the average wage was about $3,500. She was generous too and once bought him a Colt .45 for his birthday.

She had a restless nature and preferred constant activity. She enjoyed all sports, especially tennis, swimming and badminton, and was also described as a handy golfer. Tennis was her favorite game, and she was a determined player with a tenacious, never-say-die attitude. Her game was perhaps not of the most artistic kind, but it was effective, and on her own admission she gave the ball a good wallop. Always athletic and looking for new hobbies, she even took up fencing at one stage. For years she took ballet lessons with various companies and used dance exercises as a way to keep in shape.[9]

After her marriage, she was suddenly deemed an expert on the subject of matrimony and was inundated with letters from lovesick girls asking her about the secrets of finding and keeping a man. Ruth refrained from making any major pronouncements about it but gave a tongue-in-cheek ten-point plan on how to avoid arguments. Among her recommendations, she emphasized the importance of diplomacy, even though it was difficult to practice: "I would suggest that wives stay away from religion, politics and Dianetics," she advised. "Just nod and say yes or no in the right places."[10]

One of the first things she did once she started to make her name in Hollywood was to set her mother up for life. Suky even moved out to the film capital, although, of course, they did not live together. They clashed far too much for that and found that they got along much better if they lived in different houses, especially so because her mother liked to stay

Steve Cochran (left) and Roman played characters who were both trying to escape their pasts in Felix Feist's undervalued *Tomorrow Is Another Day* (1951).

up all night and Ruth was usually up at 4:00 or 5:00 a.m. in order to be ready for starting work. After Ruth married, her mother took the house in the San Fernando Valley that she had vacated.

In the meantime, Ruth's career was motoring ahead. She landed the lead in *Tomorrow Is Another Day* (1951), an excellent crime drama which gave her one of her best roles. The first part of the film required her to be a blonde, and it was certainly striking to see her as such but a relief when she became a brunette again. Her hair was considered too black to be dyed successfully because it would have meant dyeing her hair three times. Instead, she wore a wig and only a strip of hair near the temples was dyed blonde. "This wig is driving me crazy," she complained during filming. "They have to glue it to my head and it feels like.... I'm frowning all the time."[11] The progression from blonde to brunette mirrored her character's development from lost soul to solid citizen. Blondes were always seen on film as either dizzy or lethal. Quite why that should be is open to debate. Perhaps because most were bottle blondes and therefore trying to be something other than what they were. She enjoyed working with her old friend Steve Cochran, who for once had a good chance to prove his acting credentials. The role had purportedly been designed with John Garfield in mind before his untimely death, and Dane Clark was also in the frame at one stage. There was a surprisingly touching naiveté in Cochran's portrayal of an ex-con who has been behind bars since he was 13. The two actors had a shared history and had been through a lot since first meeting when they were starting out at the dawn of the 1940s. It was just reward for both of them, and they were obviously simpatico. As she observed at the time, "Steve's strong, I'm strong and it comes through. We've known each other since we were starving actors in New York. When we work together, we keep looking at each other and saying, 'Is this possible?'"[12] He knew her well and once observed, "She has complete honesty about herself and profits from both criticism and advice. She's so very definite. I don't think she could be artistically selfish if she tried."[13] He noticed a change in her in recent years; she was far less tense than she had been when he first met her: "Ruth's more relaxed because she knows greater security," he commented. "She herself is the first to admit that being too much on the defensive is merely wasting energy."[14] Despite his comparatively early death, Felix Feist had a 25-year career behind the camera beginning in 1930. Among his highlights were several efficient and once-overlooked crime dramas, including *The Devil Thumbs a Ride* (1947) and *The Man Who Cheated Himself* (1950), which are perhaps ripe for reappraisal. He also directed the sci-fi yarn *Donovan's Brain* (1953). During filming of *Tomorrow Is Another Day,* he continually urged Roman to "look sexy and earthy. You're a tramp," he would remind her before each scene.[15] Feist had a specific vision in mind and, for example, he insisted that Cochran should shave his chest, but he refused. Roman backed him up in that, and so Cochran remained hairy chested—to the approval of many fans. The good script was by Art Cohn (*The Set-Up, Stromboli*) working in combination with novelist Guy Endore, who wrote the original story. Endore was remembered for his screenplay of the classic horror *The Devil Doll* and as the author of the original novel *Whirlpool,* which was made into a decent film noir. In *Tomorrow Is Another Day* highly effective use was made of the evocative song "Deep Night" as a recurring theme at key moments in the narrative. Some of the seemingly semirural locations, including lettuce fields and roadside truckers' cafes, were in reality just a stone's throw from the Warner's lot on Ventura Boulevard.[16] She complained that she was freezing during filming of some of the nighttime scenes and cowered under blankets trying to get warm on braziers. It was worth the discomfort, and Roman drew widespread praise at the time for her portrayal of Cay Higgins. The *Motion Picture Daily* described hers as "a powerful performance that covers a wide range of emotions."[17] She brought out much of the restlessness and dissatisfaction of her character, and the scene on the hill where she confesses how lost she feels was a telling one. "I came to New York from up state," she reveals. "I was gonna be a dancer. I was a brunette. Started on my toes and wound up on my heels." It was certain there was some of her own bitter experience underlying the role. Another finely judged scene took place in the truck, traveling with her new neighbors, but where previously they were friendly, there was a noticeably tense atmosphere between them all in what was a wordless scene. Despite her fine work, the film itself was not considered of much worth at the time and was never likely to be nominated for any awards. Such B-films were churned out by the studios and dismissed almost as soon as they were finished. They have only slowly gained kudos in recent times as later generations have reassessed their cultural significance, but even now any praise for them is rather grudging. Some other interesting film noir roles were mooted for her, and Feist hoped to cast her as the lead in his next project, *This Woman Is Dangerous.* In the end, she lost out on that occasion to Joan Crawford, but it would have been interesting to have seen what Roman might have made of the role.[18]

After the success of *Strangers on a Train,* Sam Goldwyn wanted to borrow Roman for the comedy *I Saw Him First* and reteam her with Farley Granger.[19] Other intriguing but aborted projects included *Miss America,* an exposé of a beauty pageant in Atlantic City that would have teamed her with Virginia Mayo and/or Doris Day.[20] Fans of all three actresses might be disappointed that the latter never came into being. In 1952, there was a revival of interest in Roman's short story, *The House of the Seven Garbos.* Ida Lupino and Collier Young hoped to realize the idea as a feature film, but the project hit the buffers.

Roman played the love interest in *Mara Maru* (1952), a fair adventure yarn which starred Errol Flynn as an ex-Navy commander working as a salvage operator looking for sunken treasure in the Philippines. Among the good supporting cast was Raymond Burr complete with the standard issue white suit of the heavy menace in the East. This was obviously not the Flynn of his heyday, but even Flynn on the wane was good value, and his tired appearance emphasized the toughness and underlying weariness of the character, which added an elusive wistfulness to proceedings. He succumbed to a mystery virus during filming, which might have added to his jaded look. Paul Picerni stood in for him on those occasions when he was indisposed, which, according to the director, was usually after 3 p.m., by which time he had been drinking in his cabin for some time.[21] Roman also became sick when they were shooting the storm scene. It was caused by the constant rolling motion of the studio ship, which was jigged by technicians as water continually cascaded onto the actors. In addition, she injured her arm and shoulders during shooting, which required hospital treatment and caused some delays in filming. The accident happened when she fell up a short flight of stairs at the studios. In another incident, Flynn was burned in the face and singed his eyebrows. There was some location work which took place in Balboa Island and at the San Fernando Mission, where lots of excited schoolgirls converged to watch the man himself at work. Despite all their best efforts the film came across as being as jaded as its star. The gibberish title may have put some people off; the name was actually derived from that of the boat, which was in reality the twin-diesel *Malibu* loaned to the studio by a California businessman. Regardless of the title, the verdict of the critics was predictably negative. Gordon Douglas made his name for comedy shorts but enjoyed a

Mexican poster for the South Seas' adventure yarn *Mara Maru* (1952), one of Errol Flynn's last Warner Bros. films.

diverse career, and, after being hired by James Cagney for *Kiss Tomorrow Goodbye* (1950), he established himself as one of the leading directors at Warner Bros. during some of its best years. The cinematography by Robert Burks was excellent as always, and one reviewer perceptively noted that "due to its extensive deep focus photography, *Mara Maru* has a distinct, 'film noir' flavor."[22] It was the second of three collaborations between Burks and Douglas. Burks had also worked on *Tomorrow Is Another Day* and *Strangers on a Train* which marked his first encounter with Hitchcock. He was perhaps most famous for his long association with Hitchcock. Burks was cinematographer for 12 of his films and was by all accounts an important and inventive force on the master. To add to the film's credentials, the script was written by Philip Yordan, who went on to write what was arguably his best, *Johnny Guitar*, the following year. For all its apparent faults, *Mara Maru* was good escapism and the kind of thing Warner Bros. did so well. It also provided Roman with a chance to give an airing to a lavish kimono which had been a present some years earlier.[23] Her part was ill-defined, but, as sundry critics noted, she looked attractive. As ever, the music of Max Steiner was a saving grace. The film was one of Flynn's last for the

Roman showed excellent comedic timing in the charming *Young Man with Ideas* (1952) on a loan-out to Metro but was given few other chances to prove herself in the genre. Above: Publicity still showing left to right: Roman, Glenn Ford, Nadine Ashdown, Donna Corcoran.

studio and did reasonable business at the box office, perhaps largely on the lingering magic of his name alone.

Roman repeatedly petitioned her home studio to give her something different and was especially keen to do comedy, but they made only a few half-hearted attempts. She was offered a script titled *Miss Woodbury's Wolves* in which she was cast as the secretary of a law firm who has to fend off the attention of the wolves in the office. That came to nothing.[24] In the event she finally got her chance on a loan-out to Metro as the wife in the amiable *Young Man with Ideas* directed by the veteran Mitchell Leisen. It was the tale of a small-town Montana lawyer who moves with his family to California. Ruth conclusively showed that she had an aptitude for the genre. After all, she had the requisite qualities: a sense of humor and she never took herself too seriously. The film was originally known as *The Family Man* and intended as the screen debut of Russell Nype, who had left the cast of the Broadway show *Call Me Madam* in order to star. After a week of rehearsals, it was decided that Nype was not the type. He was considered too young for the role after all and was replaced by Glenn Ford. The resultant film was an appealing and typically well-made effort of the era, completed without fuss in six weeks. Leisen had an interesting career which included some effective dramas and the superior noir *No Man of Her Own*. However, his true métier was the screwball comedy of the 1930s, a style which he took well into the 1950s with only a few tweaks. Again, he displayed his familiar light touch, but for all that, *Young Man with Ideas* was only occasionally diverting. Roman proved equal to her role and especially had fun in a sequence where she gets tipsy at a party to the hearty disapproval of her husband's highbrow work colleagues. When first offered the part, she envisaged that it would be one in the Myrna Loy mold that would require her to model some classy outfits, but then she found out it was a family comedy, so at best she would only get to wear housedresses. Denise Darcel appeared in all the glamorous gowns going. Ruth was keen to try all kinds of parts: "You can always learn," she explained. "I didn't realize then that acting with children in a good family comedy can be more fun than the smart comedy I had pictured."[25] Ford sometimes gave the impression of being disinterested in the project, but, on the set, he talked about what had attracted him to play the part of a shy and uncertain husband and father, playing against type: "I hadn't done a comedy for more than three years," he revealed, "but this looked like fun and a real opportunity to act. The situations are a riot and with this cast—it was a role I couldn't miss."[26] The film was enlivened by some comical lines and a typically lively cameo from Mary Wickes as a neighbor, along with contributions from such welcome faces in support as Sheldon Leonard. The reviews were positive, and *The New York Times* commented that Roman "cuts some adroitly agile capers" in the role.[27]

Ruth continued her Metro sojourn with a promising bad girl role in *Invitation.* Unfortunately, the result was a curious mishmash of psychological thriller and sentimental melodrama which did not quite come off. It started out promisingly but veered too far away from the psychological to the sentimental. Dorothy McGuire starred as a woman who lives in the shadow of having suffered rheumatic fever in childhood, which has had the effect of weakening the heart valves. Out of the blue she announces that she will marry a man (Van Johnson) who has been going out with her friend Maud (Roman) for some time, after which Maud plots her revenge. It was an unconvincing story, but the actors did their best with a weak script. There was good support from Louis Calhern as her overprotective father and Ray Collins as the concerned family doctor. At the time the film was well thought of, and one

Dorothy McGuire and Ruth Roman pictured in an Italian lobby poster for *Invitation* **(1952). Roman enjoyed her role as a woman intent on getting revenge on her former best friend.**

leading reviewer wrote that it was "engrossing and frequently touch-ing."[28] Director Gottfried Reinhardt was born in Berlin, the son of the Austrian theater director Max Reinhardt. After moving to Hollywood, Gottfried became assistant to Ernst Lubitsch and wrote *The Great Waltz* (1938). He turned to producing and was also the producer of *Young Man with Ideas. Invitation* was his first attempt at directing, which was apparent at times. He went on to direct a handful of fairly success-ful films, including two segments of *The Story of Three Loves* (1953) and *Town Without Pity* (1961), and he also worked in West Germany. In *Invitation* Ruth's character was a bad girl of a kind who is determined to get back her man at all costs. Her role was an interesting one, but too much of the emphasis of the screenplay was on the neurosis of McGuire's character, and viewer sympathy was too heavily corralled in that direc-tion. Nevertheless, Roman spoke of how much she enjoyed playing a meanie for a change: "It's more than fun, it's a challenge. A challenge to try to prove to an audience that there's something on your side—some-thing that made you the way you are."[29] If anything, she found it harder to play good girls: "The typical nice girl in pictures is dramatically diffi-cult," she averred. "She never gets a chance to liven things up by having a good, old-fashioned tantrum. You have to struggle to keep her inter-esting without achieving the effect of too much whipped cream on top of the sundae."[30] Roman later stated that she most enjoyed making the two films for MGM, which she felt gave her more scope than anything she was being offered on her home lot. To tempt her to stay with them, Warner Bros. lined up several projects tailored expressly to suit her, but, as is the way of things, only some of the ideas bore fruit. She was touted to play a woman from the wrong side of the tracks who beats the odds to become a top doctor in an adaptation of William E. Sloan's *Not to Be a Stranger.* Unfortunately, the film progressed no further than the plan-ning stage.[31] Her name was put forward for a leading part in the women's prison drama *Caged* (1950), but, although she was a strong candidate, Eleanor Parker got the nod instead.

Despite her later reputation as something of a loner, at the peak of her career Roman maintained that she liked to be in the thick of it, chat-ting with other members of the cast and crew, catching up with every-one on set. At that time, she preferred not to stay in her dressing room because she did not like to be alone and craved company. "I relax best in a crowd," she once said. "I get a tremendous kick out of people. So why go off some place and coop yourself up? I don't want to be alone."[32] She was known for random acts of kindness and, according to more than one witness, was said to have one of the kindest hearts in Hollywood. For instance, she was moved by the plight of Tom Plant, a messenger boy at Warner Bros. who suffered severe injuries when he was accidentally shot. She remembered him because he had delivered her first fan letter on the lot. Not only did she help him out, but she also canvassed the studio and raised enough to pay for lifesaving surgery. Politically she was a lifelong supporter of the Democrats, but by and large she steered clear of politics, at least in the public sphere and avoided any pronouncements. The only time she appeared on a public platform was to endorse the candidacy of Adlai Stevenson for the presidency in 1952, along with many of her fellow stars.

On November 12, 1952, Ruth gave birth to her son Richard Roman Hall, weighing six lbs., by caesarian section. As a result, she put her career on a back burner for a while and took a long time off for maternity leave. Although the time was important for her personally, and for her family, it was also the case that a year and a half away from the

Hugo Fregonese's lively adventure *Blowing Wild* (1953) marked the end of Roman's stay at Warner Bros. Above: Publicity still showing left to right: Roman, Gary Cooper, Barbara Stanwyck, Anthony Quinn.

screen at a crucial time in her career was a decided factor in her loss of status at the studio. In her absence, Warner Bros. had almost immediately turned their attention to other starlets who they decided to build up in her stead, such as Phyllis Kirk. Kirk was not the first to be designated her replacement, and at one time Janice Rule was built up as the next Ruth Roman. On her return to filmmaking, Roman found a somewhat changed attitude awaiting her. For instance, she was lined up for *Blowing Wild* but objected to the second-lead role she was assigned and insisted on top billing. At first, she refused to do it, so risking suspension, but, in the end, she reluctantly agreed to their proposals. On the screen titles her name appeared third behind Barbara Stanwyck and before Anthony Quinn. The old-style adventure about wildcat oil drillers in Mexico during the 1930s was a likable one that was made compelling by the actors involved. Once again, Frankie Laine was pressed into service to deliver the theme song as only he could, over pictures of men on horseback entering a dusty south-of-the-border town. Roman expressed great disappointment that she was given only three scenes. Nevertheless, she made all those scenes count as the stranded American who turns her hand to dealing blackjack. She shared only one big scene with the great Stanwyck, a telling encounter in which both gave as good as they got. Further tussles between the two strong women would have been welcome, but on the whole it was one of her better movies. She loved to work with first-class actors and likened her attitude to a tennis analogy: "You play your best game with the best competition, and it's the same thing in acting."[33] Argentinian director Hugo Fregonese had a sure hand with bold adventure tales and showed his familiar sense of style and gusto. A former sports journalist from Mendoza, Fregonese studied at Columbia University and worked successfully in cinema both in Argentina and Hollywood. He was once married to the actress Faith Domergue. He made interesting, entertaining films in different genres, including westerns, historical pictures and film noirs. During the making of the film, Ruth's old fear of flying reasserted itself, and to begin with she tried to persuade Mort to drive her down to the location shooting in Mexico. Sometimes her phobia was so pronounced that she felt nervous just being at an airport. In the end she decided to try and face her fear head on and took a flight to Mexico City. Later she felt so emboldened that she took another flight to Acapulco and back. There was some talk of her taking flying lessons, but, in any event, she never entirely conquered her phobia. Her experience in the country gave her some sense of release, and she found a real liking for travel, which she felt broadened the mind. It was while working on the picture that she began to fall under the spell of Spanish culture. Her first attempts at speaking the language were encouraged by technicians working on the film, who told her they would communicate with her only if she conversed in Spanish. "Sometimes I didn't use the right words, and the boys got a laugh, but they were quick to correct me," she related. "Now, thanks to them, I can speak the language fairly well for a beginner."[34] She kept a journal of her impressions of the country, which she called *A Star Looks Down in Mexico*, an idea she hoped might become a short story.[35] During her time there, she indulged her love of shoes and bought a dozen pairs on a shopping spree in Mexico City. At Tijuana she watched her first bullfight, which she found exciting, even though things got a little out of hand and the bull almost ended up in her lap. It was on the set of *Blowing Wild* that she first met Budd Burton Moss, who was introduced to her by Anthony Quinn. At that time Moss was working as the manager of his father's restaurant The Matador in Los Angeles. At one time his father was a film editor, and his maternal uncle was the Hollywood producer Sam Zimbalist. Budd studied theater arts at the Los Angeles City and State College and served in the Korean War. He was drawn to Mexico by his fascination with bullfighting, which had all started as a teenager when he saw Rita Hayworth in *Blood and Sand*.[36] It held a similar attraction for Ruth, who fell in love with the culture of the country so much so that several months later she returned to Acapulco for a three-week break with her husband. They often spent time with Quinn, who was another bullfighting devotee.

Producers at Warner were so taken with the Cooper-Roman teaming that they proposed a further project, *A Bridge in the Jungle*, based on a novel by B. Traven, which was a sequel to his classic *Treasure of the Sierra Madre*. However, the project came to naught at that time, and it was not until about 20 years later, after Traven's death, that a version of the story finally reached the big screen starring John Huston and Katy Jurado.[37] After finishing *Blowing Wild*, Roman had lots of intriguing offers, including the chance to go to England for *The Good Die Young*, but on that occasion her role went to Gloria Grahame. Around the same time, she was going to swap assignments with Grahame in the Cold War adventure *Night People* (1953) starring Gregory Peck, but Rita Gam filled in instead.[38] The movie was mostly filmed in Germany, and, once again, it may have been Ruth's fear of flying and the time factor involved in traveling by ship that prevented her from being the successful candidate for both roles.

Her dissatisfaction with her home studio reached a watershed with her experience on *Blowing Wild*, and, shortly after, she effectively secured her release from Warner Bros. It seemed to be a mutual decision that she was no longer indispensable to their plans, just as they were not to hers. From then on, she really hoped to branch out and do all the things that she had longed to do with no constraints.

◈◈ 7 ◈◈

"The sexiest girl
in town"

"I don't like lace and furbelows. I do like the
trim-as-a-sail appearance that puts men on their
guard."
—Ruth interviewed for *Modern Screen*, 1951

Hollywood in the 1950s was obsessed with appearance, and Ruth
was considered to have the ideal figure for the Atomic Age. At that time
the required look was for an hourglass figure *vide* Ava Gardner and
Marilyn Monroe, who were considered far shapelier than some of their
predecessors in the pre-war era. While Roman never reached the iconic
status of either, she was consistently one of the most popular young
actresses of the decade. Striking, raven-haired and voluptuous, she was
a pinup like all the other starlets, but one of whom great things were
hoped of her acting. Her time at the top was soon over, but, for a brief
period, particularly in the first half of the decade, it seemed that anything was possible for her and that she would fulfill her potential.

After she made a big impression in a run of films in 1949, she was
interviewed at length by Hedda Hopper, who appeared to genuinely like
her and found her refreshingly honest. The veteran gossip columnist
singled Roman out as one of the stars to watch in the coming year and
wrote of her: "The girl of whom I'm expecting most this year is Ruth
Roman. With looks, talent, drive, she has the potentialities of a great
star. Furthermore, she's daring and intensely ambitious."[1] After such a
buildup from an established and influential Hollywood personality, it
was no surprise that fulfilling that promise was a lot to ask, especially so
because she expected no less from herself.

Ruth was selected as one of the Stars of Tomorrow for 1950 in the
Motion Picture magazine annual poll. Numerous other accolades and

Glamor publicity shot of Roman in her early days at Warner Bros.

nominations came her way such as the Press Association award for the "Fastest Climb in International Recognition."[2] Confirmation that she had finally arrived came when she appeared on the cover of *Life* magazine for May 1950. This time there was no doubting her success because they spelled her name correctly. During the decade she regularly made the cover of digest publications, including *Quick* and *Tempo* as well as many international film titles such as the popular British *Picturegoer*, the French *Cinémonde*, the Italian *Bis*, the Japanese *Kinema Junpo Motion Picture Times* and the Spanish *Garbo* (see Some Collectible Magazines). Her newfound fame meant she was called on to endorse numerous products, and her image was most often used for marketing beauty items, such as Lux soap and Lustre shampoo. The adverts appeared in all the printed media, including *Photoplay* and *Modern Screen* as well as non-film releases. She also advertised the *Hollywood Special Formula* bread for dieters, made from eight varieties of flour and the same number of vegetables, which was low in calories. Her outfit in an ad for Chesterfield cigarettes was especially chic. Smoking was de rigueur at the time, and she was a heavy smoker herself for many years. Her preferred brand was Camel non-filter. Among other products, she extolled the merits of the Stereo Realist camera, made by the

An ad for Chesterfield cigarettes from around 1950. Like many at that time Roman was a heavy smoker herself, which contributed to her famously husky voice.

David White Company of Milwaukee. It was the most popular 35 mm 3D camera of the time and was advertised in the pages of such publications as *National Geographic* under the slogan, "The camera that sees the same as you."[3] The advertising was often directly associated with a particular film in which she appeared; for instance, she endorsed Stratocruisers for Northwest Airlines around the time of *Three Secrets*, as did her two co-stars. She featured on many trading cards of the day, including cigarette cards and bubble gum and confectionary brands in both the United States and across Europe, including for the Kane Co., A & BC and Monty Gum, among others. She was one of a particularly collectible set of Greiling cigarette cards from Germany issued in 1950. An unusual product with which she was associated was a set of playing cards with a western theme that on one featured her with James Stewart in a scene from *The Far Country.*

Although she had not set Hollywood alight, she had most definitely been noticed by those who mattered most, in other words, the audience, which was global. Ruth had a big fan following, described by *Collier's* as "one of the widest and most avid ... in the movie world." A leading newspaper in Venezuela voted her the "most striking film personality of 1949."[4] Always attentive to her fans, she received about 800 letters a month, and she read every one. She tended to read them in bed after learning her lines for the next day's filming. It was a surprise for her to discover that she was a big hit among college boys when she featured in several polls and was voted the ideal girl by 35 seats of learning. A fraternity of the University of Virginia even invited her to be their housemother for a semester, but she wrote to them to tactfully decline their

offer. A university in Texas voted her the girl they would most like to be pinned to.[5] The student scientists of the Acacia Fraternity of the University of Southern California were suitably inventive and elected her as having "The Most Attractively-Arranged Molecules in Hollywood."[6]

She was always popular among servicemen and regularly appeared in magazines such as *The Army and Navy Fun Parade* as pinup girl of the month. During the Korean War, marines were fond of naming hills after their favorite stars, with Roman among them. A group of marines in a machine-gun

Roman testing out some perfume samples in a publicity still circa 1952.

79

sector near Seoul even named one of their machine guns after her. One of the boys wrote: "She talks hard and fast and has never lost an argument, and she'll fight to the end and never give up."[7] Ruth took it all in good part. Her concern for servicemen saw her take up various campaigns on their behalf, for instance, when she heard about their difficulty in phoning home to their families or girlfriends. In those days it was an expensive rigmarole to phone from distant lands. Long before telecommunications were so advanced, a three-minute call from Boston to London in 1950 would cost around $12. Before the submarine cable was laid, prices were inordinately high. Her idea was to start a fund to help them. She was allied with several charities and good causes and took part enthusiastically in charity fundraisers for servicemen, for instance, the marine reservists and their families with the "Toys for Tots" drive. In October 1950 she was elected Sweetheart of the YMCA at its 18th annual celebration before 800 young members at the Hollywood Bowl.[8] The following year she was proclaimed Easter Season Girl by the National Society for Crippled Children.[9] As though to emphasize her wide appeal, some of her other accolades included Miss Printer's Devil and Miss Streamline. In addition, she made such a hit with the Ohio State players and fans during a Rose Bowl game that she was crowned their Football Queen for the year, having won 90 percent of the votes. Oddly enough she was also revealed as a subject of infinite fascination for the retired PhDs of the National Philosopher's Club.[10]

Her appearance was a frequent subject of animated discussion. A jury of leading hairstylists decreed her one of the 12 girls with the most beautiful hair in the world in a survey for *Modern Screen.* There were other frivolous polls in which she featured, such as the world's most kissable women or who had the best legs. In the latter category, the head of the famous Hoosiers Willys of Hollywood, a true connoisseur of gams, debated the issue and decided that Ruth had the "best legs of the half-century." She was once cited as having the most sensuous shoulders (coming ahead of Virginia Mayo for once, who was said to have the most devastating back). The judges on that occasion were the boxer-turned-actor Mushy Callahan and a lady who luxuriated in the mysterious-sounding mononym of Olga, who was described in her resume as a movie bra magician. While Mushy expounded his insights into character based on anatomy, Olga declared breathlessly that the sultry Roman's shoulders were "sheer drama in motion ... vibrant with excitement disturbing the senses and dilating the eye—hitting with

A-bomb impact."[11] Ruth for her part was nonplussed. "Whew," she remarked, "it's news to me."[12] After appearing on the most kissable female list, she had a bit of fun and concocted a tongue-in-cheek top ten of the most kissable males. On her idiosyncratic list, along with Yehudi Menuhin, Kirk Douglas and Milton Berle, were several surprises. She said of the runner-up Joe DiMaggio, "He has an innate boyishness," and described University of North Carolina football star Charlie Justice as "athletic but sweet." She was clearly impressed by men who made a success in public life, and there were several politicians on the list, which was headed by Vice President Alben W. Barkley, a name all but lost to history who nonetheless served as President Truman's deputy in his second term.[13]

Ruth had clearly been noticed by leading directors too. In the late 1940s, the veteran King Vidor recognized her as the harbinger of a new trend for the fuller figure, which he welcomed, in contrast to the vogue during the interwar years. He commented: "Take a good look at Ruth Roman, and I believe any man will see what I mean. She doesn't resemble a clothespin or a pogo stick. She looks like a—well, a woman." The look itself harked back to the hourglass figure of the archetypal Gibson girl of the pre–First World War. Vidor developed his theme: "Ruth is not exactly Rubenesque yet. But she has all the qualifications and all the fundamental curves. And her basic figure is a step in the correct direction."[14] Film critic George Raborn once rated her as the All-Time Best Female Figure in one of his many lists. It was not just prominent Hollywood denizens who had noticed her. Plastic surgeon

Roman on a glamor postcard which the studios issued in large numbers in the 1950s.

to the stars Dr. Robert Allyn Franklin commented that hers was a popular look for young aspiring models and actresses seeking to improve their appearance in his Los Angeles practice. Observing her from a dispassionate and purely analytical viewpoint, he declared her to be "a very interesting type." He concluded, however, that she was "comely and characterful not pretty."[15]

Roman worked with many of the leading costume designers during the glory years at Warner Bros., including Leah Rhodes (1902–86), Milo Anderson (1910–84) and Marjorie Best (1903–97). Rhodes was chief designer in five of Roman's films, namely *Always Leave Them Laughing*, *Three Secrets*, *Strangers on a Train*, *Lightning Strikes Twice* and *Starlift*. The Texas-born designer began her career as a window dresser in her native Port Arthur. She joined Warner Bros. in 1939 and studied under Orry-Kelly. In 1950 she went to Paramount and later worked at Universal. Among others she worked on *The Big Sleep* (1946) and *White Heat* (1949). Nominated three times for an Oscar, she won for *The Adventures of Don Juan* (1948). Perhaps her most memorable designs for Roman were those for *Strangers on a Train*, some of which, for instance, the slim line skirt and blouse, were popular as patterns on the Star label. The outfits Rhodes designed for her in *Lightning Strikes Twice* raised some eyebrows at the time for their masculine and sometimes daring look. A new creation was an evening gown adorned with a vest that had a plunging neckline which appeared to cause most of the controversy. Rhodes was innovative in borrowing from the male wardrobe for some items and was at a loss to explain the fuss. "It's just a plain little old white vest," she contended, "and quite like the masculine type except that it is slashed deeply across the top and hasn't any shoulders in it and not much of anything else, really except Miss Roman." So as not to offend Hollywood sensibilities too much she conceded that a scarf could cover her shoulders. "After all," she added with a wink, "we just want to electrify people, not knock them out of their seats."[16] Milo Anderson created some of cinema's iconic looks for leading actresses, including Joan Crawford in *Rain* and *Mildred Pierce*. He was involved in over 170 films, and his career lasted 24 years (1932–56), which neatly encompassed what many consider the golden age of cinematic art. However, he is little remembered today despite his contribution to costume design. He encountered Roman in *Mara Maru* and *Tomorrow Is Another Day*. By all accounts he enjoyed designing for her, and his simple and effective costumes accentuated her particular appeal and the requirements of the different characters she played. Anderson's creations for her were generally tight-fitting and used solid color, emphasizing the neckline and bustline with no need for accessories. Her vital statistics were 36.5, 26, 34. He eulogized about her as a gift to the adventurous designer, who could let loose with swags and frills. "Ruth is a stunning example of the full-blown, shapely woman of 1951—and considerably different from the clothes-rack ladies that used to be so popular." He enthused, "She will be the sexiest woman that the screen has exhibited since the time of Jean Harlow."[17] Other designers who worked effectively with Roman included Marjorie Best, who specialized in period costumes and was designer for a number of westerns. For Roman, she was involved with *Dallas* and *Blowing Wild*, both of which had a Spanish background. Ruth also had an opportunity to work with the great MGM designer Helen Rose on *Invitation*, which saw her at her best in some of her most stylish outfits befitting the poise of her character. Rose (1904–85) was nominated many times for an Oscar and won twice for her contribution to *The Bad and the Beautiful* (1952) and *I'll Cry Tomorrow* (1955), which proved that she was adept at working in both color and black and white. Roman's only direct encounter with Edith Head was while working on *Beyond the Forest* when she got to wear some stylish outfits as befitting her character recently returned from the city.

Off-screen, Roman was different from some of her fellow stars in that she was not too interested in fashion for its own sake. She disdained mink coats, which most women her age apparently craved, at least in Movieland. The outward trappings of fame did not appeal to her. Her preference was for clothes she felt comfortable in, regardless of how she looked, which was somewhat against the grain of what was expected of a glamorous 1950s star. "I like to wear strange little things," she admitted. "If I could dress the way I wanted to, I'd look real weird."[18] True to her personality she had definite opinions on the subject. She contended, "If a gal's built right she can look sexy in slacks, toreador pants, breeches, party dresses or a wedding gown. I wear slacks all the time around the house. They're comfortable. I even wear them to the local market and other shops near our house in Brentwood. And I haven't heard any complaints yet."[19] Her one indulgence was, of course, shoes, which she had in abundance. Although in private she had her own casual style, she wore what the studio gave her to wear for the most part and understood she had a duty to look spectacular all the time. At premieres and when arriving at the airport for filming, she would don the obligatory mink.

"It's expected," she once reflected. "Stars are supposed to have more imagination about clothes, and more money to spend on them." Left to her own devices she preferred to lounge around in jeans or a peasant costume, but, after hearing several negative comments on the grapevine, she began to realize that she ought to make more effort with clothes, even on her days off. When her name began to pop up in lists of Hollywood's worst-dressed actresses, she decided to do something about it. "I used to boast about how fast I could get dressed," she commented. "Now I take my time and plan my outfit and check every detail before leaving the house."[20]

In the time before rock 'n' roll took off it was the film stars who were household names all over the world, thanks in no small part to the studios' highly effective publicity departments. This got Ruth known worldwide, but she sometimes felt she had too much exposure in the early years. During the filming of *Lightning Strikes Twice*, students from Victorville Junior High descended on the location and almost engulfed her during a photo-signing session.[21] She was always attentive to fans and had a reputation as a happy autograph signer. Such things may seem unimportant, but they mean a lot to the fans. To outsiders it looked like an effortlessly glamorous life, with a marvelous salary and the world at one's feet. However, it was tiring, and she found it difficult to be "on" all the time before the cameras, which she felt were always rolling. The schedules were far from glamorous, and much of the day was tedious, involving a lot of standing around waiting for something to happen. She grew annoyed by reports that life was one long orgy in sinful Hollywood. "Believe me," she said, "I am not in the orgy business. Who can have an orgy every night when she has to be up at 5 a. m?"[22] Being so much in the public eye sometimes brought with it unwanted attention. For instance, in May 1952, a bizarre plot emerged to extort money from herself and Doris Day. A group of men planned to lure the two stars to a house where they were to be drugged and photographed in a scheme that would demand $50,000 in blackmail. Details of the plan came to light when George Owen Yoho, one of the men involved, refused to go through with it. He claimed that two of his cohorts tied him to the bed in his hotel room and fastened two sticks of dynamite on each hand. Yoho, described as a part-time actor, lost his left hand as a result.[23] The unlikely tale immediately sounded suspicious to detectives, and it transpired that the whole episode was a hoax of Yoho's design, with the aim of landing him a Hollywood contract. The idea had probably occurred to him when he saw *Starlift,* in which Day and Roman converse with "ordinary" soldiers in hotel rooms and hospital wards. When told of the case, Roman commented, "I feel sorry for that man and I've never heard of him."[24]

The real life of a starlet was far more mundane, or at least it seemed so to her. The schedule was demanding, not only at the studio for long hours, but, in common with all other stars and starlets, she was required to spend a lot of extra time on publicity. There were hundreds of stills to pose for, interviews to attend, and extensive publicity tours required to promote her films. She was accommodating to all and sundry. Some of the tours were long and must have been draining. For instance, to plug *Champion* she visited 15 big cities and to promote *Three Secrets* another nine. At that stage, she was charm personified and proved a popular guest with management and press alike, receiving a positive response wherever she went. The itinerary for the premiere of *Three Secrets* in Buffalo was typical of these events. There was a luncheon held in her honor at the Hotel Statler, where she was met by the Mayor Joseph Mruk. Later there was another reception at City Hall. In the evening she was interviewed at the premiere of the film, which was broadcast live on the local radio station. As often on these occasions she made several extra local trips under her own steam and took the opportunity to visit the Buffalo Veterans Hospital. There was some time off for sightseeing, and in interview she related how thrilled she was to catch her first glimpse of Niagara Falls.[25] In Pittsburgh, she impressed many of the locals with her refreshing forthrightness. Veteran critic Harold V. Cohen called her "the fastest-rising young star in Hollywood" and remarked of her visit to the city: "Ruth Roman captured some goodwill for herself and some pictures around town yesterday by dint of a lot of straightforwardness, a great deal of charm and an abundance of good plain talk about the business of movies in general."[26]

She accepted all publicity as par for the course in a movie star's life but did take exception to doctored photos of herself that were once published in a magazine. She even threatened to sue the magazine in question and remarked, "I've got enough curves of my own without somebody painting some on."[27] At times the press attention became too much, and it rankled her that she was frequently badgered when she was "off duty" so to speak. Her privacy was always important to her and became more so as the years passed. "Maybe I'm anti-social," she once remarked. "I'd walk into that studio and that was it. Ruth Roman the actress. I did what I was told to do. Outside the studio I was Ruth Roman, the citizen."[28]

In the 1950s there was a great deal of attention on an actress' appearance. Although Ruth had a comparable figure to Ava Gardner and Marilyn Monroe, she was never seen as a sex goddess. In her case many commentators picked up on her elusive wholesome quality which made an interesting and unusual counterpoint to her sexiness. At the same time, she seemed sophisticated, and her natural character did not lend itself to ingénue roles. She effectively bypassed the bobbysoxer stage altogether and could never have played the type of girl-next-door roles Jeanne Crain did, for instance. Initially it was maybe not her acting ability in *Champion* that caught the attention of many of the male members of the audience so much as the way she filled out a bathing costume. There was often a vulnerability about her that made her an interesting screen actress, but she required good roles that could use both aspects of her persona. Alas, few of the parts she was given allowed her the opportunity to showcase that talent to the full. Nonetheless, she did things her way, and in the confines of the time she made an impression not just for her looks but was appreciated for her wholehearted and consistent efforts as an actress. Moreover, she was popular with the fans because she always had time for them and proved a good ambassador for her profession.

❖❖ **8** ❖❖

Freelance

> "Motion Picture work is the best way to a liberated
> education that I can think of. I've learned more
> practical things through my screen roles than I
> could have learned in four years of college. Every
> new role brings me face to face with something
> different."
> —Ruth interviewed by Leon Cutterman, 1951[1]

In September 1953, after four and a half years with Warner Bros.,
Roman finally won her escape from the studio and went freelance. This
gave her far more scope to choose what suited her, and those years saw
her at her best in some fine roles. Of special note were *The Far Country*,
Down Three Dark Streets, *Joe MacBeth* and *Rebel in Town*. At the same
time as her career was going well, her personal life was not, and her
marriage to Mortimer Hall became irretrievable.

Warner Bros. knew of her dissatisfaction with them, and in an
attempt to keep her on board drew up a new contract for her in September
1953 that allowed her to make pictures for other studios, with an
obligation to do only one a year for them. Effectively, she had won her
release and gained the freedom to freelance. On leaving she reflected,
"I'm grateful to the studio. They gave me a build-up I couldn't have gotten
if I hadn't been under contract. I admit I worked hard. I did eight
pictures in one year."[2]

A number of studios immediately sought her out. RKO wanted to
hire her for *Glacier* with Ray Milland, but as it turned out the film was
never made. The great Italian director Vittorio De Sica first considered
her for the lead in his *Indiscretion of an American Wife*, but Jennifer
Jones took the role. Notwithstanding, De Sica still had plans for Roman,
and a script, tentatively titled *Romance*, was proposed but never actually
came into being. Another interesting but sadly abandoned idea was Nat

Wachsberger's *The Tigress* in which she would have starred as a true-life 18th-century pirate, Maria Conateri.[3] Several other European ventures presented themselves, and she was sounded out for the Italian production *Ulysses* starring Kirk Douglas, but a decision was later made to use all Italian actresses instead. One of the most unusual offers she ever received was the role of Lola in the Mascagni grand opera *Cavalleria Rusticana*. Considering she could not sing a note, it seemed on the face of it a nonstarter, but actually most of the actors were miming anyway, including Anthony Quinn who was dubbed by the great Tito Gobbi.[4]

Roman had one of her best roles as an independent career woman forging her way in the Klondike in the excellent Anthony Mann western *The Far Country* (1953). Publicity shot with James Stewart and Corinne Calvet (right).

8. Freelance

The golfing picture *Cupid Under Par* for Republic was one of the few comedies among all the offers she received, but even that was not realized in any form.[5]

As it transpired, her first freelance venture after leaving Warner Bros. was *The Far Country* for Universal International. This gave her one of the most satisfying roles of her career as Ronda Castle, a strong-minded, independent woman forging her way in a remote town in the Yukon during the Gold Rush of the 1890s. Newly arrived in the isolated frontier town of Dawson, she sets up her pitch at once, the Dawson Castle, selling food, provisions, tools to the miners, and anything else they might want. Before anyone knows what is happening, she is practically running the town, much to the chagrin of the decent citizens who are trying to build a respectable community. She also appears to be in cahoots with Judge Gannon (John McIntire), a sinister individual who seeks to have everyone in his pocket. Director Anthony Mann was a master of the psychological drama, and his raft of westerns of the period have proved to have lasting influence. He had the knack of drawing layered and above all believable characters, allied to a good story and a fine cast. Some of the same actors put in appearances in several of his others and were almost like a small stock company. Stewart was the mainstay of them all. Memorable in *The Far Country* were the character actress Connie Gilchrist, who made a redoubtable figure as the plucky innkeeper Harmony, and John McIntire as the controlling Gannon. It was a keynote of Mann's work that his smaller characters were no less significant than the stars. For all the star status of Stewart, those films were essentially ensemble pieces. Ronda Castle was a great character: ambitious yet human, strong yet vulnerable. She was probably one of Roman's finest roles, which she embodied to the full. The lively screenplay by Borden Chase displayed a decided flair for character dialogue. He gave the perfect weight to humor and tragedy. Witness the scene where Stewart first arrives in Dawson with his herd of cows, and Harmony rounds on Ronda, itemizing how she ruined the miners of other towns with her "bad whiskey and fancy women." It was a great confrontation between the forces of the honest, law-abiding townspeople and the new in the form of transients and exploiters embodied in the Ronda character. The locals all agree they are tired of eating "moose, caribou and bear" and furthermore complain that "them ain't young bears, them's old bears!" Chase was a frequent collaborator with Mann and contributed the scripts for both *Winchester '73* (1950) and *Bend of the*

River (1954). All those films shared the same strong feeling for character and were also imbued with a sardonic humor. For all the great skill of Mann, it was the combined effort of director, writer, actors and technicians who together created memorable cinema. Sometimes in westerns there was a tendency to emphasize the rather clownish aspect of comedy at the expense of a good story and credible characters. The Mann westerns showed a new way forward; they were intensely dramatic and psychological, but the humor was integral to the characters and flowed naturally from them and even in response to the dire situations they encountered. Filming took place in the majestic Jasper National Park in the Canadian Rockies. There was a memorable scene of an avalanche that was actually rather too close for comfort. The Columbia Ice Fields was an area regularly prone to such phenomena. The guide warned the party of 150 that all the power equipment needed at the filming location was likely to set something off along the route. Sure enough, there was a real-life avalanche that almost caught them unawares. Roman recalled, "Let me tell you—the earth trembled! It was all we could hear. I ran like hell over a glacier which was a stupid thing for me to do. But thankfully, it all stopped after about three minutes." She later described events, "When I started to do the scene, I did hear something. This was for real. I looked up and saw the ice above where we were starting to crack. Pieces of ice as large as a room started falling out. They told me I should run under it. But all I could think of was that crazy ice cube and I ran in the other direction."[6] In the avalanche scene, Mann wanted her to scream just as the ice began to cascade, but she refused because she did not think in real life that she would scream. The terrain was hazardous even for experienced climbers, such as Bruno Engler, who worked as the principal guide and advisor for the film. Engler remembered events somewhat differently, from the perspective of an outsider in the world of filmmaking. He saw her on a moraine separated from the others when the avalanche began: "Ruth Roman was alone yelling help, help. She fell on the rocks, on this moraine and the extras scattered. The director was the farthest of all. Holy doodle, he was flying across those crevices. So, I picked up Ruth Roman. I still have a card saying Thanks for saving my Life."[7] There was a legion of stuntmen, the unsung heroes of many a film, who certainly earned their corn in what was a challenging environment. A key element was the fine cinematography by the veteran William Daniels, which did full justice to the grandeur of the scenery. He started his career in the early days of motion pictures at 15 as an assistant cameraman and was perhaps most famous for the score of Garbo films he photographed.

Costume designer Jay Morley, Jr. (1918–97) designed the wardrobe for varied fare which encompassed *The Glenn Miller Story* and *The Incredible Shrinking Man*. His creations for Ruth in *The Far Country* were especially apposite. She had the figure that suited westerns and, as Milo Anderson once observed, could carry off swags and frills with aplomb. On screen her voluptuousness made a striking contrast with the bobble-hatted, pixie-like Corinne Calvet. Off-screen it was reported by gossip columnist Jimmie Fidler that Roman and Calvet did not get along. The trouble apparently began in a nightclub when they exchanged what he called "catty" remarks about the film.[8] The two women later played down the spat. When it was claimed that they were not even speaking to each other, Calvet remarked, "Of course we are speaking. We are not close personal friends, but we certainly speak."[9] Roman was annoyed by the reports, later commenting, "Every time there are two actresses in a picture who don't pussyfoot around each other, everybody thinks there's something wrong."[10] For some undisclosed reason, the film was first released in Great Britain in July 1954 but was held back from distribution in the United States for a full seven months until February 1955. It did well internationally and in America secured decent returns at the box office of $2,500,000. The canny Stewart opted for a share of the profits and realized about $300,000.[11] Stewart and Roman worked well together on screen, and the producers of the affectionate biopic *The Story of Will Rogers* (1951) had initially thought of teaming them as Will and his wife. The film was directed by Michael Curtiz. Stewart dropped out of the running, and Will Rogers, Jr., was signed to play his own father, at which time Ruth was still inked in for the wife role, but that eventually went to Jane Wyman.[12]

Warner Bros. had wanted Roman to star in *The Girl from San Francisco* in order to fulfill her outstanding contractual obligations with them.[13] However, Universal had more ideas for her too, and after the success of *The Far Country* planned to put her in another wide-screen Technicolor western, originally titled *Echo Canyon,* with Glenn Ford. By the time it came to the screen, it was recast with Joel McCrea and renamed *Black Horse Canyon* (1953).[14] Instead, she was cast as the girl in the middle with Van Heflin and Howard Duff in the adventure *Tanganyika* (1954). Set in Africa but filmed almost entirely in the studio, this old-fashioned Saturday afternoon yarn was directed in familiar, spirited

Ruth Roman

Italian lobby poster for *Tanganyika* (1954), directed by the veteran Andre De Toth. Left to right: Van Heflin, Roman and Howard Duff.

style by the larger-than-life Hungarian émigré Andre De Toth. Roman played a stranded schoolteacher who looks after two orphans who also get left behind and are forced to trek across the jungle to reach safety. She certainly had to rough it in some scenes, such as the one where she fell—or rather was dumped unceremoniously—in the water. The dunking was an indignity she had to endure several times until De Toth was completely satisfied with the outcome. Throughout, she was naturally convincing as a capable pioneer type, equal to all challenges thrown at her. While on the set, she indulged in one of her favorite pastimes of whittling, one thing at least that she had in common with Heflin. She had always been nervous and highly strung, particularly in her early days, and found that it helped her to calm down during the inevitable long periods of boredom sitting around waiting. "When I have a heavy scene coming up, I pick up my knife and a block of wood and whittle," she explained. "It creates the entirely blank mind needed before your entrance cue." She graduated from walking stick handles to more elaborate carvings such as a replica of the Eiffel Tower. During her stint on *Tanganyika,* she found time to fashion a likeness of Winston Churchill from an offcut of Philippine mahogany, which she had come across in the studio lumber room.[15] The film suffered from an artificial feeling and, although it was augmented by stock footage, was widely considered one of De Toth's weakest efforts. It proved fairly popular in the United States but made a negative impression in some other countries, especially those in sub-Saharan Africa, on account of its demeaning presentation of native races. It was banned outright in Uganda, and there were lengthy protests by 20 African students at a university in New Delhi, India. Those students were so incensed that they marched around Connaught Circus demanding the film be boycotted. They even camped outside the residence of the prime minister, Jawaharlal Nehru. He gave them an audience, and the upshot of the meeting was that the film was pulled in India.[16]

A new direction was indicated for Roman by her role in the film noir *The Big Knife*, with Jack Palance, Ida Lupino and Shelley Winters. Shortly before traveling to Europe, she was signed up by producer Robert Aldrich and spoke about how much she was looking forward to the prospect of working with them all. However, somewhere along the way the casting was altered, and Roman's role went to Jean Hagen. Roman traveled to Turin to film *The Widow* (1955) for Lewis Milestone, by then exiled to Europe because of his problems with blacklisting. However, she was later replaced by the British actress Patricia Roc. Roman was at the height of her popularity, and many intriguing prospects came up. When a movie version of the life of boxer Jack Dempsey was mooted, it was reported that his ex-wife Estelle Taylor expressly wanted Roman to play her.[17] In the event, and despite the great raw material of Dempsey's life, no such biopic was made until a TV movie appeared in 1983, the year of his death. Other putative projects which did not come to pass for Roman included *7 Rue Pigalle* or *A Matter of Life and Death*, which was to have been filmed in Spain. There was another Africa-set yarn, *The End of the Line*, with Rock Hudson. This would appear to have resurfaced as *Congo Crossing,* with Hudson switched to *Giant* by the studio in exchange for Virginia Mayo.[18]

Roman had a central role as the leading femme, who might or might not be *fatale,* in *The Shanghai Story* at Republic. A decent espionage drama, it concerned a group of American residents in China at the time of the Korean War who are kept under house arrest because there is believed to be a spy among them. Essentially a product of its time, when the Red Scare was at its peak, it was well-acted by a fine

Cover of the Exhibitors' Campaign Book for the Red China adventure *The Shanghai Story* (1954) depicting Roman with Edmond O'Brien.

cast of familiar faces headed by Edmond O'Brien as a doctor. He and Roman made a good combination. They both had a strong presence and made up for any of the film's weaknesses. She proved an ideal counterpoint to O'Brien's jaded doctor and gave a fine portrayal of a conflicted woman, mistrusted by her fellow Americans on account of her exotic background and her apparent liaison with the hated Chinese Major. Her costume was again a key to the character: the fancy evening gowns in which she sashayed down the hotel staircase while the dowdy ex-pats looked on and wondered out loud about the source of her wealth. The costume designer was an Oscar nominee, Adele Palmer (1915–2008), who had a long career stretching back to silent days. Her other creations for Roman's character included a jazzy gold and white number, and a full-length mink stole. Several lucrative product tie-ups were suggested to theater managers, including hair salons and jewelers, to emulate Ruth's style in the film. She wore ornate chandelier earrings with multicolored rhinestones, and in Britain the craze for pendant earrings was apparently at its peak. Other ideas for publicity included linking up with local Chinese restaurants and even staging a Mahjong tournament in the week before the movie was due to play at a given theater. Every angle for sales and advertising was utilized. For instance, one image showed Roman reclining on a pouf while wearing the earrings and modeling luxurious, quilted brocade slacks and mules. Each item was linked to a particular store, and even the pouf could be had from a furniture shop. Scottish-born director Frank Lloyd (1888–1960) had a long and distinguished career and was a double award winner. He started out in silent films as an actor in 1914 but soon switched to directing. Among his 135 credits, he showed great technical proficiency and worked in a wide variety of genres from Charles Dickens adaptations to westerns and romantic dramas. He had not made a film for several years but was persuaded out of retirement because of the "screenplay and cinematic possibilities" he recognized in *The Shanghai Story*.[19] Indeed, both writers involved in the screenplay were highly accomplished in their line. Stephen Gould Fisher (1912–80) was a popular pulp writer who was much in demand in Hollywood. He adapted his own novel *I Wake Up Screaming* into a successful film and wrote the screenplay for *Dead Reckoning* (1947), among other films. Unsurprisingly, *The Shanghai Story* had several elements of the pulp novel about it, such as strongly drawn characters, shadowy villains, a cartoon-strip quality, and a touch of the lurid, which was reflected in some of the posters. During his half-century as a writer in Hollywood, Seton I. Miller (1902–74) worked with many leading directors, including Michael Curtiz and Howard Hawks. Miller's highlights included *The Adventures of Robin Hood* (1938) and *Here Comes Mr. Jordan* (1941), for which he won an Oscar. Years later at the tail end of his career he co-wrote the horror *A Knife for the Ladies* which starred Roman. Alas, despite the great potential considering the track record of all involved, Republic did not appear to have confidence in *The Shanghai Story* and held it back from release for almost a year. When it finally hit the screen, it was castigated from practically every side.[20] Despite all its faults, the film does have some elusive appeal which is difficult to explain. It was probably best summed up by Leonard Maltin, who memorably labeled it "tawdry yet intriguing."[21]

Roman did fine work in an efficient thriller, *Down Three Dark Streets* (1954). The urgent, dramatic voice of the narrator, William Woodson, set the tone for this well-made documentary-style drama which interwove three cases that an FBI agent was working on before he was murdered. There were good performances all round from a group

Spanish poster for the highly effective FBI drama *Down Three Dark Streets* (1954).

of reliable players led by Broderick Crawford as the chief investigator. Joseph Biroc's clear photography made great use of the clean cityscapes, full of light and dark. Throughout, Roman's character was required to be on the verge of breaking down without going over the edge, which she did admirably. There was one scene in which she must meet her black-mailer in a graveyard at night, which might easily have been handled in a clichéd manner but was skillfully done with a minimum of fuss. All her conflicting emotions were expressed in her visage and demeanor, but it was done with subtlety and devoid of any hysteria. This grounded her portrayal and made it more convincing. She worked well in con-junction with Crawford, who had a similar down-to-earth approach. The climactic scenes at the Hollywood sign gave another perspective on an iconic landmark, all the base metal and bare wires behind the scenes dispelling the magic of the name. Director Arnold Laven made just a handful of feature films and enjoyed a long career on television. Some of his other big-screen ventures were similarly effective crime dramas in the film noir mode including *Vice Squad* (1953) and *Slaughter on Tenth Avenue* (1957). The original working title was *Case File: FBI* from a story by Gordon and Mildred Gordon. An earlier draft of the screenplay was objected to by FBI boss J. Edgar Hoover, who, in his letter detailing the problems wrote that as it stood it was "a blueprint for extortion." He spe-cifically took offense at the depiction of wiretapping, which he felt gave too much away of bureau methods and in short gave criminals ideas. He wrote, "You not only reveal the activities of the criminal, but also reveal the countermeasures taken by the F.B.I. ... portrayed in such a way as to make it easier for a future extortionist to avoid apprehension."[22]

Ruth's private life was often difficult in that period, as she tried to balance the demands of family life and her career simultaneously. Sometimes work interfered with her domestic harmony. There were times she declined work in order to put her marriage first. For instance, Celeste Holm attempted to persuade her to join her in the cast of *His and Hers* at the 48th Street Theater, but, although strongly tempted, she said no.[23] When Sidney Kingsley wanted her to star in his new play *Lovers and Lunatics*, she reluctantly turned it down because it would have meant being away from her family for the best part of a year. In New York, she had some lucrative offers of radio shows but again rejected them because she was unable to get anyone to look after her infant son. She also maintained that her husband was all in favor of her continuing her career. "I like to work," she stated. "I wouldn't be happy if I didn't.

My husband approves, and he thinks it's wonderful."[24] There were times she appeared to want to get away. She accepted an offer to go to Turin at short notice to work on *Desert Desperadoes* and spent over three months there. By September, Mort declared that he had waited so long he was going to Italy personally to bring her back. Such long absences put a strain on their marriage, and, after she returned, the couple came close to splitting up. They reconciled and things seemed to go well for a while. In October 1954, she commented rather cryptically, "If we ever were happy, we're happy now."[25] Their troubles did not go away, and in March 1955 they had a trial separation, at which time Ruth immediately instituted divorce proceedings, citing cruelty.[26] However, shortly after, they got back together again.

On screen, she was keen to assert herself in different roles from those that she had been given during her contract days. Increasingly she wanted to be seen as a sex symbol and began to accept more roles that accentuated her physical attributes. She spoke of her frustration at some of the parts she had been assigned: "I tried to get sexy roles for years, but everybody said I was a 'great' actress and ought to concentrate on my acting ability—not on my 'figger.' I made a lot of money doing just that, but the woman inside me hasn't enjoyed it one bit!"[27]

In some ways the Anglo-American co-production *Joe MacBeth* (1955) gave her the best of both worlds: a good acting role which she could reinterpret in a sexy way for the Atomic Age. However, as a modernization of Shakespeare's tragedy *Macbeth*, the film presented something of a missed opportunity, especially so considering that it had been almost a decade in the planning. An interesting cast was headed by Paul Douglas as a gangster who wants to be kingpin but not as much as his wife Lily (Roman) does. Much of the filming took place at Nettlefold Studios at Walton-on-Thames, a famous name in the history of British cinema. Unsurprisingly, Roman caught a chill while filming some of the scenes at dusk near the Thames in her nightdress. Several familiar faces turned up, including Sid James, Bonar Colleano and Gregoire Aslan, who all did sterling work in support. For once an authentic American ambience was maintained, especially in the scale of the house by the river and the New York apartment house set. Fans of the immortal bard would enjoy seeing how the different characters and key scenes of his classic play were handled. However, Douglas was arguably a weak choice for the lead; he was too bombastic at times and approached his role in a straightforward way when it called for nuance. An early contender

A striking Italian poster for *Joe MacBeth* (1954), which gave Roman an excellent chance to shine as a modern-day Lady Macbeth in an intriguing twist on Shakespeare's classic tragedy.

for the part was Lew Ayres. Roman's role was somewhat circumscribed because it felt that so much of the emphasis was on Joe. Nevertheless, she was splendid within the confines of Philip Yordan's curiously disappointing script. She gave a modern twist to one of the great characters of literature, and it certainly caught the imagination to see Lady Macbeth floating around in a bikini. Ruth believed the lady had sex appeal; otherwise, she could never have snared the top man. She gave several interviews in which she expounded some of her ideas and observations about the role: "A girl who could make Macbeth do the things she made him do, must have had something. You know, they had sex in those days too."[28] She revealed that she had been brushing up on the bard on the journey to England and had been reading *Hamlet* as well as *Macbeth*. It was reported that she was hoping to visit Stratford-on-Avon during her stay in the country in order to get the atmosphere. At first, she was worried that the press would take offense at some of the liberties done to the national hero, but she found that by and large they took it in good part. Ever after she cherished a cartoon of herself as Lily Macbeth toting a gun, that appeared in a newspaper. Director Ken Hughes displayed some interesting touches, but overall arguably lacked the requisite vision to do full justice to the project. He was a serviceable director of low-key B-films such as *The House Across the Lake* (1954), based on his own novel. He had first made his name for several of the earliest and best episodes of the popular series *Scotland Yard.* Later he graduated to more varied fare, achieving his greatest success in the following decade with *The Trials of Oscar Wilde* (1960) and *Chitty Chitty Bang Bang* (1968). There were some genuine pieces of inspiration in *Joe MacBeth*, such as the character of the flower seller/fortune teller as the embodiment of the three witches, and the appearance of the ghost of Banky in the banquet scene was effectively handled. The scene by the river at night where Lily's desperate ambition becomes fatal was one of the best in the film, which she handled beautifully. The Thames never looked so eerie. Publicity material stressed the story was only inspired by *Macbeth*, but, in a sense, it fell between two stools. The outline and general plot were similar but differed in crucial details, and the result was thus dissatisfying both to Shakespeare devotees and modern dramatic fans alike. Oddly enough, it was banned by the censor in Singapore on the grounds that it was "unsuitable," although no specific reasons were given.[29] One critic made the crucial point that despite its flaws, it would in all likelihood send many people to seek out the original text, probably for the first time. That, after all, was what its makers and she had hoped would be the result. As she remarked in one interview, "I want people to understand that though this is modern stuff, it is meant to introduce Shakespeare to folk who mightn't otherwise get the taste. You can say it's introducing 'culture with curves.'"[30] While in England she was interviewed by Ted Ray on his television show in which she spoke about working on the film and said the transition of the play into a modern crime drama was "a fascinating and worthwhile experiment."[31]

Furthermore, she felt that the role presented her with "the most interesting challenge to come her way" so far in her career.[32] Around the same time there was some discussion about a possible British television series to be produced by her husband Mort with Ruth as star, but that failed to materialize.

Roman also appeared in a short film about the founding of the State of Israel for the United Jewish Appeal. *Man on a Bus* (1955) featured Broderick Crawford as the bus driver and Walter Brennan among the assorted passengers attempting to reach their homeland through the Negev Desert during which the bus breaks down. Each in turn related their individual stories of why they were making the journey. Its strengths included a good cast and a decent script. Crawford's laconic narration set the tone, which was maintained throughout. It was a tale simply told and made its point with far more acuity and much less fanfare than the ponderous epic *Exodus* made five years later. Black and white gave it a greater feeling of authenticity and the look of a documentary. There was no denying the sincerity with which it was presented. Director Joseph H. Lewis had a good career and made some influential movies, including *Gun Crazy* (1950) and *The Big Combo* (1955). *Man on a Bus* also had something of a film noir atmosphere, particularly with the unspecified sense of menace. Writer Stephen Longstreet was a successful author in several genres, including fiction and nonfiction. He wrote *The Jolson Story* while under contract at Warner Bros. A respected journal dedicated to its target audience judged *Man on a Bus* to be "fairly effective, both technically and story-wise" and praised the film for its "sheer entertainment value."[33] Freelancing had proved beneficial in more ways than one to Ruth. Not only did she find more varied roles that she enjoyed, but by January 1956 her salary had increased by 25 percent.

The Bottom of the Bottle (1956), sometimes known under the title *Beyond the River*, was a decent drama which utilized all the technology that CinemaScope could muster and was directed by Henry Hathaway. Joseph Cotten starred as a respected lawyer whose bad news brother (Van Johnson) suddenly appears out of the past to threaten his position in the tight-knit Texan border community. Roman played Cotten's young and disillusioned wife. The wide-screen treatment for once helped with character development, and the vast interiors of the ranch spoke for the gulf between them all. This was especially true when Cotten and Roman were discussing the parlous state of their marriage. Early titles included *The Intruder* and even *The Wrong Man*. The screenplay was adapted from a tale by Georges Simenon and was based on his experiences during the time he lived in the area in the late 1940s. Director Henry Hathaway made the picture as a favor to his friend Charles Feldman in order to fulfill the contractual obligations of producer Buddy Adler. Unfortunately, Hathaway felt he had compromised his standards for once and let it be known that he was disappointed with Adler's casting decisions. Hathaway was especially critical of the choice of affable leading man Van Johnson, who was usually cast in lightweight, boy-next-door roles. He did not consider Johnson convincing as a desperate ex-con and was also unhappy with the other choices for the leads, namely Roman and Cotten.[34] Jean Peters was the first choice of 20th Century, and Dana Wynter was among those tested, but on balance it was a good, sympathetic, dramatic role for Roman, and she was suitably impressive in conveying her character's profound disillusionment. Several leading film journals praised her conviction.[35]

When Virginia Mayo was first assigned to play the bad girl Boston

Roman enjoyed her role as the archetypal saloon bad girl in *Great Day in the Morning* (1956), a fair western directed by Jacques Tourneur. She (right) tries to attract the attention of the stranger in town (Robert Stack).

Grant in *Great Day in the Morning* (1956), she said she was tired of the same roles and opted to play the good girl instead. She later admitted that she regretted the move.[36] However, it meant that Roman was cast in the role Mayo had rejected and it fit like the proverbial glove. The story was set in Colorado on the eve of the Civil War and used a good script by Lesser Samuels, adapted from the novel by Robert Hardy Andrews. On paper, the project sounded promising, and any film directed by Jacques Tourneur was always worth watching. Unfortunately, this was one of his least satisfying films, although it was difficult to say exactly why. The actors all played their parts well, and the reliable Raymond Burr managed to breathe life into yet another formulaic heavy role as Jumbo Means, which gave him next to nothing to play with. Mayo and Roman did what they could within the confines of their respective parts, but the film arguably never really caught fire despite spirited support from Leo Gordon as an agitator. It was beautifully shot by William Snyder in full Technicolor and Superscope at locations in Silverton in Colorado, which passed for 1860s Denver. Moreover, it was fairly popular at the box office. The film had an interesting perspective on war and explored the notion that humanity could prevail whatever happens. Tourneur declared that he was personally dissatisfied with the film, which had to be truncated from the original source material of the novel to fit the studio's required running time.[37] That would most likely account for the feeling that the story was rushed somewhat, and the final third of the film especially so. Roman highly rated the costumes she got to wear, which she called "gowns that will make Gina Lollobrigida blush"[38] They were designed by Gwen Wakeling, whose career spanned five decades and encompassed biblical epic *The King of Kings* (1927) and an Elvis movie *Frankie and Johnny* (1966). Roman also mentioned in an interview that she would be doing some singing in *Great Day in the Morning* using her own voice for the first time in her career. She had taken singing lessons over the years on the off chance that she would one day land a part in a musical. However, there was no singing in evidence in *Great Day in the Morning.* She did play a few tunes on the piano during a tense card game, and at one time entered carrying an accordion but never got around to playing it. Neither leading actress appeared to be first choice of the producer, Edmund Grainger, and both Grace Kelly and Shelley Winters were sounded out. Richard Burton was approached to play the role of Owen Pentecost that went to Robert Stack. Mayo and Roman were always great value and shared some good scenes to cherish in which they were once more at loggerheads. Off stage they got along well. The famously forthright Mayo once gave her pithy, honest assessments of her fellow players and said of Roman that she was "a lovely woman, great actress."[39]

A far less trumpeted but infinitely more quietly impressive work was *Rebel in Town* (1956). Shot in monochrome, this curiously undervalued western felt at times more like a film noir. Set just after the Civil War, the tragic tale of an accidental shooting and its dramatic repercussions featured an excellent cast headed by John Payne, Roman, and J. Carrol Naish, who gave convincing and rounded portraits. Nora Willoughby was one of her best but least-known characters in whom was reflected the human response to tragedy. Here was a strong woman of a different kind to others she had played. In a sense she loses what she loved the most, and yet she keeps the family and, by extension, the wider community together by her actions in the wake of the worst kind of personal tragedy a family could suffer. Payne usually played amenable

Rebel in Town (1956) was an intelligent, underrated western which featured fine performances all around from a top-notch cast. Left to right: Roman, John Payne and Ben Cooper.

characters on screen but proved a revelation as the embittered, former Union army major-turned farmer. The screenplay tapped into the long-standing, simmering resentment on both sides of the divide. Nora encapsulated the woman's experience, weary of her husband's inability to move on from the war and fearing they will never escape its shadow. Director Alfred L. Werker has often gone unsung, but he beavered away for many years from the 1920s onwards, making interesting films including the once highly regarded historical biopic *The House of Rothschild* (1934). His varied oeuvre encompassed *The Adventures of Sherlock Holmes* (1939) and a lesser Laurel and Hardy feature, *A-Haunting We Will Go* (1942). His race drama *Lost Boundaries* (1949) was nominated for two awards, including one at the Cannes Film Festival, and the semi-documentary-style noir *He Walked by Night* (1948), co-directed with Anthony Mann, was voted Best Police Film at the Locarno Festival. He made several efficient westerns, and *Rebel in Town*, one of his best, was his penultimate film. It provided a thoughtful insight into the nature of grief and forgiveness and was sensitively done. In many ways it had more in common with some of his police dramas, and yet its resonance was far wider. It might be classed in the same category as *3:10 to Yuma* (1956) in terms of cinematic style and approach and could even be considered in a line of descent from *Fury* (1936), *The Ox-Bow Incident* (1943) and *Intruder in the Dust* (1949), strong films that transcend genre. They had comparable themes of civic responsibility and personal integrity, and some were made against the background of the McCarthy years. Although *Rebel in Town* was only a second feature, the film did not go unnoticed at the time of its release when it was appreciated by a surprisingly varied audience. It was discussed in a distinctly positive light by the century-old *Catholic World* from a moral viewpoint.[40] And there was an interesting article which compared and contrasted the film with other similar westerns of the era in *The Commonweal*.[41] The cinematography by Gordon Avil underlined the noir sensibility. Early in his career Avil was associated with King Vidor and worked in a wide variety of films, including *Shield for Murder* (1954) and *Big House, U.S.A.* that stylistically had more in common with *Rebel in Town* than some of his westerns. The sparse use of music was another noticeable element, and even the theme song by the Crew-Cuts was not intrusive. The story played out almost like a fable. It was not predictable and was ably written by Danny Arnold, an actor and producer who mostly worked in television. Much of the filming took place near Hollywood at ranches in Woodland Hills and Thousand Oaks, where a special set was built including a ranch house, a corral and a complete town.[42] Costume designer Angela Alexander (1916–2011) spent much of her career in B-movie westerns but also worked on *Whatever Happened to Baby Jane* and *The Manchurian Candidate*. Her rather austere costumes for *Rebel in Town* were particularly appropriate for the somber nature of the piece and the serious but inspiring Nora. Surprisingly, the film was practically Roman's last big-screen western, and although she had chances for others, such as *The Marauders* (1955) with Dan Duryea, that project did not transpire for her. Nor did she win the coveted role of Kate Fisher in the classic *The Gunfight at the O.K. Corral* (1957), although the competition was stiff on that occasion.[43] *Rebel in Town* has often been overshadowed by the big-budget CinemaScope and Technicolor features that were prevalent at the time but purely on its own merits has consistently received fine reviews in the time since it was made. It gave Roman one of her best roles and was an ultimately moving film that may come to be valued more as the years pass.

◈◈ **9** ◈◈

The Box
in the Corner

"I'm just plain fed up with playing tragic heroines. I
need a good comedy, and television needs one too."
—Ruth interviewed, 1959[1]

From the early 1950s, Roman tentatively entered the world of television, which was for a long time considered a poor relation of all the other mediums. She was among several big-name stars to embrace the new technology, which encouraged others to do the same. Personally, she found that it gave her greater scope in a wider range of roles than she had been offered in her career to date. Although the pace and schedule were far more hectic, she enjoyed the challenge it presented. At the same time, her movie career was still going well.

Like many of her contemporaries, her attention turned to television as the studio system began to break down, and the quality of feature film material she was offered began to decline. Although the medium could trace its history in the United States as far back as the 1920s, it was not until after the Second World War that television started to become established on a nationwide scale with the mass manufacture of TV sets. By the early 1950s, it truly came into its own and soon began to outstrip radio in terms of popularity. Roman made her debut in 1953 on an all-star telecast to raise funds on behalf of a cerebral palsy charity, the first of several charitable broadcasts. She was also announced for various other projects which are not listed in her credits.[2] The following year she made her first appearance in a drama in "The Chase" for the *Lux Video Theater*. It was based on a book by Cornell Woolrich that had been made into a successful film in 1946. In many ways it was a safe bet for television, an excellent production with a good cast by a tried-and-tested author. In 1955, she starred in "The Lilac Bush" for the *Ford Theater*, which was perhaps more interesting in terms of television striking out in a different direction from that of film. The story concerned a woman who becomes unbalanced in her grief and believes that a bush is tied to the death of her son. It was a psychological tale of a difficult subject matter which was handled with sensitivity. At that time, Roman was cautious of too much exposure on the new medium and waited to see the audience reaction to the broadcasts before she accepted more offers. As it transpired, the reception was positive, and so she gave the green light to other projects in a similar vein. Before long, many of her fellow stars did the same, and television was setting the pace for Hollywood. In a second *Lux Video Theater* episode, "Panic," she was highly effective as a woman desperately trying to escape from an obsessive man (George Macready) who stalks her. Roman later said that her appearances on the show "boosted her professional stock."[3] Most of the productions at that time were for adaptations of well-known dramas. The *Producers' Showcase* anthology series for NBC was one of the most prestigious among the early television programs. Filmed in color, episodes were broadcast every fourth Monday between 1954 and 1957 and attracted a host of big-name stars of stage and screen, including Humphrey Bogart, Katharine Cornell and Margot Fonteyn. Roman had a prominent role as Luba, a confused party office worker and practically the only woman, in "Darkness at Noon" (1955). It was a significant feature-length production and one of the only filmed versions of Sidney Kingsley's play based on Arthur Koestler's influential Cold War classic. The book was first published in 1940 and set during the Stalinist purges of the 1930s. It dealt with Rubashov, a faithful Bolshevik who is tried for treason against the government and by the whole system that he helped to create. The excellent cast was headed by Lee J. Cobb, taking over at short notice from Claude Rains, who had played the role on Broadway. The veteran Oskar Homolka was also in good form as his old comrade Ivanov. Viewers and critics alike were impressed; many found it moving, and Jack Gould in *The New York Times* hailed the production's "provocative power."[4] Some noted that the play, with its claustrophobic dark prison sets and even darker psychological themes, was especially suited to television. Roman drew praise, although one reviewer noted that her style in the first part was similar to that of Katharine Hepburn. The same observer wrote, "However, she more than compensated for this with a gripping performance in a later scene dealing with her own interrogation and condemnation."[5] After the play, as a kind of postscript comment, the then Vice President Richard Nixon gave a brief pre-recorded talk about the dangers of communism, which, considering the eloquence of the foregoing, was generally considered unnecessary. The show was an important one in terms of the rising prestige of television and set something of a benchmark for quality. It was frequently nominated for and won Emmy Awards, including Best Dramatic Series in 1956. Of the total of 37 episodes made, several have since been released on compilation DVDs in black and white, but, unfortunately, *Darkness at Noon* was not among them.

In the third season of *General Electric Theater*, Roman appeared in "Into the Night" in which she and Eddie Albert played a couple on a weekend trip who unwittingly pick up two dangerous escaped convicts (Dane Clark and Robert Armstrong). It was an atmospheric drama directed in great style by Jacques Tourneur. His special expertise with night filming was noticeable. Much of the drama took place in the dark, and there was an evocative sense of time and place, for instance, with the settings of the remote roadside gas station. Roman got to work for the up-and-coming director John Frankenheimer in "Spin into Darkness," a teleplay that also starred Vincent Price, in the highly regarded anthology series *Climax!* The story centered on Roman as a woman with a big gambling addiction who goes to work for an alcoholic who offers her money to clear her debts while under the influence but sees things in a different light the following day. Frankenheimer made his name on television and directed many installments during the show's run (1953–58) before finding major success in the following decade with intelligent and influential big-screen political thrillers. Although some of the *Climax!* series have been released on DVD, "Spin into Darkness" has alas not known to have survived. Roman also did good emotional work in the short format (30-minute) dramas that proliferated at the time, including "A Letter from the Past" for *Celebrity Playhouse* (1956) and "He Came for the Money" for *Fireside Theater* (1958).

By common consent Roman did well in her roles but spoke of her frustrations with getting the same kind of parts to play as she had in films. "I'm just plain fed up with playing tragic heroines," she once declared. "I need a good comedy, and television needs one too."[6] It was her long-held ambition to prove herself in comedy, but apart from the odd guest spot such as in a skit on *The Red Skelton Show* as the Queen of Mars, she had found little outlet to realize it on television. "I think it would be a good emotional balance for me to do comedy on television and save my emotional outbursts for motion pictures," she remarked.[7] She pointed to the highly successful comediennes on television and how so few women had been anything other than hosts of their own show, with the notable exception of Lucille Ball. Speaking for herself she found working in live television a real challenge, and even rehearsals were difficult, particularly in some of the more intense psychological roles. "It's like group psychiatric therapy," she remarked. "The pace is frenetic, and you don't get any sleep for a week. But I'm such a crazy, mixed-up kid I love it."[8] She was always the ultimate professional and put a lot of effort into whatever she did. For instance, even for her dancing routines on *The Arthur Murray Party*, the choreographer on the show recalled that she worked the hardest of all the guests.

Television has always had its critics, who were particularly snooty about the upstart medium during the pioneering years. At first, it was often dismissed as the box in the corner and looked on as a passing fad. Several big-name actors disdained it altogether. However, she defended it, pointing out that it had something for everyone. For instance, although she hated making westerns, she admitted that she enjoyed watching them, and her son Richard was a big fan of The Three Stooges. Among the other highlights of her small-screen career was her turn as a visiting actress in the first series of the ever-popular *Bonanza* in 1959. She brought a touch of glamor to the role of Ada Isaacs Menken in "The Magnificent Adah" who was based on a real-life figure. Her arrival in town causes consternation with the sons of Ben Cartwright, who seem startled that their father might ever have had an old flame. She had fun in the role, and it even gave her the chance to act a bit of Shakespeare during the stage play scene, which she did to great effect. The first series of *Bonanza* was notable for being filmed in color and because stars were paid almost double the rate of other comparable television shows. Salaries were around $7,500 per performance, whereas most offered between $3,500 and $4,000. This was a conscious decision on the part of the program's makers in order to attract big stars and thus more viewers. Among the names in that first year were Ida Lupino, Jack Carson and Ricardo Cortez. The idea certainly proved successful, and the show got off to a splendid start. It ran for 14 series in total over a period of 13 years. However, all subsequent seasons after the first reverted to the lower pay scale in order not to blow the budget altogether.[9] Roman had a great opportunity to shine in a smart comedy classic with which she was familiar when she played Liz Imbrie in a well-received two-hour version of *The Philadelphia Story* (1959) on NBC. Oddly enough, Diana Lynn played Tracy Lord, the Kate Hepburn role. It must have been a curious experience for Ruth to act with the new Mrs. Mortimer Hall. Also among the cast was Mary Astor, with Christopher Plummer as Mike Connor. Ruth also took part in *At Random*, a late-night, open-ended discussion show in which a panel of diverse people sat around a low table and talked about anything that came to mind. The program was the brainchild of host Irv Kupcinet, always known as Kup, a columnist of the *Chicago Sun-Times*, and was broadcast live on WBBM in Chicago. His idea was for "variety, spontaneity, and a lively and sophisticated discussion."[10] It began at midnight and finished whenever the participants felt like it, often at about 3 a.m. Among the other guests on that opening show in February 1959 were Sidney Poitier, Congressman James Roosevelt of New York, and Sammy Davis, Jr. Subjects ranged from Hollywood, U.S. presidents, race relations, attitudes of foreign nations towards America, and the water table. Over the weeks and years, Kup would continue to try and assemble an unexpected mix of guests to generate lively debate. Among the famous names who appeared were Alfred Hitchcock, Jimmy Hoffa and Malcolm X. It ran for 27 years in various formats on different channels and won several Emmy Awards.[11] Essentially a low-budget production, it pointed to a new direction, and its revolutionary approach tested the boundaries of where the medium could go. The blueprint would be emulated many years later to memorable effect on British television in the Channel Four show *After Dark.* Certainly, by the end of the 1950s, television had proved it was more than a passing fancy, and before long the box in the corner moved into the center of the entertainment world. Filmmakers, the studios, theater managers and distributors were all concerned by just how far television was advancing at the expense of the movies. Some of the figures were alarming; for instance, it was estimated that weekly cinema attendance had fallen from 45,000,000 in 1957 to 40,000,000 in 1958. In Ruth's case, she had made such an impression in her first seven years on television that she was awarded a star on the Hollywood Walk of Fame in recognition in February 1960. Sadly, the powers that be failed to acknowledge her 40 years in cinema, which ought to have counted for something.

At the same time as her television career was beginning to take off, her screen career was going well and still seemed to promise much. *Five Steps to Danger* (1956) was an intriguing but overlooked Cold War

Pressbook cover for the appealing espionage thriller *Five Steps to Danger* (1956), pairing Roman with Sterling Hayden (right).

thriller which had more than a touch of film noir style about it. Sterling Hayden starred as a man on a fishing vacation whose car breaks down and is offered a lift to Santa Fe by a mysterious femme in the tantalizing shape of Roman, with no questions asked. The plot could have continued in the expected crime drama fashion but instead veered into espionage territory involving a search for a hidden transcript sought by the enemies of the state. Clever in its way, the meanderings of the story were made credible by the fine work of the two leads, who ensured the journey was an enjoyable one. There was great use of landscape, and lovers of period style would admire the cars and such details as the design of the roadside diners. Eagle-eyed viewers might recognize the 1956 Lincoln Premiere Convertible that she was seen driving. There was good use of contrasts, for instance, between the rural idyll of the fishing lodge to which the couple escape and the international complications of politics that encircle them. The scene in the philosophical judge's house was a highlight. Director Henry S. Kesler also wrote the screenplay, adapted from the 1948 novel *The Steel Mirror* by Donald Hamilton which had first been serialized in the *Saturday Evening Post*. Critics at the time lined up to lambaste the film, but it was no more outlandish than any other espionage yarn, and a good deal more engaging, not to say comprehensible, than most. Kesler made just a few features but showed a deft touch at times and later did sterling work on television. The cinematography by Kenneth Peach was notable for its crispness. His expertise was gained over a long career which practically began with *King Kong* (1933) and included the Disney animal adventure *The Incredible Journey* (1963), and he too worked extensively on television. Taken on its merits, *Five Steps to Danger* was undemanding fun. The two leads made an appealing couple, and the story of their growing romance kept the whole thing ticking along at a brisk pace with some suspenseful scenes along the way. Set designers took special pains to recreate interiors of nuclear power plants with all the paraphernalia of the Atomic Age. Roman showed her skill at portraying a possibly disturbed woman whose sanity is in question for much of the time. The film was first released in Britain in November 1956 but for some reason did not make its American debut until January 1957. Even then it did not get a great deal of attention because it never found its way into many of the bigger movie theaters. It has only been in the years since that it has been rediscovered to an extent thanks to its issue on DVD and especially in the restored version on the Blu-ray format, but even now it is something of a forgotten item from the Cold War era that deserves to be seen again by all those who enjoy classic films. It would make a good subject for comparing and contrasting with contemporary efforts, such as *Shack Out on 101* (1955), which was, if anything, even more far-fetched but no less appealing for all that.

❖❖ 10 ❖❖

Disaster at Sea

"Actresses are always being asked to give their advice on dozens of subjects. I have worked pretty hard learning how to do my job, but that certainly hasn't qualified me to give advice on love, fashions, or how to bake beans."[1]

For Ruth, 1956 was a far more dramatic year off-screen than it was on. After almost six years of marriage, she secured a divorce from Mortimer Hall and entered into a third marriage shortly after. She was aboard the luxury liner SS *Andrea Doria* with her young son when it sank off Nantucket in an incident that made headlines all around the world and which caused her to re-evaluate her life.

Her marriage to Hall had been rocky almost from the outset, and they had numerous trial separations and reconciliations over the years. They separated for the final time in November 1955, at which time she commented, "Mort and I have tried very hard to work things out, but we haven't been able to. There are no hard feelings. It's just that we both feel we would be happier separated."[2] There was inevitably some acrimony that was reflected in court, which heard how he often belittled her in front of her friends. Her longtime friend Janet Stewart described how this upset Ruth so much that she would flee from the room in floods of tears.[3] Ruth said her husband would go away for long periods without saying where he had been. "If I questioned him, we'd have a violent argument," she related. "He told me I was stupid and said he wished he'd never married me."[4] Divorce proceedings were instituted in March 1956 on the grounds of mental cruelty. Hers was sometimes described as a "quickie" divorce. She was given custody of their son, Richard, then three and a half, and awarded $500 a month in alimony. Among other requests she also sought permission to resume the name Roman afterwards. Hall quickly obtained a Mexican divorce and married another

114

actress, Diana Lynn. Ruth soon started dating again after her divorce, and her name was linked with several men, including the actor Brad Dexter, ex-husband of Peggy Lee. There was also a much-publicized romance with the Bulgarian count José Dorelis, a 60-year-old perfumier who wore a monocle and was once married to the socialite Dolly O'Brien. For several months Ruth was seen around town with the singer Michael Rayhill. There was even talk of marriage. However, she spent most of her time with Budd Moss, and it was a near tragedy that brought them ever closer together.

In July 1956, she was traveling on the Italian luxury liner SS *Andrea Doria* on its journey from Italy to New York when the ship collided with a Swedish liner, the *Stockholm*, off Nantucket Sound in darkness and fog. Ruth had joined the ship at Cannes with her son and his nanny, Mrs. Grace Els. Blithely unaware of the catastrophe afoot, Ruth was dancing in the Belvedere Room at the time of the collision. It was gala night, and the party was in full swing as everyone was celebrating the end of the journey. People were exchanging contact details, and Ruth and others were singing a boozy chorus of "Arrivederci Roma." Suddenly the collision happened. "It was just like an explosion. Like a very big firecracker," she explained.[5] Everyone knew something terrible had happened and immediately went to their cabins, as she did too. It was hard not to think of the sinking of the *Titanic* 44 years before. However, she said that there was no mad rush or sense of panic. She kicked off her shoes and ripped her jax dress at the sides so she could move more freely. In many ways she surprised herself with her own calmness and sense of purpose; in her double cabin 82–84 she got into her life jacket and helped Dickie and Mrs. Els into theirs. All the while she chivied Dickie along with the story that they were all going on a picnic. When on the deck, she found a balloon and blew it up for Dickie, continually cajoling him with talk of the picnic. Eventually his turn for the lifeboat came, and he was lowered into one. He started crying, and she reassured him all would be well as she put him into the boat. She took to the rope ladder to make her way back up to fetch Mrs. Els. Unfortunately, the lifeboat set off before she was only halfway up the ladder. Despite her calling out to the crew, she could not attract their attention, and the boat left without her. Her last sight was of a smiling Dickie holding his balloon and talking about his picnic as the boat moved away. She was forced to return to the ship and, along with Mrs. Els, await another boat. The hours seemed to drag by, and all the time the ship was listing, and she was worrying about Dickie.

Mrs. Els was equally distraught but stoic. In time they finally got in a lifeboat from the *Île de France* and were taken to safety. Forty-six people lost their lives in the disaster. The ship sank in 11 hours. The *Stockholm* was not so badly damaged and managed to rescue over 500 of the survivors. After Ruth and Mrs. Els safely reached the shore, they went to the Warwick Hotel where Ruth waited for news of her son in a suite of rooms provided by her mother-in-law, Dorothy Schiff. Meanwhile, back in Los Angeles, Budd Moss had contacted her on the ship the day before but had not heard anything for hours. He heard purely by chance on the radio about the disaster and immediately made his way across country to be with Ruth, taking a nine-hour flight. He was on hand in New York shortly after she arrived and proved a great support to her at that time. Mort, still then officially her husband, did not go because he said he did not see the point in traveling there unless there was blood. His mother, Dorothy, turned up at the hotel, and there was a rather embarrassing encounter between her and Budd. Budd was a tower of strength to Ruth, who was beside herself with worry. He comforted her and Mrs. Els, who was also badly affected by the whole traumatic experience. Eventually word came through that Dickie was safe and would be reunited the following morning at the quayside. After a fitful night's sleep, Ruth made her way to wait for her son on the shore, and those photos of her and the other relatives being reunited were all over the newspapers. For his part, Dickie thought it was all a great big adventure and was only sad to lose all his toys, but he was soon given some more toys in his own special case. In what was still the age of the great ocean liner, the *Andrea Doria* sinking made headline news worldwide. It was one of the top five news stories of 1956. There were numerous lawsuits launched, but the question of blame was never entirely established. It would appear there were navigational errors made on both ships. Despite her near miss, Ruth never lost her faith in the liners and always preferred to travel by sea rather than air. In retrospect, what stood out to her most about her experience was the strength of character and sense of calm among the passengers and crew during the whole ordeal. She remembered the small acts of kindness by such people as a waiter who took time out to heat milk for the little children, and the many unbidden kindnesses of total strangers. Above all, she was reassured by the resolution and resourcefulness of people. It reaffirmed her faith in humanity.[6]

In the immediate aftermath of the incident, the opera singer Eleanor Steber, whom she had known previously in Europe, invited Ruth,

Left to right: Roman, Moss and the singer Eleanor Steber at Long Island shortly after the *Andrea Doria* disaster, 1956 (courtesy Budd Burton Moss).

Budd and Dickie to stay with her and her friend Mitch Miller at Long Island. Eleanor had a friend through whom they found a lovely house on Cape Cod where they stayed for a while. It was a wonderfully relaxing time for Ruth after her recent trauma, and Budd recalled their time there fondly when they took walks along the beach together with Dickie.

Everyone knew about the *Andrea Doria* incident, and they were kind and concerned about her. When they met people in the local shops, they were all respectful of her privacy and just wanted her to know how happy they were that she and her son were safe. Ruth was especially touched by a letter she received from the great writer and stage actress

Moss and Roman during their honeymoon, Portofino, Rapallo, Italy, 1956 (courtesy Budd Burton Moss).

Cornelia Otis Skinner, who had a beach lodge nearby where she often went to retreat from the world and work on her plays. The letter was hand-delivered by her husband Alden Blodget. Skinner invited Ruth and Budd to use the lodge whenever they liked. They took her up on her thoughtful offer, and despite the lack of amenities—the place had no electricity—they loved the house on the beach where they spent many idyllic hours. Budd recalled it ever afterwards as one of their happiest times together. For Ruth, the *Andrea Doria* incident was a real turning point. She began to see things clearer and re-evaluate her life. As a consequence, she and Budd became ever closer. He was there when she needed him most and helped her through the trauma of it all. She was keen to finalize the divorce with Hall as soon as possible, which was finally granted on October 14, 1956.[7] For Ruth and Budd, their priority then was to marry. Budd was 26, seven years her junior. His father owned The Matador restaurant in Los Angeles. His parents were uncertain about his marriage on two counts: the fact she was a Hollywood actress and especially on account of the age gap. Budd reassured them that everything would work out fine.[8]

Ruth had long wanted to travel and particularly desired to explore Europe. As far back as 1951 she had been invited to London by Laurence

Roman and Moss (third and fourth from left) at their wedding reception with unnamed guests, 1956 (courtesy Budd Burton Moss).

Olivier and Vivien Leigh for the Festival of Britain. Her fear of flying had often prevented her from traveling, and at that time she was in the midst of her Warner Bros. career, churning out films. She did get to visit France in 1955 when she finally fulfilled her ambition to see Paris from the top of the Eiffel Tower. Keen to renew acquaintance with the old world, she wanted a honeymoon to remember, and in November 1956, she and Budd booked a passage to Europe on the *Beranger,* a Norwegian freighter. They had hoped to be married on board ship by the captain in the truly romantic fashion beloved of old movies, but the law as it stood prevented him from doing so. Failing that, they decided to marry at San Cristobal. Out of the blue, they were invited to wed at the Panama Hilton Hotel in Panama City as the guests of Anne Henriquez, who had met Ruth in Europe some years before. Anne was the daughter of the owner of the Westphal-Larsen line in the city. There was a festival atmosphere that morning as the ship was greeted by an escort of tugboats blaring their horns and shooting out spray. The Panamanians gave the happy couple a day to remember, and there were many guests waiting to meet them on their arrival at the Hilton. At the wedding ceremony itself on November 8, 1956, the vice president of Panama acted as the official witness.[9] The service was conducted in Spanish and English, and everyone did all they could to make it a joyous and memorable occasion. Afterwards, there was a short reception complete with a mariachi band and later a poolside party for 25 guests before Mr. and Mrs. Budd Moss rejoined the ship and continued their journey across the Atlantic to Europe.

Happy days in Spain: Roman with Moss and son Richard pictured at a bullring in Seville, 1956 (courtesy Budd Burton Moss).

10. Disaster at Sea

Their trip to Europe began in Belgium, from where they moved on to Paris and relished the sights of the city of lovers, enjoying trips down the Seine. The honeymooners spent Christmas and the New Year in Switzerland, where it was reported that Dickie would attend school. They traveled on to Spain and later toured the south of France, dawdling in Nice, Cannes and Monte Carlo. In Italy they visited Rome, Portofino and Rapallo, among other cities, then returned to Spain. Ruth especially loved Spain, and they felt so much at home there that when the chance of a short-term lease on a three-story house in Madrid came up, they immediately said yes. They even found a wonderful nanny for Dickie called Mercedes, who became indispensable to them. Ruth and Budd spent a lot of their time with the great matador Luis Miguel Dominguez and his wife and saw hundreds of bullfights. The spectacle and intense drama of the bullring was something which appealed to them both. At one stage, Budd even tried to become a bullfighter. He was closely instructed by Dominguín, but despite all his training he soon discovered how hard it was to master. It was something which took years of practice. "He was a noverillo, not a matador," explained Ruth helpfully, "but he wasn't very good at it."[10] All he got for his trouble were some bruises the size of dinner plates that he could feel for ages afterwards. Had he continued he would surely have risked serious injury. Wisely, he decided it was just as thrilling—but far safer—as a spectator sport.

Ruth did not neglect her career during her journeyings and indeed had several offers while in Europe, including a series for Italian television that would be dubbed into Spanish and sold to the North American and British markets. That particular idea did not come about. Personally, she found European men far more romantic than her countrymen and had special praise for the Italians. As she commented during the Venice Film Festival, "Let's give the Italians their due. They've made a national pastime of flirting and they've polished their technique to a degree our men have never approached."[11] During those years she traveled all over and visited many countries. Her travels broadened her outlook, and combined with her experience on the *Andrea Doria* she felt she had gained a new perspective on life and particularly on herself: "I realized that I was too impulsive," she reflected. "I admire the reserve of the European women. From them I learned that I could enjoy listening as well as talking. I think that's a step toward maturity." Ruth and Budd tarried around the Mediterranean, and at one stage they chartered a yacht in which they explored the Aegean.

Moss and Roman at the premiere of *Five Steps to Danger* in Madrid, 1957 (courtesy Budd Burton Moss).

During her stay in Europe, she received an excellent offer from Nicholas Ray for the leading and only female role in *Bitter Victory* (1957). It was one of her more interesting entries of the later 1950s, at least to connoisseurs of the art of film, and she was especially flattered that Ray had sought her out, having been impressed by his *Rebel Without a Cause* (1956). The story of a wartime raid on Rommel's desert HQ, *Bitter Victory* marked her last starring role for some time. Shot in monochrome, most of her scenes were filmed at the Victorine Studios in Nice. There was some location work in the Libyan Desert, but she was not involved there. The film has gained a large reputation thanks in no

122

small part to Jean-Luc Godard's eulogy in *Cahiers du Cinema*. Godard wrote, "It is not cinema; it is more than cinema."[12] The Franco-American film had an international cast and employed several British actors. In addition, it was shot with the cooperation of the British army and a military advisor, Col. C.F. White, DSO.

Budd recalled several entertaining episodes during their time spent filming in Nice. One time the cast and crew were invited to a night out at Le Krazy Horse, a small-scale, backstreet nightclub/strip joint in the

French poster for *Bitter Victory* (1957), which had a sometimes troubled making but has come to be regarded as one of Nicholas Ray's finest films.

old port area of town. It was a night to remember, or forget as the case may be. Budd described it as a terribly tacky show and said the whole experience was like something "straight out of a bad Fellini movie."[13] The girls entertained in their own inimitable way in the small, sweaty club, dancing provocatively and performed a striptease act to martial music played loud and brassy while the customers ogled them and guzzled champagne. Both Curd Jürgens and Richard Burton were in their element, especially Burton, who grandly announced to the girls backstage after the show that they must all come out to the studio tomorrow where he would get them parts in "his" film. Surprisingly, they took him up on the offer, arriving promptly at 9:00 a.m. at the studio gate. After a long wait, Burton eventually appeared and managed to placate them—as well as the studio guard. During the following week Burton entertained each one of the girls in his dressing room, giving strict instructions that they were not to be disturbed because they were working on the script.

The making of the film has frequently been characterized as difficult by some of those involved. It was a long shoot on location in trying circumstances, and everyone became fractious after being cooped up together in one place for too long. Burton was frequently bored

Moss and Roman at the Hotel Splendido, Portofino, Italy, 1956 (courtesy Budd Burton Moss).

and drinking, and once he even got into a fight with Nigel Green over nothing in particular. Screenwriter Gavin Lambert placed many of the problems at the door of the autocratic Producer Paul Graetz and his insistence on casting Jurgens. In the early stages of planning, Ray had envisaged Burton as Brand with Moira Shearer as his wife and Montgomery Clift as the captain. The casting of the German star Curd Jürgens has frequently been criticized, but he was a good actor adept at roles of a psychological nature. Changes were constantly made to the script as it was ongoing. Ray also became disillusioned with the film as time went on. Much of the revival in its reputation was on account of European reviewers, who took to it from the first, led by Godard. The film had a limited release at the time. It was shown in selected cinemas in France and Britain and was premiered at the Venice Film Festival, in August 1957, which Roman attended personally. It was one of 15 titles nominated for the Golden Lion award that year but lost out to Satyajit Ray's *Aparajito* (1957). The version of *Bitter Victory* that most audiences viewed suffered a number of cuts according to Nicholas Ray, who said the British distributors insisted on losing 11 minutes, mostly in the last part, so cutting the running time down to 90 minutes. Another version lost about seven minutes.[14] In whatever version, it did not make its American debut until March 1958, but, even then, bypassed most movie theaters and is as a consequence far less well known in the United States. Only in recent years has it come to wider attention with its release on DVD and Blu-ray. Nick Ray specifically asked for Roman, perhaps with an eye to the American market; she was then at the height of her fame, and he told her how much he admired her work. Budd noticed excellent chemistry between Burton, Ruth and Ray as they worked without fuss on their scenes. *Film Bulletin* praised the "poignant and trenchant performances" of the three leads.[15] There was arguably something lost in translation from page to screen that made the finished picture rather less than engaging to some observers. Many blamed the international approach that weakened its attempt at realism, feeling that Jurgens in particular was miscast, whereas others felt that everyone was miscast and even the original idea of using Clift would likely have seemed puzzling. Any criticism of Roman's contribution carries far less weight considering how little she was required to do. She was seen at the beginning and end, but the main body of the movie was centered on the personal conflict between the two men and its philosophical discussion on the definition of bravery. In truth, few of the players involved

were satisfied with their part in it. Christopher Lee, who appeared as a
sergeant, reflected this general dissatisfaction when he later wrote that
the actors finished the production "in the certain knowledge of having
shared in a failure."[16] Time has proven his observation to be only partly
the case, and it was on balance a qualified success. It was Ruth's last
starring role of the 1950s, and it would be another five years before she
returned to the big screen.

Instead, she continued her perambulations around Europe, with
Budd doing most of the driving. Her son, Dickie, was reportedly fluent
in Italian, French and Spanish by the end of their long sojourn. Their
aim was for him to continue his schooling in America on their return.
By the time they did go back to the States, at the tail end of 1957, she had
several offers awaiting her, and *Seven Is for Sinners* was trumpeted as
the film that would entice her back to movies. The Mexican-set court

The Italian-made, religious-themed *Desert Desperadoes* (1959) took several years to reach the screen and is today her most elusive title. A scene
showing Roman with Akim Tamiroff as the wily merchant.

drama would likely have co-starred her with a young, up-and-coming actor Robert Horton, but the idea was not realized.[17]

Her last released film of the 1950s was *Desert Desperadoes* (1959), an Italian-made biblical picture which was known as *La Peccatrice del Deserto* in Italy and *The Sinner* in Great Britain. It was directed by the Hungarian Steve Sekely, who went on to direct a fair version of the John Wyndham sci-fi classic *The Day of the Triffids* (1962). Filmed at the Fert Studios in Turin and on location in Egypt, the making of *Desert Desperadoes* was a saga in itself, and it actually took over five years to reach the screen. Production began in June 1954 but after a few months stalled for a while because of financial problems. Filming started again, and Roman was called back to shoot more scenes several times. Prior to her long stay in Europe in 1956 she was required to stop over in Paris to work on extra scenes with co-star Akim Tamiroff and also to dub the film into English. The finished movie was set to premiere in 1957 but was not finally released in the United States until 1959. Even then, it had limited release. RKO was the original distributor but was itself in the process of ceasing business, and so distribution was put into the hands of States Rights companies in the United States.[18] After so much buildup, the film practically sank without trace outside of Europe. Much of the advance publicity centered on the risqué nature of the venture and the fact that it was just too hot for Hollywood. The emphasis was that this could only have been made in decadent Europe. Roman helped the cause with some of her statements, such as "My figure's always been sort of hidden but brother, it isn't in this picture."[19] At one stage it was even stated that the film was considered too hot for the Italian censors. Whether that was mere hyperbole, the publicity may have worked against the interests of the film in America because it did not get much attention outside Europe and even there received little fanfare. Ruth, for one, felt it ought to have stayed forgotten. It was made at the height of the biblical epic phase, the so-called "Sword and Sandal" craze. Besides Roman and Tamiroff, there were several well-known Italian names among the cast, including Otello Toso and Arnoldo Foà. Roman showed to good effect as an apparently helpless woman stranded in the middle of the desert, and the arc of the story showed the effect she has on those she encounters, particularly a Roman soldier and a wily merchant. Her character was of the typically slippery kind familiar from many a biblical fable. She and Tamiroff received all the praise going for their strong characterizations. The music of Mario Nascimbene was another appealing feature. The film was produced by Venturini and the U.S. producer John Nasht. It was Roman's last starring role for some time and a largely disappointing end to what was undoubtedly her finest decade in cinema. *Desert Desperadoes* has never been officially released on DVD and is probably her most elusive movie. She dismissed it as high camp, and the vibrant color posters put it in that category, although it was actually shot in black and white.

Ruth and Budd enjoyed their time in Europe immensely. They reckoned they had covered about 30,000 miles during their year-long travels. In an ideal world they would love to have stayed longer. American stars were increasingly looking abroad for steady work as the studio system at home was in the process of breaking down, and there was good money to be made in Europe. Many treated it as a tax break. For her it was a marvelous holiday, with the added bonus of an interesting role in a Nicholas Ray film. In some ways the time she spent away from America was another setback to her Hollywood screen career, but she was less concerned about that, having found a greater sense of perspective. Many stars gravitated to Europe at that time but found that on their

Roman and Moss enjoyed traveling in Europe for over a year. In a small bistro in Paris, 1957 (courtesy Budd Burton Moss).

return they were out of circulation and the good parts failed to come their way or were offered instead to upcoming players who were on the spot. By then television was coming into its own. As the 1950s ended, so too, effectively, did the big-screen careers of several established stars. The 1960s would prove a tough time for many who had been around 20 or 30 years. Roman, in common with most, concentrated on television, and, as a result, her cinema career was effectively over. After 1957 she made only nine films, most of which failed to trouble the scorers.

❖❖ 11 ❖❖

Triumph on Tour

"Ruth Roman, Bronx accent and all, is an appealing Gittel, capturing the quicksilver moods of
the character, so brash and worldly-wise as to the
seamier side of Manhattan, but underneath all tenderness and yearning and childlike in her poignant
simplicity."[1]

Ruth and Budd returned to the United States in December 1957,
after well over a year in Europe. As compensation for her declining
screen career, the decade nonetheless ended on a personal high for her
when she found unexpected success on stage in a year-long nationwide
tour of the hit play *Two for the Seesaw*.

Hitherto, her theatrical career had been negligible, but she jumped
at the chance to do something different and challenging. She had several
offers of Broadway successes and was invited to New York to watch all
three of the possibilities and decide which one to choose. Budd accompanied her. As far as she was concerned, there was no contest as soon
as she saw William Gibson's *Two for the Seesaw*. The story of an unlikely
love affair between a repressed and depressed Nebraskan lawyer and a
dizzy ex-dancer from Brooklyn had been a runaway success since it was
first produced on Broadway starring Anne Bancroft and Henry Fonda.
Bancroft was a close, personal friend of Roman and knew it would suit
her. They were similar in some ways and were often offered the same
roles during their Hollywood careers. More often than not, Bancroft
had lost out to Roman. Bancroft was even convinced that when she first
auditioned for the part of Gittel, Ruth would get there ahead of her. The
two were comparable, but Bancroft had a far more successful and substantial career, particularly on stage. Once she was given the script,
Ruth could not wait to get going. Budd recalled: "Ruth, Arthur Penn and
producer Fred Coe spent the next three days working on the script. On

130

the fourth day, Ruth and the stage manager got up on the empty stage and ran the play, stopping and starting a dozen times. Finally, Arthur Penn said, 'Let's run the last two scenes of the play again.' I was sitting quietly in back of the theatre in a very dark section.... God, Ruth was good. In such a brief time, with a script in hand that she barely needed to look at, she had the play almost memorized ... and with a perfect accent right out of the Bronx. When they finished, Ruth and Arthur walked backstage and sat there for another twenty minutes. Director Arthur Penn walked out and said to Fred, who was sitting alone in the third row.... 'Let's call Marty Baum and tell him that his client Ruth Roman is going to Chicago!'"[2]

She joined the National Road Company production in September 1958, which toured all across the United States and also went to Canada up until the summer of 1959. It was in many ways a demanding play because it had only a small cast and was essentially a two-hander, with William Lynn, and both actors were required to be on stage for most of the time. Ruth had nine costume changes but had less than 30 seconds off stage in total. At first, she found it exhausting but in time got used to the pace and enjoyed the experience immensely. It was a hectic tour during which they visited some cities for a week and others for two weeks. Many venues were sold out, such as Milwaukee, Philadelphia and Detroit. The performance was given twice a day, matinee and evening. Budd and Marie Cote accompanied Ruth for some of the time, and Cote frequently acted as childminder to Dickie. It was an exciting time for Ruth, who was carried forward by the sheer momentum of the performance, the adrenaline rush of a live show, not to mention all the attention and acclaim surrounding it. The reception across the country was uniformly warm. In Oregon, Budd and Ruth took time out to do some fishing and gave tickets for the show to some of the people they met there who taught Ruth how to fish for sea trout. She was chuffed when she caught a three-lb. trout. In Pittsburgh, veteran drama critic Harold Cohen praised her honesty in the role and especially noted the way that after the first act she "comes brilliantly alive and her Gittel takes hold and rings true."[3] In the same city, Kaspar Monahan commented: "Ruth Roman, Bronx accent and all, is an appealing Gittel, capturing the quicksilver moods of the character, so brash and worldly-wise as to the seamier side of Manhattan, but underneath all tenderness and yearning and childlike in her poignant simplicity."[4]

Too often she felt the parts she played on screen were too tragic and did not have enough humor in them. The balance of wit and humor in *Seesaw* was one of the things she loved about it most. Above all she found the role of Gittel a gift, with its perfect combination of comedy, drama and pathos: "When will such a fabulous part for an actress be written again?" she enthused. "There is such a definite growth in the character, and how fortunate to be able to play her." Here was someone she thoroughly understood and could use her own personal experience to bring to life. "Gittel is someone I can understand, since I've known people like her. I was raised in a Jewish family myself. I always talked with my hands, anyway. They used to have to cut me down in the movies." The script they used was an altered version of the original, with the intention of bringing out more of the tragic aspects inherent in the piece. Ruth considered the ways in which her interpretation differed from that of Anne Bancroft. She said that Bancroft was "fun, fragile, more pixie-like" and that she was "more dramatic, earthier."[5] She got so used to using the New York accent that she found herself speaking that way in real life. The tour was a great personal triumph for her. Although she was frequently tired by the end of it, she came into her own in the role. The tour finished at the Biltmore Theater in Los Angeles, and among the audience were a great many of her old friends and peers from Hollywood. By then she was exhausted most nights and was relieved when it finally came to a close. Of the final night at the end of the long tour, Budd recollected: "The last performance had to be somewhat sad for Ruth and Jeffrey, but they played it like opening night. A great audience ... and Ruth got another standing ovation. The curtain came down and we all hugged and cried and said our farewells. I had picked up a couple of bottles of champagne and everyone promised that we would all meet again in Los Angeles for lunch or dinner in the near future ... we never did."[6]

To her great joy in Chicago, she was nominated for a coveted award by the Sarah Siddons Society. Established in 1952, the Society was composed of critics and devoted theatergoers and was named in honor of the famous 18th-century actress. Each year the award was given to the outstanding performance in a production in Chicago. Roman appeared at the Michael Todd Theater that season, and her name was on a long list of 47 nominees. To her great delight she won the award, which was presented to her by Hedda Hopper. She had remained on cordial terms with Hopper over the years, who seemed generally well disposed towards her, although they were only ever acquaintances and never knew each other socially. The award was a great achievement for Ruth and meant a lot to her because it was from the real doyens of theater. Roman was only the seventh actress to win the prize, following in the footsteps of Helen Hayes, Deborah Kerr and Shirley Booth.[7] Flushed with success, Ruth felt emboldened to take on more ambitious projects and hoped to get a chance at a Broadway play. It was reported that *The Fanny Brice Story* beckoned. All her time was taken up with the tour, and each night she was exhausted, more so as the tour progressed, of course. She had an offer for a film in Italy but turned it down because she wanted some time to recharge, but she was tempted by more local prospects, such as the chance of a play at the Palm Springs Playhouse for producer-director Eric North.

The original play of *Two for the Seesaw* had been a decided hit and ran for almost two years, not to mention the tours that ensued. There were several similar productions on the road at any one time. Film producers soon recognized the potential for a movie version, and in 1962 the Mirisch Company bought the rights to the play for $350,000. It was bought expressly for Elizabeth Taylor. Paul Newman was lined up for the male lead. The obvious idea was to cash in on their successful teaming in *Cat on a Hot Tin Roof.* However, Taylor was too tied up with *Cleopatra*, and so other actresses came into the frame, and Newman was also busy. Several big names were hopeful of netting the role, among them Debbie Reynolds. Even so, by the time Robert Wise was hired as director, the casting of Robert Mitchum and Shirley MacLaine had already been settled. Mitchum was clearly miscast as the buttoned-up conservative attorney, but MacLaine was the girl of the moment after her outstanding success in *The Apartment* (1960). It was that success which the film's makers hoped to cash in on and hopefully repeat. For all that, the movie version of *Two for the Seesaw* met with only qualified approval at the time and viewed now seems something of a period piece. The rather downbeat tone and lack of any real action meant that on balance it was probably best suited to a night at the theater and did not readily lend itself to the big-screen treatment. The spark was missing, that elusive electricity that can come only from a live performance. At almost two hours, it also tested the patience of audiences in what was still practically a two-actor play, despite the inclusion of supporting actors who were not in the original and additional scenes to attempt to open out the action. Nevertheless, it would have been an ideal project for Roman to have proven her acting ability. By then she was falling out of the reckoning where big roles were concerned. In her career she had learned to accept all her many disappointments, but after playing the role for the best part of a year to great notices, she could count herself especially unlucky that she was not chosen or seemingly even considered for the role. Gittel was someone with lots of flaws and contradictions but who was at heart a decent if misunderstood woman, and Roman knew her inside and out. Had she been cast in the movie it might have given her screen career a great fillip just when it needed it most, opened up new opportunities for her, and maybe even surprised the critics so much that they might have had to revise their opinion of her.

◈◈ **12** ◈◈

"Did you know Rod La Rocque?"

> "Nobody was falling down to say hello to me when I got back. My agent told me that in five years a whole new group of directors was on the scene. They thought Ruth Roman worked in silents or had dropped dead."
>
> —Ruth interviewed, 1967[1]

Boyed by her stage triumphs and constantly employed on television, Roman also made a few more films in the early 1960s. Her personal life continued to be unsettled, and the decade began with the breakdown of her third marriage.

In the early months of 1960, Ruth and Budd moved into different wings of the house they shared. By June, they separated altogether, and he moved out of the house the following month. Publicly she maintained that the split was amicable. "We made the decision four or five days ago," she said in July, "and Budd has moved out. There is no bitterness between us but I feel it is better for me to get a divorce."[2] He recalled events differently and related that things had been going sour for some time. The trouble arose just as he was beginning to establish himself as an agent in his own right, and he was naturally excited about the way things were happening. After getting to know one of the foremost agents in Spain during their stay there, he had first begun to find his vocation during the year-long theatrical tour of *Two for the Seesaw*. While Ruth was engaged in the play, Budd made the first steps into launching his own career. Before long, he was being sought out by many of the leading players of the era. Each evening, when he returned home, he was full of stories about his encounters with Frank Sinatra and how he had found work for Mia Farrow. His other clients on his growing

135

list included Cyd Charisse and Rita Hayworth. For someone who truly loved old Hollywood he was in his element. As he enthused about the way everything was opening up for him, Ruth was far less enthusiastic and asked pointedly, "That's great, but what have you got for *me*?" He contended that he had found her lots of TV work, but she said that what she really wanted was good roles in movies. "Where are the features?" she demanded to know. Her big-screen career was floundering, and he was not able to secure anything that suited her; either the parts were too small or for low-budget ventures that did not interest her. Sometimes she was required for only five lines of dialogue. She felt that she had introduced him to her friends and contemporaries in Hollywood and got him launched on the road to success but that he had not helped her in return. Matters came to a head when he missed a promised dinner engagement because he had been waiting around at the studio for Mia Farrow, who had turned up late. When he finally arrived home several hours later, he noticed smoke rising from the chimney. He had a feeling something was wrong because it was still summer. Inside, he found her ritually burning all his $500 bespoke Harry Cherry suits on the open fire. Each one had the trademark cherry red silk lining and had already been shredded prior to their incineration. He was completely stunned and watched speechless as the beautiful handmade suits were consigned to the flames. Later he remarked, "I guess it's over for us," to which she replied smartly, "Gee, whatever gave you that impression?"[3]

She filed for divorce but was further disappointed to discover that they were not legally married because of a technicality; she had not officially divorced Hall when she married Budd. Her initial reaction was, "Does that mean I don't even get any alimony now he's rich?"[4] In the end, the suit was changed to one for annulment, which was finally granted on August 10, 1960. Money became a concern for her, and in June 1962 she returned to court to try to get an increase in support from Mortimer Hall. He had since married the actress Diana Lynn and had several other children.[5] Under the original settlement, it had been agreed that she would receive $1 a year token alimony and $500 a month for support of their son, Dickie. She believed she had been tricked into settling for a deal that suited Hall in the first trial. In court she declared that her living conditions were considerably altered since then now that she was no longer married. She reckoned that she spent about $2,000 a month looking after the household and the menagerie, which included a cat, a dog and a parrot. In addition, she detailed how her earnings had fallen substantially in the previous five years from $79,637 in 1956 to $59,788 in 1961. Consequently, she calculated that she needed more for day-to-day expenses and specifically wanted payments to her son increased to $1,200 monthly to cover all her outgoings.[6] When asked about her current house at 1225 Cliff Drive, Laguna Beach, that she had bought in 1960, she contended that she "doesn't live in a shack" but that it was "not what you would find in Brentwood."[7] Visitors described it as a large, comfortable and well-appointed house. Hall's lawyer claimed that she was living too extravagantly and that $1,200 was far too much for a ten-year-old boy. He pointed out that Hall's income had also fallen to a level below hers. The judge ruled in Hall's favor, and Ruth did not get any increase in alimony. In the aftermath of the end of her marriage to Budd, her name was sometimes linked to that of others, including the stage actor Buddy Rudolph. Throughout the years she remained a close friend of Paul Davis, whom she had known ever since her time in New York. Ruth was not a heavy imbiber but was what Budd called a "two-scotch drinker." After that she became quite difficult. Janet Stewart and Eleanor Steber were two of her closest friends and drinking buddies whom she saw regularly at one time. Even in her heyday she was not a big partygoer, although she was occasionally spotted at informal get-togethers. One such was a golfing-inspired party given by Muriel and Abe Lipsey, friends she had known in Europe who frequently entertained. The party took place at the Garden Room of the Racquet Club where Roman was among the 30 or so guests who attended, along with Hedy Lamarr, who happened to be the Lipseys' house guest that week.[8] Ruth always helped friends out when they were down on their luck. For instance, in 1960 when Helen Walker lost everything in a house fire, Ruth and others, including Dinah Shore and Vivian Blaine, rallied round and helped to organize a benefit for her.[9] Budd was later engaged briefly to another actress, Carolyn Jones. He went on to great and much-deserved success in his career, and among his many serendipitous matches was that of Elizabeth Montgomery with her role in *Bewitched*.

Ruth's film career continued in desultory fashion. The pictures she made during the decade were on the whole rather low-key but gave an insight into some of the changes taking place in society during what would be a turbulent period. Offers trickled in for her. She was one of those considered for a leading role in *Sleeping Partner* by William E. Barrett, who went on to write *Lilies of the Field*, but nothing came of the idea.[10] After almost four years she returned to the screen in *Look in Any*

Jackie (Roman, left) flirts with Gareth (Jack Cassidy) in a scene from *Look in Any Window* (1961), a study in the ennui of the moneyed classes and a generation with a lack of moral direction or genuine interest in what their children were doing.

Window (1961), a curious period piece about dissatisfied rich people in suburban Los Angeles during a heatwave. The star was teen idol Paul Anka as a peeping Tom who wears a mask while spying on the neighbors, especially the nubile girl-next-door, Gigi Perreau. Roman played his bored and restless mother, with Alex Nicol as his dipsomaniac father and Jack Cassidy as her lover. It was promoted with several sensationalist taglines, including "The shades are open ... and their morals are showing!" Anka had first come to widespread fame with his number one song "Diana," which he followed up with numerous further hits. He was not known as an actor but brought a suitably oddball, moody quality to the role. The film was the only one ever directed by William Alland and was made on a shoestring—which at times was all too apparent. The screenplay was written by Lawrence E. Mascott, who mostly wrote for television and who was later nominated for an Oscar for one of his documentaries. His effort in the Alland film was largely lacking in humor, although some of the conversations between the two cops employed

12. *"Did you know Rod La Rocque?"*

to keep tabs on the shenanigans of the idle rich seemed unintentionally funny. Perhaps Alland's most famous but unknown acting role was as the reporter who tries to discover the truth about Rosebud in *Citizen Kane* (1941), unknown because he was never actually seen by the audience. He was mostly recognized for his work as a producer and as a writer of westerns and science fiction films. Among his credits, he was said to have contributed to the original idea for *The Creature from the Black Lagoon*. Despite its flaws, there was enough in *Look in Any Window* to suggest that Alland might have made some interesting films as director. The cast was well chosen. Roman in particular showed the requisite ennui of the disappointed woman of a certain age as though born for the role. The film was essentially the study of a dysfunctional family and by extension a critique of an increasingly dysfunctional society. There were several piquant scenes of acute embarrassment which revealed the characters as on the whole unpleasant and unsympathetic. Rather surprisingly it was shot in black and white, when the fashion of the time was increasingly for bright, if not garish, color. However, that decision was one of its strengths and lent the picture almost the quality of a documentary at times. Soon after the movie was released, Roman was tested for another mother role in *Flowers in the Attic* (1962), but that went to Gene Tierney instead.

On screen, Roman was next seen in a markedly different role in the obscure Spanish film *Milagro a los Cobardes* (1962), which translated as *The Miracle of the Cowards*. It was filmed in monochrome at the Estudios Ballesteros in Madrid, and although it took place largely in a dusty courtyard, clever use was made of limited sets on different levels. A philosophical religious piece, it might almost have been a television play. The story concerned a group of people whose lives have been affected directly and indirectly by the miracles of Jesus, who gather just as He is about to be put on trial. They want to rescue Him from the Romans, but they find that although the spirit may be willing the flesh is weak. An interesting idea, it was brought to life by a capable cast, and despite a tendency to wordiness at times, made its point well. Roman was spirited and almost Lady Macbeth–like in her portrayal of a disillusioned but determined woman who feels she still has the fire of youth but is surrounded by weak men. There were some discrepancies; for instance, Roman was not yet 40 when the film was made and was still attractive, so Javier Escrivá, who played her son, looked too old for the role and was in fact only eight years younger. Such minor considerations apart, the

Poster for one of Roman's least-known films, the thought-provoking *A Milagro do los Cobardes* (1961) made in Spain.

film presented a different kind of challenge for her and was interesting from that point of view. Such chances came along rarely at that stage of her career. All the actors were dubbed, and her voice was done by Mercedes Mireya, who, during her 20-year career, often dubbed for international actresses, including Alida Valli and Anita Ekberg. Mireya did well to capture the timbre and tone of Roman's voice and helped make the characterization successful. The film won two awards at the National Syndicate of Spectacle in Spain: one for its composer and a special award for the film itself. Writer-director Manuel Mur Oti was a fascinating figure of Spanish cinema who won many awards for his work over a 30-year period, beginning with *Um Hombre ya por el Camino* (*A Man in the Road*) (1949). Among his most noteworthy films were *Cielo Negro* (*Black Sky*) (1951) and *Fedra* (1956). The collaboration with Roman came about when Oti happened to be having dinner with producer José Luis Renado one day, and they decided, purely on the off chance, to give her a call. It so happened that she answered personally and accepted their offer at once. She was always happy for a chance to return to her beloved Spain, and during her stay she took the opportunity to take an extended vacation in Malaga. Oti had always admired her work and enjoyed working with her. He also noted that although she was not a fluent Spanish speaker, she quickly latched on to all that was being said and seemed to understand what was going on. He was extremely happy with the result and declared that *Milagro a los Cobardes* was one of his favorites among all the films he had made.[11] Alas, the movie had limited exposure outside Europe and even there made little impact. The appetite for religious subjects had markedly waned since the peak years in the late 1950s, and such philosophical treatments were never likely to find a wide audience. Nevertheless, *Milagro a los Cobardes* does not deserve its obscurity and would reward the patient viewer.

By the mid–1960s, her big-screen career had effectively ground to a halt. Hollywood always had a problem when an actress hit 40—a problem which men did not suffer. The sexist and long-held assumption that an actress was only worth watching if she was in a bathing costume still held sway, and good roles for mature women were few and far between. Roman was a good example. In the early 1960s she still looked great and by then knew her craft intimately. She had improved as an actress and was winning awards for her stage roles, not to mention acclaim for her television work. Like all those others of her generation, she ought to have been getting good offers from all over. Instead, her talents were left to wither on the vine, and her hard-won expertise was largely frittered away in some poor fare. Studios were just not making the kind of films that could use her qualities, or, if they were, they had forgotten her name, and she was by then probably considered as a television actress, as though the two mediums were mutually exclusive. Not only was the fare poor, but she appeared to have lost interest in her career as such. Her last film for almost a decade was *Love Has Many Faces* (1965), an attractively shot but ultimately empty escapade. Acapulco and Mexico City looked great, and the sea was a deep azure, all the bodies were bronzed and the outfits immaculate, but the scenario was preposterous. The story was supposed to be about the murder of a man washed up on the beach, but the screenplay almost entirely revolved around Lana Turner and Cliff Robertson lounging around on a boat or at a mid-century modern beach house attempting to be meaningful. Roman was chosen by producer Jerry Bresler for the role of Margot Eliot, the proverbial "older woman" looking for kicks and finding them briefly with the impossibly conceited, aging, gigolo Hank Walker (Hugh O'Brian). On some of the posters, her character was described thus: "Margot, she came to Acapulco for the auction where the 'beach boys' go after the highest bidder." Her friend and fellow lady-of-a-certain-age bidding at the said auction was played by Virginia Grey, with whom she had first appeared at the beginning of her career. Walker came across as too much of a caricature and the kind who give Americans abroad a bad name, particularly with his casual denigration of the Mexicans. Although supposedly much younger than Ruth, they were practically the same age, and with his weather-beaten face, he looked older if anything. Edith Head was the sole designer for Turner's gowns at the cost of $1,000,000. The rest of the cast had to fend for themselves in the wardrobe department, but at least they saved a lot of expense on shirts for the men. When Roman arrived for filming, she realized she had brought with her the wrong kind of clothes, so she went into Acapulco and bought what she thought was fashionable and that suited the character as she saw her. Turner, in full diva mode, was keen to ensure that the camera should be on her as much as possible and partway through production made known to the director her displeasure that Stefanie Powers and Roman were getting far too much attention. Hence, a lot of Roman's scenes were cut out, which pushed her further into the background. She always maintained that it was a bad movie. It seemed to promise more at the beginning, when Walker works his well-worn chat-up lines on the jaded but susceptible Margot: "Haven't I seen you around?" he says to her. "It's possible," she answers laconically, "I've been there!" Director Alex Singer was a schoolfriend of Stanley Kubrick and even worked as assistant director on *The Killing*. He made a few feature films as director but spent most of his later career working in television. In the light of this and some of his other films, such as *A Cold Wind in August* starring Lola Albright and *Psyche 59* (1964) with Patricia Neal, the critic Andrew Sarris wrote, "Perhaps Singer has become the poet of the rejected woman while commercially exploiting the subject of the fallen woman."[12] During filming Ruth was among the guests at a lavish birthday party given in Acapulco by Armando Sotres, an old amigo of Lana Turner. She presented Lana with a bouquet of flowers. The overall verdict on *Love Has Many Faces* was perhaps best summarized by Judith Crist who wrote, "For connoisseurs of perfectly awful movies."[13] For all that, Roman's own contribution had merit. Margot was one of her most exposed characters, well-drawn and human. There were several leading roles she could have played in the 1960s. However, memories in Hollywood are notoriously short, and it appeared that she was just not in the forefront of the minds of casting directors. Hence, the big movie offers just did not come along.

Television gave her steady work throughout the period, and she was a familiar face of the medium. At the dawn of the decade, she was lined up for her own series, *The World of Lisa Boston* for ABC. The premise announced that she would star as "the curious and intrepid editor of a women's magazine, who travels the world in search of material, accompanied by a conservative male photographer."[14] John Greene and Phil Shuken were the co-writers, both of whom were well-known names on television who were involved with several hit series. Greene was the creator of *My Favorite Martian* and wrote many episodes of *Bewitched* among others. Shuken wrote for *Mister Ed* and *The Beverly Hillbillies*. It all sounded promising, and the feeling was that it would give her career the new direction it needed. *Lisa Boston* was to have been shot on film and involve glamorous location shooting. Unfortunately, although the pilot may have been made, the promising idea did not materialize, and Roman never had her own TV vehicle. Instead, she had to make do with guest spots on the big shows of the time. She appeared in many of the staples such as *The Naked City, The Untouchables* and *The Defenders*. In *The Untouchables* episode "Man Killer" she was highly effective as a tough dame who tries to strike out on her own in her husband's cab business running narcotics after his untimely demise. In a typically engrossing episode of *The Defenders,* she impressed as a woman accused of murdering her abusive husband. The strong script was the work of Reginald Rose, and among the cast was a young Dustin Hoffman in one of his earliest appearances. Roman renewed acquaintance, in a roundabout way, with Hitchcock in the anthology series *The Alfred Hitchcock Hour.* In "What Really Happened?" she starred with Gladys Cooper and Anne Francis. The series began in 1955 as *Alfred Hitchcock*

Presents. It ran for ten years, and from the 1962 season it was renamed. Throughout the run, Hitchcock acted as host and producer. "What Really Happened?" was a disappointing, conventional courtroom drama that held little suspense and gave no opportunity for any of the leading actresses to shine. Roman also had the obligatory spot in the first series of the guest-heavy *Burke's Law* (1963), but she was somewhat lost in the crowd in a scene near a swimming pool. She had one of her best roles in an installment of the popular semi-anthology series *Route 66* as Alma Hawkes, a troubled woman just released from prison into a small, coastal community after a long sentence for murdering her father. The episode in which she appeared, "In the Closing of a Trunk," also starred Ed Begley as her bitter uncle and featured some excellent location work at Corpus Christi in Texas near the ferry terminal and along the Gulf of Mexico. It was a difficult part for Roman, who was poignant at times as the disturbed Hawkes, and she ably conveyed the tragedy of her character while generally avoiding hysteria. The role had originally been intended for Joan Crawford. The script by Stirling Silliphant and Herbert B. Leonard was first class. They handled the story and characters with intelligence and sensitivity. The writing and production values were of a consistently high standard throughout the series, which ran for four years on CBS (1960–64) with a theme tune composed by Nelson Riddle. The show's freewheeling format meant that it covered a wide spectrum of stories and unlike some shows was not confined to studio sets or to one city but involved a different location every week. *Breaking Point* was another interesting series that broached contentious subject matters. It was essentially a psychiatric version of *Dr. Kildare*, and each drama centered on an emotional crisis. Although it ran for only one season in 1963–64, it attracted many established stars and some stars in the making and proved to be influential in pushing the boundaries of TV drama in terms of what was acceptable for discussion. In "Who is Mimi, What is She?" Roman played a fading film star who has problems with an obsessive fan who lives vicariously through her. It proved an intriguing insight into the nature of fame, fandom and problems of self-esteem.

The competition for good television roles was surprisingly tough, and it was sometimes the case that new directors and producers did not remember who she was. Once someone asked her if she knew the old silent screen star Rod La Rocque, to which she replied smartly, "I haven't been around THAT long!" Hence, she had to effectively start at the beginning again and attend auditions, take lunches at studio commissaries and get to know the directors. Doing so brought dividends, and she was especially pleased to land a coveted role in the perennially successful *Dr. Kildare* in 1963. It was the first of two appearances she made in the series, both two-parters. The second was the following year in an episode titled, "A Candle in the Window," which was written by Rita Lakin and directed by Sydney Pollack. Roman played a nurse whose reaction to her husband's death surprises everybody. She was widely praised for her poignant performance that even made Pollack cry. He thought she was unlucky not to have been nominated for an Emmy, but the reason seemed to be a technicality because there was then no category for two-part stories.[15] She passed through most of the series of the time in which she did sterling service, including an installment of *Bus Stop* with Wendell Corey. She turned up as an aerialist in the circus drama *The Greatest Show on Earth* but as ever could not be induced to fly to the location shooting in Florida and preferred to take the train. She was reunited with Milton Berle as his long-distance wife in a seamy political drama, "The Candidate," which drew much praise for its honesty. She had a good role in an episode of *The F.B.I.*, which was concerned with a spy ring and a secret Cobalt Bomb, that also featured Gene Hackman as a fellow conspirator. Roman played a respected and much-loved woman in charge of an orphanage who is not quite what she seems to be. The part had been especially desired by Bette Davis. Among other highlights Roman had a sizable sympathetic role in a rather convoluted installment of *The Name of the Game* (1968) starring Robert Stack and featuring the veteran Victor Jory as a mafia boss. She also showed to good effect as a faith healer who believes she can help a sportsman regain his equilibrium in an episode of the perennially popular *Marcus Welby, MD* (1969).

In the middle of the decade, she finally landed a leading part in a TV series when she was cast in a regular role in *The Long, Hot Summer* (1965–66). She beat several other actresses for the part, including Gale Robbins. The premise sounded promising; the story was based on William Faulkner's homage to Tennessee Williams, with up-and-coming actor Roy Thinnes, herself, and Edmond O'Brien as stars. As Minnie Littlejohn she had a decent and prominent role as the longtime admirer and confidante of "Boss" Will Varner (O'Brien). For his part, O'Brien was full of praise for Roman, with whom he always enjoyed working. He had previously cast her in an episode of his own series, *Sam Benedict.*

He remarked perceptively, "As an actress, Ruth taps the right note; she can give it to you in color."[16] Unfortunately, *The Long, Hot Summer* was beset by problems from the beginning, which culminated in O'Brien dramatically quitting partway through the run, thoroughly dissatisfied with the way his role was being sidelined. He felt all the young characters were being given too much prominence. He was replaced by Dan O'Herlihy at short notice, but the writing was on the wall, and the series limped through to its end in the spring of 1966 before being taken off the air. Roman featured in 21 of the 26 episodes and gave a strong performance throughout. However, her character weaved in and out of the drifting narrative, which often lacked continuity. As time went on, she featured less often. In common with some of the other characters, Minnie failed to develop satisfactorily. More than likely there was not enough strength in the original idea to stretch to a series. The show has not stood the test of time and would seem to have disappeared without a trace. It has never been officially released on DVD and nor has it been considered important to Faulkner enthusiasts.

Roman contributed memorable performances to some of the popular fantasy series of the era, which gave her the opportunity to explore different kinds of roles. In an episode of the first season of the highly regarded sci-fi series *The Outer Limits* (1964) she played a scientist on a moon base faced with curious aliens that looked like huge eyes inside a globe. Despite the program's low budgets, the makers were inventive with special effects. For example, the eyes of the aliens were constructed from old New York street lanterns. Fellow cast member Tim O'Connor recalled that Roman turned to co-star Alex Nicol between takes and remarked wryly, "Isn't it wonderful to be a star!"[17] The series proved influential to a whole generation, and horror maestro Stephen King rated it as one of the best of its kind ever made. Espionage was another popular area for television in the Cold War era, and Ruth had a prominent role in an installment of the playful and innovative series *I Spy*, which starred Robert Culp and Bill Cosby as government agents. In "Let's Kill Karlovassi" Roman was the local bigwig who has a seemingly unpleasant assignment waiting for the duo. It was one of the best regarded episodes, not least for its cast, which included veteran character actor Walter Slezak as the seemingly affable engineer Karlovassi of the title. The man-of-the-moment British actor Peter Wyngarde played Roman's right-hand man in one of his few American appearances. In most of his roles Wyngarde was the dashing lead with all the women in his thrall, but in the episode Roman's strong character was in the driving seat, and the dynamic of their relationship was one of the main points of interest. The award-winning series was known for its lavish budgets and exotic filming locations, which this time took place in Greece. Due to her fear of flying, which she never overcame, she often turned down such work. However, she decided to make the journey the safe way, even if it was via the scenic route. She began by taking a train from Los Angeles to New York, thence a ship to Italy and from there a train to Greece. *I Spy* was never shown in Britain. *The Girl from U.N.C.L.E.* was a short-lived spin-off of the iconic series *The Man from U.N.C.L.E.* Stefanie Powers played the eponymous heroine, with Leo G. Carroll and Noel Harrison the other regulars. Although it lasted only one season (1966–67), the show attracted many big-name guests during its run, including such diverse personalities as Joan Blondell, Boris Karloff, and Stan Freberg. Roman appeared in "The Furnace Flats Affair" (1967) towards the end of the run and had fun as Dolly X, a villainess who can literally throw people about. It was all terrific period camp jollity, and the episode also featured a typically eccentric cast, including Peggy Lee and Percy Helton. Roman was often seen in such feisty roles at that stage, which she relished. Her guest spot in *Mission: Impossible* gave her a good part as a vain and power-hungry Eva Peron–type in a fictional Latin American country who hopes to pick up where her late dictator husband left off. The plot of "The Elixir" (1968) hinged on her overarching desire to look younger, but it was striking how attractive she still looked, particularly in the fresh and clean-cut color cinematography of Keith C. Smith and wearing the stylish costumes by the Swiss-born designer Sabine Manela. Manela worked on the program for three years and had had long experience prior to that in B-movies. Her input into the aesthetic of the show ought not to be overlooked. The hairstyles of Adele Taylor were another factor, particularly in the look of Roman's character, which those interested in the era's fashion would surely admire.

Although acting remained her one abiding interest, she was often torn about her motivation as she found more peace of mind away from the mad whirl of Hollywood and enjoyed her own company at Laguna Beach. "I walk on the beach," she reflected, "and don't even think about acting. Then a nice role comes along and I wonder why I don't act all the time."[18] She tried to keep in shape and practiced yoga every day but did not play sports as much as before. If she found she was gaining weight, she reverted to a buttermilk-only diet, which she found reduced her weight in a matter of days. In addition, she developed a yen for Chinese vegetables and sometimes experimented with high-protein diets.[19]

As an interesting diversion, she occasionally returned to the stage in road tours of several plays, including *Plaza Suite, The Killing of Sister George,* and *The Night of the Iguana.* In March 1965, her good friend Mercedes McCambridge fell ill and had to drop out of a University of Utah production of *Candida.*[20] At short notice, Roman agreed to take

Publicity photograph of Roman, who eased comfortably into character roles as the decade progressed.

her place and by all accounts did full justice to Shaw's assertive heroine. The play's director noted how patient and attentive she was to the partially student cast during rehearsals, giving generously of her time and experience.[21] A first-night critic commented, "Miss Roman demonstrates great range, grace and fluidity as the personification of the 'new woman' who manages the men in her life for their own good."[22] She expressed the hope that she might tour with the play and tackle other great roles such as *Medea.* This seemed to rekindle her interest in stage work, and shortly after she revisited her old favorite *Two for the Seesaw.* She received especially fine notices for her portrayal of Martha in *Who's Afraid of Virginia Woolf* with Wendell Corey during a fortnight run at Melodyland. Several critics noted how she took the essentially unlikable character of Martha and invested her with humanity. She also appeared with John Vivyan in *Beckman Palace* at the Ivanhoe Theater, Chicago, in August and September 1967.[23] Memories of her time working with Vivyan may not have been among her most precious. He complained that his female co-stars on stage were always jealous of his reviews and said that Roman was "the worst of them all."[24] Nevertheless, she was always a trooper, and even a car accident on the way to the theater one night could not prevent her from appearing. Ever the professional, she leaped from the burning wreck and made it to that night's performance as though nothing was amiss, so determined was she never to disappoint her public.

❖❖ 13 ❖❖

Whatever Happened to Ruth Roman?

"I'm really a hermit at heart and thoroughly disinterested in the Hollywood social scene. They pay me to act, not go to parties. I did all that years ago. And there are some things you don't want to experience twice."[1]

After a decided lull in her career, Roman returned unexpectedly to the limelight in the early 1970s in an oddball horror film. This led to a resurrection of kinds for her. During the decade, she was constantly employed on television to good effect in some of the best remembered programs of the age.

At the start of the 1970s her big-screen career remained in abeyance and she was seen far more on television. She appeared in several prominent TV movies, which were then becoming popular, including *The Old Man Who Cried Wolf* (1970). It had good production values and was one of the most highly acclaimed of its kind at the time of its release. Edward G. Robinson starred as a man who witnesses the murder of a friend (Sam Jaffe) but is unable to convince anyone else that it has happened. It was a solid thriller in its way with well-judged performances from a fine cast, particularly Robinson, and Martin Balsam as his loving son. Roman shone in her brief scenes as a barfly who latches onto Robinson in a pawnshop, airily assuring him that she knows all the men in the vicinity but not the women. The indifference and hostility of the city, even of schoolchildren and the police, towards the elderly was brought home forcibly, although the story itself descended into conspiracy theory and was ultimately improbable. There followed other thrillers in a similar mien, such as *Incident in San Francisco* (1971), which was set in the world of newspapers. It had a good cast, including other old timers such as Dean Jagger. About a year later producer Martin Gabel initiated a series based on the format but switched the location to a police precinct. Thus began *The Streets of San Francisco*, one of the best-loved TV series of the 1970s. Roman was listed among the cast of *S.R.O.* (1971), filmed in Dallas, Texas, starring Rosey Grier and co-directed by Rory Calhoun. The story of down-and-outs and drug addicts would appear to have been based on the novel by Robert Deane Pharr, but only a few sources make any mention of the film, and there is some doubt if it was ever completed or released.[2]

After an eight-year hiatus, Roman made a striking return to the big screen in the horror movie *The Baby* (1973). This genuine oddball entry in the genre took as its premise an extreme case of arrested development in which she played Mrs. Wadsworth, the mother of an adult man still treated like a baby. It was too disturbing to be considered comedy and nor was it intended as social comment. The director was Ted Post from a story by Abe Polsky. Post had a long career and first made his name on television, especially with countless episodes of *Gunsmoke* for seven years. It was while working on that show that he got to know Clint Eastwood and proved to be a major influence on the actor's career. The two often collaborated on features, including *Hang 'Em High* (1968) and most notably *Magnum Force* (1973). Post's other films of note included an influential critique of the Vietnam War, *Go Tell the Spartans* (1967) and *Beneath the Planet of the Apes* (1970). By common consent, *The Baby* is regarded as his most unusual and atypical work. He initially took a lot of persuading to get on board with the project. As he recalled in an interview: "I hated it when I did it ... my friend who was a social worker wrote it and he wanted me to do it. So, for two cents and a nickel we did it. And much to my amazement it won all kinds of ... things."[3] The story was written by Abe Polsky, who had also worked briefly in television. Rather more disturbing than the film was the fact that it was based on true-life events. Post had tried since at least 1968 to get his script produced, and although he eventually found a company who agreed in principle to do it, they encountered too many problems. The first hurdle was the controversial subject matter itself, which they did not think would find favor among the viewing public. The second was how to assemble a cast. Both obstacles proved too difficult to surmount, and the company pulled out of the project. At one stage the producers Hal Landers and Bobby Roberts announced that they intended to collaborate with the director William Castle on the project, but that too did not transpire.⁴ After some years Polsky persuaded a reluctant Post to get involved, and the film finally got the green light. At a film seminar in the 1990s, Post revealed that the original script was "so shocking that he decided to shoot the film in a 'flat,' realistic manner in order to defuse its exploitational qualities."⁵ Even by the standards of a 1970s' horror exploitation, *The Baby* managed to offend a lot of people at the time. Now it would most likely offend just about everyone, and it is hard to imagine that it could be made today. The whole idea of iconic actresses let loose in horror films was set in train by the classic *Whatever Happened to Baby Jane?* (1962) starring Bette Davis and Joan Crawford. That worked on so many different levels, as a knowing black comedy and pure Grand Guignol. However, often the ones that came after were essentially parodies of the genre. A swift follow-up *Hush, Hush Sweet Charlotte* (1964) reunited Davis with Olivia de Havilland. It proved popular, and filmmakers saw the potential in the notion and lo, the hag horror bandwagon was up and running. There followed a whole raft of similar fare of varying quality which put fading Hollywood stars through the horror ringer with such titles as *Straitjacket* (1965) and *Berserk* (1967), both of which starred Joan Crawford, whose career had practically gone full circle from the early days when she appeared in Lon Chaney pictures. Later there was *Whatever Happened to Aunt Alice?* (1969), with Geraldine Page and Ruth Gordon, and *Who Slew Auntie Roo?* (1972) starring Shelley Winters. They became increasingly exploitative and camp, not to say banal, but they appealed to the prevailing taste and are now considered genuine cult classics. It was curious that faded male stars were seldom subjected to such treatment. As for the actresses concerned, the films did little to halt the slide for them, rather the reverse—they hurried them along the downward path. The later careers of Davis and Crawford showed the law of diminishing returns. In contrast, some actresses did find more rewarding roles as time went on, and, if they lived long enough, they could enjoy several renaissances in their careers. Ruth Gordon was a case in point. She became known to a new generation with her appearance in *Rosemary's Baby* (1968) which re-ignited attention in her at the age of 72 and led to many more offers for parts in films that were critically acclaimed and are still talked about today, such as *Harold and Maude* (1971).

The Baby found its audience in the intervening years and would always appeal to those drawn to the truly bizarre. It must rank high in

13. Whatever Happened to Ruth Roman?

After many years away from the big screen, Roman made a remarkable return in the curious psychodrama *The Baby* (1973). Above: Roman at right, with, from left, Marianna Hill and Susanne Zenor as her two daughters.

the "hag horror" pantheon. Critics have often been at a loss as to know what to make of the film itself. With its cast largely made up of strong women, it has sometimes been considered a subverted parody of the so-called "woman's' films" of the Hollywood heyday. It might as easily be viewed as a cynical comment on the rise of the feminist movement. It is striking that although most of the personnel involved behind the camera were men, none of those men who were seen on the screen registered in any way.

Roman's performance as Mrs. Wadsworth was extraordinary by any standard. Here writ large was the monstrous epitome of all her disappointed women, a woman so let down by men that she refuses to let her son become a man at all. It was malignant mother love turned in on itself. Her costume was another important aspect of the character: the denim jeans, shaggy wigs, shapeless jumpers, garish colors and baggy kaftans, which were so redolent of that era. The initial visual impact when she first appeared on the verandah of the house flanked by her two equally disturbed daughters was striking. The costumiers employed on the film were Shirley Brewton and Frances Dennis, who had worked in similar low-budget ventures for most of their careers and excelled themselves in this instance. Roman's performance has frequently been called over the top and high camp, but those descriptions miss the true

153

essence of it. On the contrary, the key to her success in the role was that she played it dead straight. She admirably displayed what critic Richard Scheib accurately described as "a real malicious flintiness as the matriarch of the show."[6] Her conviction made the darkly comic moments all the funnier. It was all about her timing. Certain lines she uttered seemed incongruous, but because they were not played for laughs, they seemed funny in the circumstances. The film's ambiguity might be seen as its main weakness but could as easily have been its strength. In some ways it could leave an audience feeling queasy. The soundtrack by Gerald Fried created the right atmosphere, with the use of interesting contrasts such as the childlike lullaby melody played on music box chimes and the unsettling, sometimes startling counterpoints of menace from interjections on the cello and violin. A particularly memorable scene was Baby's birthday party, with the typically 1970s-sounding music in overdrive, which increased the sense of uneasiness if anything. Fried has had an impressive career, which began with a number of Stanley Kubrick films, including *The Killing* (1956). He worked extensively on television and was nominated for several Emmy Awards, winning for *Roots*. The soundtrack of *The Baby* was released in 2019 by Caldera Records of Germany and includes an audio commentary by the composer along with detailed liner notes.[7]

The Baby was in some respects not a horror film per se and nor was it truly concerned about the plight of the unfortunate title character. It was presented in such a way that made the audience complicit in viewing the Baby merely as a freak, to be treated in the same pitiless way as the freaks of old sideshows, even tormented by his sisters with cattle prods. It was ultimately this lack of humanity at the heart of the film that left viewers all the poorer. Ultimately, Mrs. Wadsworth could be seen in a different light, and at least she has some kind of attachment to the Baby. In the world it describes most of the cast are freakish; it is just a matter of scale. Ideas of normality are subverted. The anonymous period interiors of the Wadsworth house resemble something from a David Lynch set. A similar sinister feeling pervaded, a feeling of unease. There was no telling just what might happen in bland suburbia. This was a prevailing theme of the 1970s in many ways, *vide*, *The Stepford Wives* (1975). No one can say what might be hidden in those nondescript rooms. One of its other weaknesses was the distinct lack of any sympathetic character. The social worker (Anjanette Comer) ultimately comes across as even more unappealing than the Wadsworths, with her overly neat appearance and her unhealthy interest in the case. Marianna Hill, who played daughter Germaine, was an often-underrated actress who had a solid career on film and especially television. Involved in the entertainment business from childhood, she knew everyone, including Ruth. Hill remarked, "Ruth Roman was great because I remember when I was a little girl, she would come over to our house. She did a movie right down the street from my dad's ranch.... She was working nearby, and she would come over and hang out with mommy and have girl talk and so I knew her from the time I was a kid." Hill was drawn to the project because it was so weird. She remarked, "It was absolutely nutty, but so enjoyable."[8] After her remarkable return to the screen, Roman was inundated with offers. Predictably, these were all for similar roles. None of those that followed were as memorable or as oddly substantial as Mrs. Wadsworth. Along with all the other titles in the cycle, *The Baby* is now firmly established as a genuine cult classic. However, Ruth was heartily dismissive of it at the time and readily admitted that it was the one film of hers that she would gladly burn.

At first glance, her movies from the 1970s vie with each other for the title of the most dubious film. A run of low-budget horrors did nothing to enhance her reputation apart from show that she was game for anything. They did highlight the paucity of good roles for any decent older actress in the decade. From the outside it looked as though she had simply given up on her career altogether or maybe had seen the futility of it all. *The Baby* was quickly followed by *The Killing Kind, Impulse* and *A Knife for the Ladies* (1975). Ruth was apparently "entranced" by her role in *The Killing Kind*, although it is hard to see why. She played an attorney whom the psychopathic main character Lambert (John Saxon) blames for having landed him in prison for ten years. Roman literally went through the mill for her art, for her big scene where she was forced to drink a whole bottle of liquor while he exacted his terrible revenge. The director Curtis Harrington was dissatisfied with how it was coming out, and so she had to do lots of retakes, which required her to down several gallons of tea-colored water. Despite such difficulties she was apparently unfazed. As the press book commented, "A born trouper, Miss Roman made no complaint when her scenes shot until five o'clock in the morning for several nights in a row." The director must have had a sadistic streak because he made several other veteran actresses suffer ignominies, especially Ann Sothern, who was obliged to consume vast quantities of Dr. Pepper and popcorn, both of which she loathed.[9] Of the two, Sothern landed the far more rewarding part as the blithely indulgent mother of the disturbed man, and Roman definitely drew the short straw. Despite her prominent billing her screen time was minimal and hardly worth the effort. She was wasted in a role that anyone could have played, and it is difficult to see what attracted her to it. Harrington was an avant-garde director with long experience in Hollywood who made something of a specialty in the hag horror genre and was also responsible for *Who Slew Auntie Roo?* and *What's the Matter with Helen?* (1971). *The Killing Kind* made little impression on its release, which, according to Harrington, was entirely the fault of the distribution company, Media Trend Productions. The movie became more widely known when it was released on VHS video in 1987 and in the years since has gained a devoted following, with several other reissues on disc. The 2007 DVD version of *The Killing Kind* released by Dark Sky Films includes an interview with Harrington.

Impulse was constructed around William Shatner as a smooth-talking con man psychopath who ingratiates himself with women to divest them of their assets. Roman played a wealthy widow who acts as matchmaker to her daughter until she realizes that Shatner may not be the ideal son-in-law. She seemed surprisingly sanguine on first appearance despite the sleazy scenario and helped to ground the film in any sort of recognizable reality before it completely unraveled. She even managed to keep a straight face opposite Shatner's frequently oddball and barnstorming performance. Director William Grefé remains little known outside the cult circles of exploitation horror but feted within them as a minor potentate. The original shooting schedule was for 12 weeks, but to save money most of the photography was completed in only 15 days. Some reports suggested that 12 days of filming solely involved Shatner and that the rest of the cast were required for just three. The budget was around $250,000, which, to put it in context, was half that of *Champion* 25 years earlier. Grefé's girlfriend Jennifer Bishop played Ruth's daughter, and the veteran actress took a liking to her. Bishop was dark and striking, and Ruth said she reminded her of herself when young. With her wealth of experience, she even compensated for some of Grefé's lack of expertise. "She taught me how to get close-ups which Grefe didn't care about," recalled Bishop, "And she looked after my wardrobe. She was really quite like a mother hen to me."[10]

Continuing the theme, Ruth next popped up in the murder mystery *A Knife for the Ladies*, which was essentially yet another horror movie that followed the same worn track as the others, only switched to a western setting. The story concerned a private detective (Jeff Cooper) who is called on to investigate a series of murders of prostitutes in a once-prosperous mining town. It featured Jack Elam as a grizzled sheriff with the usual assortment of defensive and reactionary townsfolk. The direction by Larry G. Spangler was generally poor and the pacing disconcerting. For the most part it was slow-paced but with sudden outbursts of seemingly gratuitous violence. Of its kind it could have been a lot worse, and at least some of the leading personalities were more sketched in than was usual in such lurid fare. Roman had near star billing but not a great deal of screen time. However, she made her time count as an influential town matriarch and a crucial character in the story. When first introduced, interviewed by the detective, she wears severe mourning dress as she talks about her late and much beloved son. Considering she has lost her son, she appears unnaturally calm and composed but with hints of a far less attractive personality lurking underneath if questioned too closely. Filming took place at the Old Tucson Studios in Tucson, Arizona. There were two versions made: an explicit one aimed at the European market and a less gory version for American consumption. An edited version is also known under the misleadingly jocular title *Jack the Ripper Goes West*, which made it sound like a lost Abbott and Costello movie.[11] Roman had by now so cornered the market as a harridan of horror that she was finding it difficult to get work in any other genre on the big screen. Some sources also list *Dead of Night* (1976), a made-for-TV anthology of three separate tales, among her credits. If she did appear in this, her scenes must have been deleted.[12]

Television continued to give her more scope, and she featured in several movies, including *Go Ask Alice* (1973) about teenage drug addiction. Despite receiving high billing her role as a psychiatrist was only a small one. Occasionally she had a more substantial part, such as that as a circus owner in *Punch and Jody* (1973), which reteamed her with Glenn Ford over 20 years after *Young Man with Ideas.* The story revolved around an aging drifter (Ford) reluctantly forging a relationship with a daughter he never knew he had. It felt like the pilot for a TV series, but despite its promise it did not get any takers. Roman was at ease as a straight-talking veteran of the big top, and her scenes with Ford were some of the most relaxed. It was pleasing to see her in a sympathetic part for a change against the run of most of her termagant roles in the decade. She played yet another formidable matriarch in an episode of the feature-length western series *Hec Ramsey*, starring Richard Boone, that bore some striking similarities with *A Knife for the Ladies* both in setting and storyline.

In 1973 she had another chance for a regular role in a TV series, this time a comedy, which she hoped would elevate her from the horror trough. For a long time, she wanted to prove she could make a success in comedy but despite all her attempts had never been given much chance. *Cops* was set in a low-crime, suburban precinct and featured Ruth as the object of affection for a group of beat cops. The cast was headed by Vincent Gardenia as the captain, recently transferred from a tough city neighborhood. A short movie pilot was made, and, if the reception was favorable, a series was a distinct possibility. "I play a wise-cracking meter maid," she revealed in an interview at the time. "So far as I know that particular brand of character hasn't been tried yet." She was pleased to find a chance for a regular role in a comedy series at last but at the same time was reluctant to leave her beloved Laguna Beach location for long periods: "I'm concerned about the show in a way," she revealed. "If it's a hit that means I'll have to move in from the beach. But that's alright, I have another house here in town. Still, I'll miss the privacy."[13] The show's creator, Jerry Belson, had a track record of success on television, for instance with *The Odd Couple*, but *Cops* was not the expected hit, and so no series ensued.

Ruth was happily settled in Laguna Beach in her comfortable house overlooking the Pacific where she was to remain for the rest of her life. She entered a more settled and contented phase, having largely come to terms with the disappointments of her career. By then she appeared more comfortable with her fame or lack of it. Although she was never the subject of iconic artwork by Andy Warhol like some of her contemporaries, she did feature in the art of another minor pop artist, the neo-Dadaist Ray Johnson, a collagist who frequently referenced popular culture in his work. One particular composition of his was described in a leading art journal as, "Populated in addition by ducks, elephants, sea horses and Ruth Roman."[14]

When she was 53, Ruth entered into a surprise fourth marriage. On May 4, 1976, in a civil ceremony at Clark, Nevada, she married William Ross Wilson, a businessman and realtor. Little is known about him, and most of her friends only heard about it afterwards.[15] Unlike her previous marriages, this one was far more low-key, as suited her life at that point.

13. *Whatever Happened to Ruth Roman?*

However, they did not live together as a couple for long and separated after a short time, although they never actually divorced. She characterized herself as essentially a loner who prized her own privacy. She was a homebody and as time passed discovered the delights of cooking. Her son Dickie inherited her love of the sea and spent much of his spare time sailing on a boat he had bought and studying maps. He was never enamored of Hollywood to say the least. They had an up-and-down relationship like every mother and son. "I like him," she once remarked. "Mothers must love their children. But they don't always love them."[16] She described their relationship as resembling that of Auntie Mame and her nephew. Ruth and Budd had stayed in touch, despite their split, and he even put work her way when he could. He always got along well with Dickie. Even today, Budd still keeps in touch with him.[17]

Ruth's big-screen movie decade was rounded off by *Day of the Animals* (1977), also known as *Something Is Out There.* The screenplay asked pointedly which species was the more dangerous, animals or man. The answer clearly was man, especially in the guise of Leslie Nielsen stripped to the waist in full psychopath mode. The film carried a serious message about the damaging effects of aerosol sprays on the ozone layer, at a time when environmental concerns were beginning to be debated. The story followed the trials and tribulations of a party of hikers who are besieged by aggressive wildlife, particularly eagles, as they go up into higher altitudes. The special effects have often been derided, but the photography was of good quality. For two-thirds of the running time the screenplay was plodding and surprisingly wordy, with plenty of bickering among the party. Roman played a woman from the city who has a difficult relationship with her son (Bobby Porter). Her role required her to be neurotic and unglamorous, usually at one and the same time. Presumably Shelley Winters was busy that week. Ruth must surely have lamented the sharp decline from her Hollywood heyday, which reduced her to traipsing through a forest in the pouring rain looking bedraggled and hysterical wearing a cagoule and grappling with an unbalanced Nielsen. Arguably the best thing about the movie was the soundtrack by the great Lalo Schifrin. Writer-director William Girdler made six films in a nine-year period, of which *Grizzly* (1976) was perhaps the best known and most successful. *Day of the Animals* turned out to be his penultimate film, as he was killed in a helicopter crash the following year at age 30.

Despite her bruising decade on screen in which she had been

murdered more times than she might care to remember, Ruth remained philosophical about herself and her career. She saw things more in perspective, and to her that once so important career was now a distant third on her list of priorities, after her son and love of travel.

Television kept her constantly employed and gave her a chance to escape the horror straitjacket. She guested in episodes of the hardy perennials of the decade, including *Gunsmoke, The Virginian, Ironside, Cannon, Harry O, Faraday & Company* and *The Mod Squad.* The remarkably hardy *Gunsmoke* ran for 20 years in total. Roman appeared twice in the series to good effect. In "Coreyville" (1969) she played one of two feuding women who practically run a small town. The other woman was Nina Foch, and both had markedly changed from their previous appearance together in *Young Man with Ideas.* Roman was invited back to *Gunsmoke* a couple of years later in 1971 for the two-parter "Waste," which at a combined two hours essentially came across as a TV feature movie. This time she played a world-weary madam who protects her dwindling down-on-their-luck coterie of girls and has her own sense of honor. Filmed in Kanab, Utah, some fans of the show consider it to have been among the best stories of the later seasons.[18] Roman was restrained and rather sinister, although criminally underused, in "Once Upon a Chilling," an installment of the cult paranormal series *The Sixth Sense*, which could never compete with *The Twilight Zone.*[19] In the *Ironside* episode "Gentle Oaks" (1971) she was impressive as the head nurse of a sanitarium where a series of suspicious deaths have been reported. Seemingly agreeable and approachable, she reveals a much darker side. Among the supporting cast, the veteran character actor John Carradine was a standout as an eccentric but observant inmate of the home. *Cannon* was a great showcase for the skill of the dependable character actor William Conrad as a private eye in a fondly remembered Quinn Martin production that ran for five seasons (1971–76). In "Flashpoint" (1974) he was hired to investigate a series of rapes and murders in a small town and had to face the hostility of the local community which has already decided on the guilt of an accused boy. Roman presented another in her gallery of strong women, this time as an indulgent mother of a disturbed young man (Kristoffer Tabori). It was a complicated mother/son dynamic as always. *Faraday & Company* began as a feature-length Wednesday Night Movie on NBC starring the likable Dan Dailey as an old-style detective. Roman turned up in that show married to fellow veteran Howard Duff. Although it looked as though a possible series was in the offing, only three further episodes were made, perhaps because of oversaturation of the maverick detective format in the era. Roman enhanced an episode of the semi-mystical *Kung Fu* (1974) titled "A Dream Within a Dream" as the puzzled wife of a banker who is found hanging in mysterious circumstances and then even more mysteriously disappears. The series frequently won awards, but that particular installment was rather slow and lacking in action.[20] *The Mod Squad* was a counterculture crime series that had its origins in the fervent late 1960s and ran for five seasons during which it attracted an impressive roster of star names. Roman appeared in an episode about a threatened former child star in which she was married to Dane Clark, their third appearance together. She was also seen in the Angie Dickinson series *Police Woman* (1976). In "The Disco Killer" she gave a well-judged performance as an ex-Big Band singer and mother of an estranged daughter who is a witness to a murder. It gave her some good scenes with Dickinson.

Being something of a recluse, Roman seldom appeared in the pages of the popular press in those years, except for the occasional "Where are they now?" queries. She was also seen at the odd premiere, such as that for *The Great Waltz* (1972). There was one curious incident that made headlines in Britain. It was reported in *The Times* of London that a jealous British actress, Betsy Nemes (35), ripped Roman's fur coat which was valued at $3,000. It seemed that Nemes was spurred to spoil it because of the attention that her boyfriend Kimberly Moffat (44), a businessman, was paying to Roman. Moffat, described as a friend of Miss Roman, arrived home at Holly Tree Gardens, Rayleigh, Essex, on New Year's Day 1973 to find Nemes dancing naked on the lawn. Nemes said in court that she was carrying his child and declared, "I thought I would get my own back by hitting him where it hurts."[21] It seems an odd story considering Ruth's avowed dislike of fur coats.

Her last television movie of the decade was the acclaimed all-star western *The Sacketts* (1979). Based on two popular novels by Louis L'Amour, the four-hour production was shown in two parts and followed the fortunes of three brothers after they leave the family home in Tennessee and head to Santa Fe. Roman popped up in a one-horse town as Rosie, a blousy but sprightly saloon keeper with a past who happens to be an old amour of Ben Johnson. The movie remains a favorite among western fans for its crossover of the classic and modern eras, encapsulated in its impressive cast, with the classic era represented by, among others, Glenn Ford, Mercedes McCambridge and Gilbert Roland, and the modern by Tom Selleck and Sam Elliott. Although rather rambling, it fulfilled many of the requirements of aficionados of the genre, with action, suspense, tension, interesting characters and plenty of gunplay. There was some attractive location shooting, and much of the filming took place in Arizona, including at Salt River, Patagonia and Mescal, among others.

On balance, the 1970s proved a time of mixed blessings for Ruth, as it was for many of her contemporaries. Although she re-established herself on the big screen, it was solely in low-budget horrors. Television gave her far more opportunity to display her ability as a character actress and continued to offer more in the following decade.

$\diamond\diamond$ **14** $\diamond\diamond$

The Short Goodbye

"I feel you have to have a sense of humor. It can
save the world. It can save you."
—Ruth interviewed by Ellie Schultz[1]

In the 1980s Roman made a final big-screen appearance and continued to prosper on television, with roles in *Dallas* spin-off *Knots Landing,* and especially found her niche as a recurring character in *Murder,
She Wrote.* She retired at the end of the decade and lived out her remain-
ing years in comfortable seclusion at Laguna Bay.

Roman celebrated her 60th birthday in December 1982 but had
long since ceased to be concerned about playing glamorous roles. She
would never countenance the idea of having a facelift, although she
understood those women who did so and fully supported them in it.
Besides, she had become a sought-after character actress and liked the
idea that she was still recognizably herself. Her attitude to her career
was far more ambivalent than it had been, and by then she let it be
known that she viewed acting largely as a hobby. When asked by an
interviewer around that time what she considered her ideal role, Ruth
answered that she had not found it yet. The decade started with yet
another chance at what might have become a regular series. She had
a prominent part as one of the warders in *Willow B: Women in Prison*
(1980), a pilot for a show that was billed as the American answer to the
cult Australian series *Prisoner: Cell Block H,* or even the British *Within
These Walls.* It was an interesting idea, and Roman could have become
a key character as one of the sadistic prison guards if the makers had
stuck to the same blueprint as the highly successful Australian series,
which covered all kinds of daring subjects during its run, including drug
addiction and lesbianism. The film also bore a superficial resemblance
to another TV movie, *Women in Chains* (1972), that starred Ida Lupino

as a brutal officer, a part not dissimilar to the role she had played in *Women's Prison* (1955). Unfortunately, *Willow B* sometimes followed the line of least resistance and softened its approach, so it came across as mere pastiche. The ABC network was wary of the entertainment value of even slightly controversial subjects on prime-time television in those days and, according to the show's producer, did not give it a fair hearing. In many ways it was an opportunity missed. Carol Lynley was one of the stars and recalled that she had been looking forward most to getting to know Ruth, but the cancelled series put paid to any chance of that.[2]

By the beginning of the 1980s, Roman's movie career appeared to have ended to all intents and purposes. The odd, interesting offer came along, and producers had not forgotten her entirely. For instance, Roger Corman wanted her to play a spaceship captain in his fantasy science fiction opus *Galaxy of Terror* (1981), but the part went to a little-known actress Grace Zabriskie, who later found fame in *Twin Peaks*. After some five years away, Roman made a return to feature films in the mystery thriller *Echoes* (1982). The premise involved an artist, Michael (Richard Alfieri), who begins to be plagued by recurring nightmares about a 19th-century love triangle. What might have been an intriguing ghost tale was slow and often self-indulgent. The dark, moody photography and discordant one-note organ music did not lift the consistently downbeat feeling, and the story was not strong enough to hold interest. Star Alfieri also wrote the screenplay and went on to win awards for his work, but not on this occasion. He often collaborated with the director Arthur Allan Seidelman, who began his career with the cult movie *Hercules in New York* (1970) but found his greatest success on television. In *Echoes*, Roman played Michael's mother and brought her customary skill to bear in her brief scenes which served to establish the scenario in a recognizable reality. Among the cast was Mercedes McCambridge as an art dealer and the veteran Gale Sondergaard as a medium. It turned out to be the final film appearance of them all and was a disappointing end to three good Hollywood careers. *Echoes* made little impact at the time on the big screen and soon found its way to the then-flourishing straight-to-video market.

Roman still turned up in guest spots in the shows of the day, including an episode of the ever-popular *Fantasy Island* set on a Pacific island where people are granted their wishes, but at a cost. "My Fair Pharaoh" starred Joan Collins as a woman with a secret desire to be Cleopatra. (Collins famously auditioned for the part of Cleopatra in the

1963 film but lost out to Elizabeth Taylor.) Roman was cast in a small role as the husky-voiced queen bee of the harem, who brooks no nonsense. It proved to be a turning point for Collins, whose career was then somewhat stymied. Producer Aaron Spelling saw her in the episode and was suitably impressed, so much so that he offered her the role of Alexis Carrington Colby in the era-defining *Dynasty*. The soap opera was one of the biggest shows on TV at the time, which once drew audiences of almost 60,000,000 viewers. Collins was ever afterwards assured of superstar status. There was no such reward for Ruth, but later in the decade she did get an offer for another soap in a similar vein, which she accepted. She appeared in two seasons of *Knots Landing*, a successful spin-off of *Dallas*. Sylvia Lean was a subsidiary character, the mother of arch-schemer Peter Hollister (Hunt Block). The initial run was for seven episodes, with the option of more depending on how things worked out. Her character was well received, and in total she featured in 21 installments between 1986 and 1987, her longest stint in a series since *The Long, Hot Summer* 20 years previously. Many welcomed her appearance in a prominent production after years of relative obscurity. Some fans were especially alarmed by a storyline in which her son tried to murder her. At the time several viewers wrote in to say they found the scenes upsetting even by the standards of soap opera shenanigans. All in all, *Knots Landing* put her in the public eye once more and gave her a good salary. Ruth was ever the trained professional, and, during filming of the series, she noticed many changes from the days when she was a Warner Bros. contract player. "You wouldn't believe some of the behavior now on the set," she remarked. "If you had done those things then that happen now, you'd have been thrown out on your ear."[3] Another glamorous star of the 1950s and contemporary of Roman's appeared in the soap opera, namely Ava Gardner, the year before.

It was not until the end of her career that Roman found one of her best roles on television as Loretta Spiegel, the gossipy hairdresser, in several episodes of *Murder, She Wrote*. She was to the manor born dishing the dirt with many of her generation, Angela Lansbury and the girls, especially Julie Adams, Gloria DeHaven and Kathryn Grayson in the beauty salon. Loretta was such a warm and believable character who fit in perfectly with the cozy Cabot Cove community. Often, she gave Jessica clues to her cases. Garrulous but well-meaning, she made such an impression that it was surprising to discover that she only appeared in three episodes. Spotting the old-time stars was one of the highlights of the fondly remembered show. Lansbury became the producer and so exercised a lot of influence, which led her to send many invitations to her old friends from her Hollywood days who were struggling to find work. In fact, it was Budd Moss who got Ruth the role in the show, and casting director Ron Stephenson was only too pleased to oblige. She made her debut during the fourth season in 1987. The story, titled "If it's Thursday, It Must Be Beverly," centered on an amorous sheriff's deputy who spends his spare time entertaining the lonely ladies of the community, many of whom happen to frequent the beauty parlor. The episode established the parlor as the place to find out what is really happening in town, and it was great to see some of the old favorites and contemporaries of Lansbury in their element. Roman next appeared in two episodes of the following season (1989). In "The Sins of Castle Cove" a novelist creates havoc when she writes a scorching *Peyton Place*-type tell-all bestseller. All the townsfolk of Cabot Cove believe it is a thinly veiled attack on them. Naturally, Loretta and the girls are in the thick of the melee, and the installment saw the gossipy gang going great guns. In various polls conducted of the entire series, "The Sins of Castle Cove" has always rated highly. Her final episode, "Town Father," was about yet another local scandal, this time involving a mayor alleged to have a secret wife. The crew at Loretta's salon put the world to rights, agreeing that what the place really needs to sort it out is a woman mayor. All three of the episodes in which the gang appeared together were considered some of the best of the 12-year run by those who admire *Murder, She Wrote*. Alas, the beauty parlor did not feature again, and many viewers missed both the place and its regulars. Of the ladies, only Julie Adams as a real estate agent was seen in later episodes. All three of the installments in which Ruth appeared were entertaining, gave her some good lines and allowed her to show her humor. Often Loretta tried to persuade Jessica to go for the same poodle perm that she sported herself. The comical interplay between her and the other veteran stars was one of the chief joys of the show. In various novelizations based on the franchise, the parlor and its inhabitants often featured. Ruth's final episode, "Town Father," turned out to be the last thing she ever did. Coincidentally, it also turned out to be the final appearance in any medium of Kathryn Grayson.[4] In 1991, according to an article in *Film Review* magazine, it was reported that Roman had just completed one more film, her first in eight years, titled *When in Rome*, although no further details were given. No such movie has come to light, and it is possible that if it was made, it was never actually released or was issued under a different title.[5]

After retiring from performing, Ruth disappeared from the spotlight altogether to live quietly, based mostly at her beloved house in Laguna Beach. It was her favorite place to be. She craved the simple life and loved nothing more than to walk barefoot on the beaches, watch the sunsets, or spend hours fishing in rock pools. She valued her privacy greatly and seldom if ever gave interviews, nor did she work the chat show circuit. In many ways, she was far happier away from the glare of publicity. As she once remarked, "I'm a solitary person—almost a hermit."[6] For most of her life she enjoyed good health, and despite her years of heavy smoking she was only ill towards the latter end. She died peacefully in her sleep on September 9, 1999, at the age of 76. A few days later there was a small, private funeral service, and at dusk her son, Richard, scattered her ashes in the ocean, according to her wishes, at the Laguna seafront where she had spent so many happy hours.[7]

Epilogue

> "To achieve maximum success, one has to blend something very personal with a good characterization. To be a real success you have to be yourself as well as an actress."
> —Ruth interviewed, 1953[1]

Ruth Roman is known to classic cinema buffs but is probably not a familiar name to the wider public. If she is recalled at all, it is perhaps for her appearance in *Strangers on a Train* or for her extraordinary portrayal of Mrs. Wadsworth in the cult horror *The Baby*. I hope this appreciation of her life and work shows that there was far more to her than those films imply and inspires people to look again at her body of work to discover her anew.

Most of her screen work is available to view; only a few titles remain elusive. A fair proportion of the television programs and TV movies in which she appeared from the 1960s onwards can be seen on DVD, Blu-ray or from other sources. Some of the 1950s teleplays are far harder to find, but a few have been released in some format, particularly installments of classic series such as *Bonanza*.

Her best films, in terms of her own performance and the strength of the films themselves, include at least two of her westerns, *The Far Country* and *Rebel in Town*. *Strangers on a Train* was the one undisputed classic in which she appeared, and, while it was hardly her best role, the film itself is indispensable. She gave strong portrayals of interesting and varied characters in *Tomorrow Is Another Day*, *Lightning Strikes Twice*, *Champion*, *Down Three Dark Streets* and *The Window*. She proved adept at comedy in *Young Man with Ideas* and could easily have done more. She was able to give the right balance to dramatic roles such as those in *Three Secrets*, *Bitter Victory* and *Always Leave Them Laughing*. Her later career fell away like so many of her contemporaries, but she was by then not unduly concerned about it, having come to terms with her own disappointment. There will always be a cult following for such films as *The Baby* despite her own dismissal of it. She made up for any cinematic disappointments with her fine work on television.

She was adept at playing strong women and often literally and metaphorically speaking her characters wore the trousers, as Lily MacBeth, for instance, or even as a more ostensibly romantic character such as that in *Lightning Strikes Twice*. It is hard not to think that the roles she best suited were those that included at least some part of her own persona and tapped into her own feelings about stardom. As she acknowledged, her finest characterizations were those that had some part of herself in them.

Her years as one of the last Warner Bros. contract players in some ways saw her at her highpoint, but the studio did not always use her talents wisely, and their idea to groom her as the next Bette Davis was a mistake. Davis was their most profitable star and left a massive gap that no one could fill. There could never be another Bette. Instead, they should have boosted Ruth as a distinct personality in her own right, discovered her strengths and played to them.

Her tenacity of spirit was one of her most admirable characteristics. Acting was her life from childhood on and her one abiding interest. Considering her early experience, it was no surprise that she often came across as a tough dame. In order to survive, it was necessary to develop a hard exterior and steel oneself for the fight. Her experiences in New York and Hollywood up until her late 20s definitely toughened her. Despite being repeatedly told that she was not good enough, not sexy enough or "the wrong type,"

Publicity still of Roman from *Lightning Strikes Twice*, 1951.

169

she persisted through all the false starts, dashed hopes and recurring disappointments to achieve stardom during an era when the competition was arguably at its greatest. It took her years to get where she wanted to be, but when she got there, it may not have been all she had hoped for, and after all that striving, it was soon over. While she never reached the dizzy heights of some of her peers, she almost got there and by her own lights achieved more than she has previously been given credit. All her effort deserved a more tangible reward, but that she achieved what she did was testament to her own innate spirit of self-belief and never-say-die attitude. That alone deserves to be acknowledged. She might have benefited from having an influential producer or director interest themselves in her career. A powerful advocate or ally could have made a big difference to her chances of success. In any event, success is relative, and she always preferred to go her own way. Suffice it to say that filmgoers recognized her worth, and she maintained a devoted following. Throughout it all she stayed true to herself and the dreams that had carried her forward in the first place. By following her own star, she achieved honest success on her own merits. Her career was by no means a failure and was only a disappointment from her own perspective, considering how she dreamed it would be when she started out. Late in life she looked back with a far more philosophical attitude. She summed up her feelings: "Thank God for giving me a career—or a hobby as I call it—in acting. It's so much fun.... I've had such a ball."[2]

Appendix

Filmography

Stage Door Canteen. Dir.: Frank Borzage. Scr.: Delmer Daves. Cast: Judith Anderson, Tallulah Bankhead, Ray Bolger, Ralph Bellamy, Helen Hayes, Katharine Hepburn, Katharine Cornell, Helen Hayes, Johnny Weissmuller, Yehudi Menuhin, Ethel Waters, George Raft, Gypsy Rose Lee, Ethel Merman, Paul Muni, Cornelia Otis Skinner, Xavier Cugat, Django Reinhardt, Kenny Baker, Alfred Lunt, Lynn Fontanne, George Jessel, Dame May Whitty, Gracie Fields, Jean Hersholt, Harpo Marx, Django Reinhardt, Benny Goodman, Count Basie & Orchestra, Sam Jaffe, Allen Jenkins, Betty Lawford, Peggy Moran, Otto Kruger, Helen Parrish, Ed Wynn, Merle Oberon, Lloyd Corrigan, Jane Darwell, William Demarest, Virginia Grey, et al., Ruth Roman (Girl, Uncredited). Principal Artists Productions, United Artists (Distributors), 1943.

Ladies Courageous. Dir.: John Rawlins. Scr.: Doris Gilbert, Norman Reilly Raine, from the novel by Virginia Spencer Cowles. Cast: Loretta Young, Geraldine Fitzgerald, Diana Barrymore, Evelyn Ankers, Anne Gwynne, Philip Terry, David Bruce, Lois Collier, Samuel S. Hinds, June Vincent, David Bruce, Richard Fraser, Frank Jenks, Janet Shaw, Kane Richmond, et al., Ruth Roman (WAF, Uncredited). Walter Wanger Productions, 1944.

Since You Went Away. Dir.: John Cromwell, Edward F. Cline, Tay Garnett, David O. Selznick. Scr.: David O. Selznick, based on the novel by Margaret Buell Wilder. Cast: Claudette Colbert, Jennifer Jones, Joseph Cotten, Shirley Temple, Monty Woolley, Lionel Barrymore, Robert Walker, Hattie McDaniel, Agnes Moorehead, Alla Nazimova, Albert Basserman, Gordon Oliver, Keenan Wynn, Guy Madison, Craig Stevens, Florence Bates, Dorothy Adams, Walter Baldwin, George Chandler, Dorothy Dandridge, John Derek, Steve Dunhill, Rhonda Fleming, Ruth Roman (Envious Girl at Railway Station, Uncredited), et al. Selznick International Pictures, 1944.

Song of Nevada. Dir.: Joseph Kane. Scr.: Gordon Kahn, Olive Cooper. Cast: Roy Rogers, Dale Evans, Mary Lee, Trigger, Lloyd Corrigan, Thurston Hall, John Eldredge, Forrest Taylor, George Meeker, Emmett Vogan, LeRoy Mason, Bob Nolan, Ken Carson, Sons of the Pioneers, William B. Davidson, Frank McCarroll, Alexander Pollard, Bob Reeves, Helen Talbot, Tom Steele, Si Jenks, Shug Fisher, Bob Burns, Jack O'Shea, et al.; Ruth Roman (Dancer, Uncredited). Republic Pictures, 1944.

Storm Over Lisbon. Dir.: George Sherman. Scr.: Doris Gilbert, Dane Lussier, from a story by Elizabeth Meehan. Cast: Vera Ralston, Erich Von Stroheim, Richard Arlen, Otto Kruger, Eduardo Ciannelli, Robert Livingston, Mona Barrie, Frank Orth, Sarah Edwards, Alice Fleming, Leon Belasco, The Aida Broadbent Girls, Ed Agresti, Georgia Davis, Gino Corrado, Bud Geary, Vincent Gironda, George Humbert, Manuel Paris, Alphonse Martel, Fred Rapport, Lester Sharp, Karen Randle, Victor Travis, Ruth Roman (Checkroom Girl, Uncredited), et al. Republic Pictures, 1944.

Appendix

Harmony Trail aka *White Stallion*. Dir.: Robert Emmett. Scr.: Frank Simpson. Cast: Ken Maynard, Max Terhune (& his dummy Elmer Sneezeweed), Glen Strange, Ruth Roman (Ann Martin), Gene Alsace, Eddie Dean, Robert McKenzie, Chas King, Bud Osborne, Al Ferguson, Dan White, Fred Gildart, Jerry Shields, John Bridges, John Cason, Tex Cooper, Chick Hannan, George Morrell, Warner Richmond, James Sheridan, et al. Maddox Productions, 1944.

The Affairs of Susan. Romantic drama. Dir.: William A. Seiter. Scr.: Richard Flournoy, Laszlo Gorog, Thomas Monroe, from their novel. Cast: Joan Fontaine, George Brent, Dennis O'Keefe, Walter Abel, Rita Johnson, Don DeFore, Mary Field, Byron Barr, Francis Pierlot, Lewis Russell, Grace Albertson, Ralph Brooke, Douglas Carter, Natalie Draper, Renee Dupuis, Frank Faylen, Alice Fleming, Almeda Fowler, Joel Friend, Sam Harris, Warren Hymer, Milton Kibbee, Teala Lauring, Mira McKinley, Harold Miller, James Millican, Mavis Murray, Gordon Richards, Marjorie Silk, Audrey Young, Eddy Waller, Larry Steers, Robert Sully, Jane Starr, Cyril Ring, Ruth Roman (Girl at Bright Dollar, Uncredited), et al. Hal Wallis Productions, 1945.

She Gets Her Man. Comedy. Dir.: Erle C. Kenton. Scr.: Warren Wilson, Clyde Bruckman, Ray Singer, Dick Chevillat. Cast: Joan Davis, William Gargan, Leon Errol, Vivian Austin, Milburn Stone, Donald MacBride, Cy Kendall, Emmett Vogan, Eddie Acuff, Virginia Sale, Ian Keith, Maurice Cass, Chester Clute, Charlie Hall, Olin Howland, Harold Godwin, Kit Guard, George Lloyd, Howard M. Mitchell, William J. O'Brien, Max Wagner, Pierre Watkin, Charlie Whitney, George Lynn, Sam Flint, et al., Ruth Roman (Glamor Girl, Uncredited). Universal Pictures, 1945.

Jungle Queen. Serial of 13 Episodes: (1) "Invitation to Danger" (2) "Jungle Sacrifice" (3) "The Flaming Mountain" (4) "Wildcat Stampede" (5) "The Burning Jungle" (6) "Danger Ship" (7) "Trip-Wire Murder" (8) "The Mortar Bomb" (9) "Death Watch" (10) "Execution Chamber" (11) "The Trail to Doom" (12) "Dragged Under" (13) "The Secret of the Sword" Dir.: Lewis D. Collins, Ray Taylor. Scr.: George H. Plympton, Ande Lamb, Morgan B. Cox. Cast: Edward Norris, Eddie Quillan, Lois Collier, Ruth Roman (Lothel—the Jungle Queen), Clarence Muse, Tala Birell, Douglass Dumbrille, Cy Kendall, Clinton Rosemond, Lumsden Hare, Lester Matthews, Napoleon Simpson, Budd L. Buster, Emmett Smith, Jim Basquette, Oliver Blake, Edmund Cobb, Jack Curtis, Cyril Delevanti, Robert R. Stephenson, John Merton, Wilton Graff, John George, Charles Wright, Louis Adlon, Herbert Clifton, Harry Cording, George Eldredge, Bobby Hale, George Reed, William Yetter, Sr., Colin Kenny, Arno Frey, Gene Garrick, Peter Helmers, John Meredith, Robert Lewis, Ivo Henderson, Boyd Irwin, Walter Bonn, Leslie V. Conant, Ray Turner, Ted Billings, Fred "Snowflake" Toones, et al. Universal Pictures, 1945.

See My Lawyer. Comedy. Dir.: Eddie Cline. Scr.: Edmund L. Hartmann, Stanley Davis, from the play by Richard Maibaum & Harry Clork. Cast: Ole Olsen, Chic Johnson, Alan Curtis, Grace McDonald, Noah Beery, Jr., Lee Patrick, Franklin Pangborn, Gus Schilling, Edward S. Brophy, Richard Benedict, William B. Davidson, Stanley Clements, Mary Gordon, Ralph Peters, Carmen Amaya, George Chandler, Vernon Dent, Kate Harrington, et al., Ruth Roman (Mud Girl, Uncredited). Universal Pictures, 1945.

You Came Along. Romantic drama. Dir.: John Farrow. Scr.: Robert Smith, Ayn Rand, from a story by Robert Smith. Cast: Robert Cummings, Lizabeth Scott, Charles Drake, Julie Bishop, Kim Hunter, Robert Sully, Helen Forrest, Rhys Williams, Franklin Pangborn, Minor Watson, Howard Freeman, Andrew Tombes, Grace Albertson, Brooks Benedict, Margaret Brayton, Jean Carlin, George M. Carleton, Nancy Brinckman, Lucy Cochrane, Frank Faylen, Ruth Roman (Gloria Revere, Uncredited). Eddie Hall, Jane Hazard, James Millican, William B. Davidson, Tom Dillon, Elaine Riley, et al. Hal Wallis Productions, 1945.

Incendiary Blonde. Musical biopic. Dir.: George Marshall. Scr.: Claude Binyon, Frank Butler. Cast: Betty Hutton, Arturo de Córdova, Charles Ruggles, Albert Dekker, Barry

Appendix

Fitzgerald, Mary Philips, Bill Goodwin, Edward Ciannelli, Maurice Rocco, The Maxellos, Catherine Craig, Billy Curtis, Harry Hayden, Carlotta Jelm, Billy Lechner, Charles C. Wilson, William A. Boardway, Billy Bletcher, Anne Carter, Lane Chandler, Catherine Craig, Jimmie Dundee, Francis Ford, Patricia Farr, James Flavin, et al., Ruth Roman (Chorine, Uncredited). Paramount Studios, 1945.

Time to Kill. Short armed services training film about the value of education available from the Armed Forces Institute. Cast: George Reeves, Barry Nelson, Don Hanmer, Jimmy Lydon, Don Taylor, DeForest Kelley (Peter), Betty White, Ruth Roman (Peter's Girl), William Forrest, Arthur Kennedy (Narrator). First Motion Picture Unit, United States Armed Forces, 1945 (22 minutes of the film can be viewed at the Internet Archive *https://archive.org/details/Time_to_Kill_1945*).

Gilda. Drama. Dir.: Charles Vidor. Scr.: Joe Eisinger, Marion Parsonnet, Ben Hecht, from a story by E.A. Ellington. Cast: Rita Hayworth, Glenn Ford, George Macready, Joseph Calleia, Ludwig Donath, Steven Geray, Joe Sawyer, Gerald Mohr, Robert Scott, Donald Douglas, Sam Appel, Symona Boniface, Argentina Brunetti, Jean de Briac, Eduardo Ciannelli, Ernest Hillyard, Forbes Murray, et al., Ruth Roman (Girl, Uncredited). Columbia Pictures Corp., 1946.

Without Reservations. Comedy. Dir.: Mervyn LeRoy. Scr.: Andrew Solt, based on the novel by Jane Allen, Mae Livingston. Cast: Claudette Colbert, John Wayne, Tom DeFore, Phil Brown, Anne Triola, Frank Puglia, Thurston Hall, Dona Drake, Fernando Alvarado, Charles Arnt, Louella Parsons, Griff Barnett, Jack Benny, Raymond Burr, Tom Chatterton, John Crawford, Cary Grant, Lisa Golm, Will Wright, et al., Ruth Roman (Girl in negligee, Uncredited). RKO Radio Pictures, 1946.

A Night in Casablanca. Comedy. Dir.: Archie L. Mayo. Scr.: Joseph Fields, Roland Kibbee. Cast: Groucho Marx, Chico Marx, Harpo Marx, Sig Ruman, Lois Collier, Charles Drake, Lisette Verea, Lewis Russell, Dan Seymour, Frederick Giermann, Harro Meller, David Hoffman, Paul Harvey, Mary Dees, Philip Van Zandt, Eugene Borden, et al., Ruth Roman (Harem Girl, Scenes Deleted). Loma Vista Productions, Inc., 1946.

The Web. Crime drama. Dir.: Michael Gordon. Scr.: William Bowers, Bertram Millhauser, from a story by Harry Kurnitz. Cast: Edmond O'Brien, Ella Raines, Vincent Price, William Bendix, Maria Palmer, John Abbott, Fritz Leiber, Howard Chamberlin, Tito Vuolo, Wilton Graff, Robin Raymond, Gino Corrado, Patricia Alphin, Russ Conway, William Haade, Dick Johnstone, Ethan Laidlaw, Jack G. Lee, Ralph Montgomery, et al., Ruth Roman (minor role, Uncredited). Universal Pictures, 1947.[1]

Night Has a Thousand Eyes. Mystery drama. Dir.: John Farrow. Scr.: Barré Lyndon, Jonathan Latimer, from the novel by Cornell Woolrich. Cast: Edward G. Robinson, Gail Russell, John Lund, Virginia Bruce, William Demarest, Richard Webb, Jerome Cowan, Onslow Stevens, John Alexander, Roman Bohnen, Mary Adams, Douglas Spencer, et al., Ruth Roman (Secretary in Prosecutor's Office, Uncredited). Paramount Pictures, 1948.

The Big Clock. Crime drama. Dir.: John Farrow. Scr.: Jonathan Latimer, from the novel by Kenneth Fearing. Cast: Ray Milland, Charles Laughton, Maureen O'Sullivan, Elsa Lanchester, Rita Johnson, Harold Vermilyea, Dan Tobin, Henry Morgan, Richard Webb, Elaine Riley, Luis van Rooten, Lloyd Corrigan, Frank Orth, Margaret Field, Bobby Watson, Frances Morris, James Burke, Virginia Duffy, Mary Currier, et al., Ruth Roman (Secretary at Meeting, Uncredited). Paramount Pictures, 1948.

Good Sam. Comedy drama. Dir.: Leo McCarey. Scr.: Ken Englund, from a story by Leo McCarey & John Klorer. Cast: Gary Cooper, Ann Sheridan, Ray Collins, Edmund Lowe, Joan Lorring, Minerva Urecal, Clinton Sundberg, Louise Beavers, Dick Ross, Lora Lee Michel, Bobby Dolan, Jr., Matt Moore, Netta Packer, Ruth Roman (Ruthie), Carol Stevens, Todd Karns, Irving Bacon, William Frawley, Harry Hayden, Pat Davis, Florence Wix, Scott Seaton, Almira Sessions, Dick Wessel, Gary Owen, William J. O'Brien, Ida

Appendix

Moore, George Ovey, Ted Mapes, Anne O'Neal, Helen Foster, James Horne, Jr., Joe Hinds, Johnny Duncan, Oliver Blake, Sedal Bennett, Jane Allan, Florence Auer, Ruth Brennan, Charles Ferguson, Kay Garrett, Marta Mitrovich, Francis Stevens, et al. Rainbow Productions, Inc., 1948.

Belle Starr's Daughter. Western. Dir.: Lesley Selander. Scr.: W.R. Burnett. Scr.: George Montgomery, Cast: Rod Cameron, Ruth Roman (Cimarron Rose), Wallace Ford, Charles Kemper, William Phipps, Jack Lambert, Edith King, Fred Libby, Isabel Jewell, J. Farrell MacDonald, Chris-Pin Martin, Larry Johns, Kenneth MacDonald, Christine Larsen, Henry Hull, Bill Kennedy, Lafe McKee, John "Skins" Miller, "Snub" Pollard, Dorothy Vernon, Terry Wilson, Joe Phillips, William Ruhl, Johnny Reese, Hank Patterson, John "Skins" Miller, Carol Henry, Harry Harvey, Ralph Bucko, Bob Burns, Steve Darrell, Tex Cooper, Bill Kennedy, Lafe McKee, et al. Alson Productions, 1948.

Champion. Drama. Dir.: Mark Robson. Scr.: Carl Foreman, from the story by Ring Lardner. Cast: Kirk Douglas, Arthur Kennedy, Marilyn Maxwell, Paul Stewart, Ruth Roman (Emma), Lola Albright, Harry Shannon, Esther Howard, Luis Van Rooten, John Day, Ralph Sanford, Bill Baldwin, Sam Balter, Paul Dubov, Joe Gray, Jimmy Dundee, George Meader, Tim Ryan, Charles Sullivan, Hilda Simms, Court Shepard, Ralph Montgomery, Hal March, Mike Lally, Jack Perry, Forbes Murray, Chuck Hamilton, Mushy Callahan, Sayre Dearing, Polly Bergan, Ralph Brooks, Charles Sherlock, et al. Screen Plays/Stanley Kramer Productions, 1949. (Nominated for six Academy Awards. Roman nominated as Most Promising Newcomer—Female, for the Golden Globe Awards.)

The Window. Drama. Dir.: Ted Tetzlaff. Scr.: Mel Dinelli, based on the Cornell Woolrich novella *The Boy Cried Murder.* Cast: Barbara Hale, Arthur Kennedy, Bobby Driscoll, Paul Stewart, Ruth Roman (Jean Kellerson), Richard Benedict, Anthony Ross, Tex Swan, Lee Phelps, Eric Mack, Johnny Kern, Lloyd Dawson, Charles Flynn, Budd Fine, Ken Terrell, Brick Sullivan, Edgar Small, Carl Saxe, James Nolan, Lee Kass, Tom Coleman, Tom Ahearne, Richard Benedict, et al. RKO Radio Pictures, 1949.

Beyond the Forest. Drama. Dir.: King Vidor. Scr.: Lenore J, Coffee, from the novel by Stuart Engstrand. Cast: Bette Davis, Joseph Cotten, David Brian, Ruth Roman (Carol Lawson), Minor Watson, Doris Drake, Regis Toomey, Sarah Selby, Frances Charles, Ann Doran, Creighton Hale, Eve Miller, Sherman Sanders, Olan Soule, Harry Tyler, Dorothy Vernon, Mary Servoss, Frank Pharr, Charles Jordan, Bess Flowers, June Evans, Judith Wood, Eileen Stevens, Jack Kenny, Hallene Hill, Bobby Henshaw, Jim Haward, Hal Gerard, James Craven, June Evans, Joel Allen, Gail Bonney Ralph Littlefield, Buddy Roosevelt, Mary Servoss, Bobby Henshaw, et al. Warner Bros., 1949.

Always Leave Them Laughing. Comedy musical drama. Dir.: Roy Del Ruth. Scr.: Melville Shavelson, Jack Rose, from a story by Max Shulman, Richard Mealand. Cast: Milton Berle, Virginia Mayo, Ruth Roman (Kay Washburn), Bert Lahr, Alan Hale, Grace Hayes, Jerome Cowan, Lloyd Gough, Iris Adrian, Ransom Sherman, Wally Vernon, Cecil Stewart & His Royal Rogues, O'Donnell & Blair, Max Showalter, The Moroccans, Arabella, Marion Colby, Kit Guard, Stuart Holmes, Bill McLean, Charles Meredith, Raymond Roe, Iphigenie Castiglioni, Mary Castle, Lorinne Crawford, Duke Johnson, Eddie Parks, Ralph Sanford, Al Hill, Karl "Killer" Davis, Eileen Howe, Flo Farmer, Al Lackey, Mike Lally, Charles Kisco, Johnny Kern, Sid Kane, Ben Jade, Lorinne Crawford, Mary Castle, George Bruggeman, Richard Avonde, John Breen, Edward Biby, Carmen Clifford, Marion Colby, Garrett Craig, et al. Warner Bros., 1949.

Stars Take to Chinchilla for Winter. Pathé newsreel. Actresses model chinchilla coats, including Alexis Smith, Eleanor Parker, Ruth Roman, Patricia Neal. (Ruth in a cape). British Pathé, 1949.

Barricade. Western. Dir.: Peter Godfrey. Scr.: William Sackheim, inspired by *The Sea Wolf* by Jack London. Cast: Dane Clark, Raymond Massey, Ruth Roman (Judith Burns),

Robert Douglas, Morgan Farley, Walter Coy, George Stern, Robert Griffin, Frank Marlowe, Tony Martínez, Ben Corbett, John Halloran, George Lloyd, Jack Montgomery, Leo Anthony, George Bell, Art Felix, Al Haskell, Douglas Kennedy, Ted Mapes, Frank Mills, Sailor Vincent, Artie Ortego, Steve Stephens, Kansas Moehring et al. Warner Bros., 1950.

Colt .45. Western. Dir.: Edwin L. Marin. Scr.: Thomas Blackburn. Cast: Randolph Scott, Ruth Roman (Beth Donovan), Zachary Scott, Lloyd Bridges, Alan Hale, Ian MacDonald, Chief Thundercloud, Stanley Andrews, Charles Evans, Nolan Leary, Kansas Moehring, Hal Taliaferro, Mary Stewart, William Steele, Buddy Roosevelt, Barry Regan, Robert Karnes, Warren Fiske, Charles Ferguson, Carl Andre, Victor Adamson, Monte Blue, Tex Cooper, Ben Corbett, Walter Coy, Franklyn Farnum, Art Miles, Hal Taliaferro, Buddy Roosevelt, Howard Negley, Nolan Leary, Jack Mower, Zon Murray, et al. Warner Bros., 1950.

Breakthrough Has Impressive Hollywood Premiere. Pathé newsreel. Stars attend premiere, including Joan Crawford, Frank Lovejoy, David Brian, Patricia Neal, Gordon MacRae, John Agar, Ruth Roman, with Jack L. Warner, Harry M. Warner. British Pathé, 1950.

Three Secrets. Drama. Dir.: Robert Wise. Scr.: Martin Rackin, Gina Kaus, Cast: Eleanor Parker, Patricia Neal, Ruth Roman (Anne Lawrence), Frank Lovejoy, Leif Erickson, Ted de Corsia, Edmond Ryan, Larry Keating, Katherine Warren, Arthur Franz, Billy Bevan, Eleanor Audley, Peter Brocco, Ralph Brooks, Nana Bryant, John Dehner, Frank Fenton, John Morgan, Duncan Richardson, William Tannen, Willard Waterman, Bill Welsh, Mervin Williams, Charles Sherlock, Gilman Rankin, Ralph Montgomery, Mary Alan Hokanson, Ross Elliott, Lester Dorr, Christian Drake, Tim Graham, Edmund Glover, George Lynn, Duncan Richardson, Lou Marcell, Frank Wilcox, Janet Warren, Rory Mallinson, et al. A United States Pictures Production, 1950.

Dallas. Western. Dir.: Stuart Heisler. Scr.: John Twist. Cast: Gary Cooper, Ruth Roman (Sonia Robles), Steve Cochran, Raymond Massey, Barbara Payton, Leif Erickson, Antonio Moreno, Jerome Cowan, Reed Hadley, Gil Donaldson, Billie Bird, Hal K. Dawson, Will Wright, Joe Dominguez, Gene Evans, Al Ferguson, Byron Keith, Anne Lawrence, Cactus Mack, Slim Talbot, O.Z. Whitehead, Chalky Williams, Monte Blue, Bob Burns, Dolores Corral, Adrian Crossett, Jimmy Dime, Mike Donovan, Steve Dunhill, David Dunbar, Tom Fadden, Wen Wright, Blackjack Ward, Glenn Thompson, Cap Somers, Slim Talbot, Mitchell Rhein, Bob Reeves, Zon Murray, Cactus Mack, Ann Lawrence, Frank Kreig, Larry McGrath, Fred Kelsey, Philo McCullough, Charles Horvath, David O. McCall, Alex Montoya, Richard Neill, Dewey Robinson, Bob Reeves, Robert "Buddy" Shaw, William Steel, et al. Warner Bros., 1950.

Warner Pathé News #30. "Ruth Roman Opens Marines 'Toys for Tots' Drive" Newsreel. Warner News Inc. MP 1045. November 30, 1950.

Lightning Strikes Twice. Crime drama. Dir.: King Vidor. Scr.: Lenore Coffee, from the novel by Margaret Echard. Cast: Richard Todd, Ruth Roman (Shelley Carnes), Mercedes McCambridge, Zachary Scott, Frank Conroy, Darryl Hickman, Rhys Williams, Kathryn Givney, Nacho Gallindo, Ralph Byrd, Frank Cady, Nina Parry, Henry Sharp, Gordon Nelson, Harold Miller, Marya Marco, Ned Glass, Marjorie Bennett, Frank Mills, Jack Mower, Sumner Getchell, Tom Wilson, Fred Rapport, Bill Walker, Helen Winston, Franklin Parker, Jack Perry, John Pickard, Joaquin Garay, Eileen Coghlan, Albert Cavens, Irene Calvillo, Leo Cleary, et al. Warner Bros., 1951.

Strangers on a Train. Thriller. Dir.: Alfred Hitchcock. Scr.: Raymond Chandler, Czenzi Ormonde, Whitfield Cook, Ben Hecht, adapted from the novel by Patricia Highsmith. Cast: Farley Granger, Ruth Roman (Anne Morton), Robert Walker, Leo G. Carroll, Laura Elliot, Patricia Hitchcock, Marion Lorne, Jonathan Hale, Norma Varden, Howard St.

John, John Brown, Robert Gist, Murray Alper, Monya Andre, Dick Wessel, Dick Ryan, Georges Renavent, Wayne Rogers, Odette Myrtil, Roland Morris, Edna Holland, Harry Hines, Al Hill, Robert Haines, Chalky Williams, Howard Washington, Laura Treadwell, Joe Warfield, Robert B. Williams, Shirley Tegge, Brick Sullivan, Janet Stewart, Charles Sherlock, Dick Ryan, Suzanne Ridgway, Georges Renavent, Anthony Redondo, Minna Phillips, Paul Panzer, Spec O'Donnell, Barry Norton, Charles Meredith, Ralph Moody, Louis Lettieri, George Magrill, Perc Launders, Fred Kelsey, Stuart Hall, Al Hill, et al. Warner Bros., 1951.

Tomorrow Is Another Day. Crime drama. Dir.: Felix Feist. Scr.: Art Cohn, from a story by Guy Endore. Cast: Ruth Roman (Catherine "Cay" Higgins), Steve Cochran, Lurene Tuttle, Ray Teal, Morris Ankrum, John Kellogg, Lee Patrick, Hugh Sanders, Stuart Randall, Bobby Hyatt, Harry Antrim, Walter Sande, Mari Aldon, John Bond, Morgan Farley, Lynn Millan, Suzanne Ridgway, Fred Aldrich, Bill McLean, Emile Meyer, Richard Reeves, Tom Wilson, Terry Frost, William Gould, Tom Greenway, Jack Stoney, Gregg Sherwood, Lynn Millan, Kenner G. Kemp, Rosemary Knighton, Jim Hayward, Bobby Hale, Vincent Graeff, Edward Hearn, Philip Carey, Fred Aldrich, Barbara Bestar, Bud Cokes, Frank Donia, Ralph Littlefield, et al. Warner Bros., 1951.

Warner Pathé News #90. "Ruth Roman Sounds New 'Mail Call'" Newsreel. Warner Pathé, June 28, 1951.

The Screen Director: The Movies and You #12. Short documentary film about the work of a director. Dir.: Richard L. Bare. Cast: Richard L. Bare, Lewis Martin, Edward Biby, Phyllis Coates, Michael Curtiz, John Ford, Leo McCarey, Ida Lupino, Frank Capra, Roy Del Ruth, Vivien Leigh, Elia Kazan, Burt Lancaster, Bess Flowers, Jane Wyman, William Wyler, Tennessee Williams, John Wayne, et al, Ruth Roman (Herself), seen in "Staged Archive" footage. Academy of Motion Picture Arts and Sciences, Warner Bros., 1951.

Starlift. Musical drama. Dir.: Roy Del Ruth. Scr.: Karl Lamb, John D. Klorer. Cast: Doris Day, Gordon MacRae, Virginia Mayo, Gene Nelson, Ruth Roman (Herself), Janice Rule, Gary Cooper, James Cagney, Dick Wesson, Ron Hagerthy, Richard Webb, Hayden Rorke, Howard St. John, Phil Harris, Virginia Gibson, Frank Lovejoy, Jane Wyman, Louella Parsons, Patrice Wymore, Randolph Scott, Noonan & Marshall, LeRoy Prinz, Ann Doran, Robert Hammack, Ellanora Needles, Joe Ploski, Stan Holbrook, Mary Adams, Don Beddoe, Rodney bell, Robert Board, Andy Brennan, James Brown, Dolores Castle, Albert Cavens, Lyle Clark, Richard Crenna, Ann Doran, Tommy Farrell, Elizabeth Flournoy, Creighton Hale, Gene Hardy, John Hedloe, William Hudson, Robert Karnes, Dorothy Kennedy, Herb Latimer, Peter Marshall, Ellanora Needles, Joe Ploski, Gordon Polk, Frank J. Scannell, Bonnie Lou Williams, Joe Turkel, Dale Young, Rush Williams, et al. Warner Bros., 1951.

Invitation. Drama. Dir.: Gottfried Reinhardt. Scr.: Paul Osborn, from a story by Jerome Weidman. Cast: Van Johnson, Dorothy McGuire, Ruth Roman (Maud Redwick), Louis Calhern, Ray Collins, Michael Chekhov, Lisa Golm, Diane Cassidy, Stapleton Kent, Barbara Ruick, Norman Field, Matt Moore, Pat Conway, Alex Gerry, Lucille Curtis, Bette Arlen, Larry Harmon, Kenneth Nelson, George Robotham, Lyn Wilde, Barbara Billingsley, Edward Clark, Andre D'Arcy, Arno Frey, Zacharias Yaconelli, Hal Taggart, Fred Nurney, Eloise Hardt, Sam Harris, Joe Gilbert, Ottola Nesmith, Albin Robeling, Bert Davidson, Andre D'Arcy, et al. Metro-Goldwyn-Mayer, 1952.

Mara Maru. Adventure. Dir.: Gordon Douglas. Scr.: N. Richard Nash, from a story by Philip Yordan, Sidney Harmon & Hollister Noble. Cast: Errol Flynn, Ruth Roman (Stella Callahan), Raymond Burr, Paul Picerni, Richard Webb, Dan Seymour, George Renavent, Robert Cabal, Henry Marco, Howard Chuman, Nestor Paiva, Michael Ross, Al Kikume, Paul McGuire, Ted Lawrence, Ben Chavez, Millicent Patrick, Leo C. Richmond, Otto Reichow, Ralph Soncuya, Don C. Harvey, Alfredo Santos, et al. Warner Bros., 1952.

Appendix

Young Man with Ideas. Comedy. Dir.: Mitchell Leisen. Scr.: Ben Barzman, Arthur Sheekman. Cast: Glenn Ford, Ruth Roman (Julie Webster), Denise Darcel, Nina Foch, Ray Collins, Mary Wickes, Bobby Diamond, Sheldon Leonard, Dick Wessel, Carl Milletaire, Curtis Cooksey, Karl Davis, Fay Roope, John Call, Russ Conway, Lawrence Dobkin, Sam Flint, Helene Millard, Isabel Randolph, Helen Spring, Nella Walker, Will Wright, Marshall Bradford, Lela Bliss, Monya Andre, Rudy Baron, Rodney bell, John Zaremba, Wilson Wood, Emmett Vogan, John Trebach, Eddie Lou Simms, Tom Monroe, William Newell, Barry Norton, Ruth Lee, Paul Kruger, et al. Metro-Goldwyn-Mayer, 1952.

Screen Snapshots: Hollywood Night Life. (Short) Dir.: Ralph Staub. Cast: Ralph Staub (Commentator), Dick Haymes (MC), Cecil B. DeMille, Dore Schary, Doris Day, Ronald Reagan, Ruth Roman (Herself), Frank Sinatra, Virginia Mayo, Jeffrey Hunter, Barbara Rush, William Holden, John Hodiak, Anne Baxter, Richard Widmark, Ann Blyth, Terry Moore, Michael O'Shea, George Murphy, Alan Dexter, et al. Columbia Pictures, 1952.

Blowing Wild. Adventure drama. Dir.: Hugo Fregonese. Scr.: Philip Yordan. Cast: Gary Cooper, Barbara Stanwyck, Ruth Roman (Sal Donnelly), Anthony Quinn, Ward Bond, Juan Garcia, Ian MacDonald, Richard Karlan, Ted Mapes, Allen Pomeroy (Stunts). United States Pictures, Warner Bros., 1953.

Tanganyika. Adventure. Dir.: Andre De Toth. Scr.: William R. Cox, William Sackheim, Richard Alan Simmons. Cast: Van Heflin, Ruth Roman (Peggy Marion), Howard Duff, Jeff Morrow, Joe Comadore, Noreen Corcoran, Naaman Brown, Edward C. Short, Murray Alper, Daniel Elam, Jester Hairston, Morgan Roberts, Maxie Thrower. Universal International Pictures, 1954.

The Far Country. Western. Dir.: Anthony Mann. Scr.: Brandon Chase. Cast: James Stewart, Ruth Roman (Ronda Castle), Corinne Calvet, Walter Brennan, John McIntire, Connie Gilchrist, Jay C. Flippen, Harry Morgan, Steve Brodie, Chubby Johnson, Royal Dano, Kathleen Freeman, Connie Van, Robert Wilke, Paul Bryar, Gregg Barton, John Doucette, Carl Harbaugh, Don C. Harvey, Terry Frost, Ted Mapes, Eddie Parker, Stuart Randall, Chuck Roberson, Guy Wilkerson, William J, Williams, Eddy Waller, Allan Ray, Damian O'Flynn, Angeline Engler, Robert Foulk, Eugene Bordon, Chester Hayes, Harry Wilson, Jack Williams, Dale Van Sickel, Marjorie Stapp, Dick Taylor, Cap Summers, Paul Savage, Victor Romito, Anton Northpole, John Mackin, Russell Meeker, Forbes Murray, Ethan Laidlaw, George Huggins, Mike Lally, Walter Lawrence, Don C. Harvey, et al. Universal International Pictures, 1954.

The Shanghai Story. Drama. Dir.: Frank Lloyd. Scr.: Steve Fisher, Seton I. Miller, from a story by Lester Yard. Cast: Ruth Roman (Rita King), Edmond O'Brien, Richard Jaeckel, Barry Kelley, Whit Bissell, Basil Ruysdael, Marvin Miller, Yvette Duguay, Paul Picerni, Isabel Randolph, Philip Ahn, Frances Rafferty, Frank Ferguson, James Griffith, John Alvin, Frank Puglia, Victor Sen Yung, Janine Perreau, Richard Loo, David Chow, Donald Curtis, Gil Herman, Eddie Lee, Tommy Lee, Joseph Kim, W.T. Chang, Edwin Luke, Frank Wong, Guy Way, James B. Leong, Wong Artane, Weaver Levy, Beal Wong, Harold Fong, Richard Wang, et al. Republic Pictures, 1954.

Down Three Dark Streets. Crime Drama. Dir.: Arnold Laven. Scr.: The Gordons, Bernard C. Schoenfeld, based on the novel *Case File: FBI* by the Gordons. Cast: Broderick Crawford, Ruth Roman (Kate Martell), Martha Hyer, Marisa Pavan, Casey Adams, Kenneth Tobey, Gene Reynolds, Jay Adler, Claude Akins, Suzanne Alexander, Myra Marsh, Joe Bassett, William Johnstone, Dede Gainor, Milton Parsons, William Woodson, Alan Dexter, Jack Daly, Alexander Campbell, Leonard Bremen, Sydney Clute, Michael Fox, Harry Wilson, Charles Tannen, William Schallert, Stafford Repp, Milton Parsons, John Indrisano, Bill McLean, Arthur Gardner, Larry Hudson, et al. United Artists, 1954.

Joe MacBeth. Drama. Dir.: Ken Hughes. Scr.: Ken Hughes, Philip Yordan. Cast: Paul Douglas, Ruth Roman (Lily MacBeth), Bonar Colleano, Gregoire Aslan, Sidney James,

Appendix

Harry Green, Minerva Pious, Walter Crisham, Theresa Thorne, Philip Vickers, Kay Callard, Robert Arden, George Marco, Mark Baker, Bill Nagy, Sheila Woods, Nicholas Stuart, Johnny Ross, Robert O'Neill, Shirley Douglas, Victor Barling, Beresford Egan, Louise Grant, Launce Maraschal. Columbia Pictures, 1955.

Man on a Bus. (Short) Dir.: Joseph H. Lewis. Cast: Broderick Crawford, Ruth Roman (Rachel), Walter Brennan, J. Carrol Naish, Rosemary de Camp, Kim Charney, Peter Leeds, Dorothy Neumann, Robert Dix, Eda Reiss Merin, David Leonard, Richard Hale, John Qualen, Peter Brocco, Paul Bryar, Henry Corden, Charles Regan. United Jewish Appeal/Metro-Goldwyn-Mayer, 1955.

The Bottom of the Bottle aka *Beyond the River.* Drama. Dir.: Henry Hathaway. Scr.: Georges Simenon (from his novel), Sydney Boehm. Cast: Van Johnson, Joseph Cotten, Ruth Roman (Nora Martin), Jack Carson, Margaret Hayes, Bruce Bennett, Brad Dexter, Peggy Knudsen, Nancy Gates, Jim Davis, Margaret Lindsay, González-González, John Lee, Todd Griffin, Ernestine Barrier, Henry Morgan, Walter Woolf King, Sandy Descher, Mimi Gibson, Kim Charney, Frances Dominguez, Maria M. Valerani, George Trevino, Joanne Jordan, George Anderson, Oscar Humberto Stevens, Martin F. Gerrish, Louise Truax, James Torrington, Leonard Sweeney, Jr., Shirley Patterson, Rosa Rey, John Doucette, Grizzly Green, Orlando Beltran, Alma Beltran, Arthur Hansen, Jr., Robert Adler, Carleton Young, Lee González, et al. Twentieth Century–Fox, 1956.

Great Day in the Morning. Western. Dir.: Jacques Tourneur. Scr.: Lesser Samuels, from the novel by Robert Hardy Andrews. Cast: Virginia Mayo, Robert Stack, Ruth Roman (Boston Grant), Alex Nichol, Raymond Burr, Leo Gordon, Regis Toomey, Carleton Young, Donald MacDonald, William Phipps, Burt Mustin, George Wallace, Dan White, Peter Whitney, Syd Saylor, Cap Somers, Kermit Maynard, Mitchell Kowall, Lane Chandler, George Huggins, Pierce Lyden, Frank Mills, Rudy Bowman, Fred Carson, Peter Whitney, George Wallace, Dan White, Sailor Vincent, Ray Spiker, John Roy, Robert Robinson, Dennis Moore, Frank Mills, John Pedrini, Earl Parker, Pierce Lyden, George Huggins, George Ford, Al Haskell, Duke Fishman, Fred Carson, George Ford, et al. Edmund Grainger Productions, 1956.

Rebel in Town. Western. Dir.: Alfred Werker. Scr.: Danny Arnold. Cast: John Payne, Ruth Roman (Nora Willoughby), J. Carrol Naish, Ben Cooper, Ben Johnson, John Smith, Mary Adams, James Griffith, Bobby Clark, Cane Mason, Joel Ashley, Jack Perrin, Jimmy Noel, Kermit Maynard, Ralph Bucko, Fred Aldrich, Herman Hack, Ivan Bell, Fox O'Callahan, Cecil Combs, Don Happy, Fritz Ford, Ray Jones, Joe Phillips, Tom Smith, Chalky Williams, Jack Lowe, Jack Tornek, Jimmy Noel, Ernesto Molinari, Earl Parker, Jack Perrin, Carl Matthews, Richard LaMarr, et al. Schenck-Koch Productions, Bel-Air Productions, 1956.

Five Steps to Danger. Crime Drama. Dir.: Henry S. Kesler. Scr.: Henry S. Kesler, from *The Steel Mirror* by Donald Hamilton, Turney Walker. Cast: Ruth Roman (Ann Nicholson), Sterling Hayden, Werner Klemperer, Richard Gaines, Charles Davis, Jeanne Cooper, John Mitchum, Peter Hansen, Karl Lindt, John Merrick, Ken Curtis, Harry Hines, Tom McKee, Bert Stevens, Sidney Clute, Leonard Bremen. Henry S. Kesler Productions, Grand Productions, 1956.

Bitter Victory. War Drama. Dir.: Nicholas Ray. Scr.: Rene Hardy, Nicholas Ray, Gavin Lambert, Paul Gallico, Vladimir Pozner, from the novel by Rene Hardy. Cast: Richard Burton, Curd Jürgens, Ruth Roman (Jane Brand), Raymond Pellegrin, Anthony Bushell, Alfred Burke, Christopher Lee, Sean Kelly, Nigel Green, Andrew Crawford, Raoul Delfosse, Ramon de Larrocha, Harry Landis, Fred Matter, Christian Melsen, Ronan O'Casey, Sumner Williams, Joé Davray. Columbia Pictures, Transcontinental Films, Robert Laffont Productions, 1957. Nominated for a Golden Lion at the Venice Film Festival, 1957.

Appendix

Desert Desperadoes aka *La Peccatrice del Deserto.* Biblical drama. Dir.: Steve Sekely, Gianni Vernuccio. Scr.: Victor Stoloff. Cast: Ruth Roman (The Woman), Akim Tamiroff, Otello Toso, Gianni Musy, Arnoldo Foà, Alan Furlan, Nino Marchetti, Gianni Glori. Venturini-Express-Nasht, 1959.

Look in Any Window. Drama. Dir.: William Alland. Scr.: Laurence E. Mascott. Cast: Paul Anka, Ruth Roman (Jackie Fowler), Alex Nichol, Gigi Perreau, Carole Matthews, George Dolenz, Jack Cassidy, Robert Sampson, Dan Grayam, Jacqueline Kluger, Norman Winston, Ray Reese, Jim Jacobs. Scott R. Dunlap Productions, 1961.

Milagro a los Cobardes. Biblical drama. Dir.: Manuel Mur Oti. Scr.: Manuel Mur Oti, Manuel Pilares. Cast: Ruth Roman (Ana), Javier Escrivá, Leo Anchóriz, Carlos Casaravilla, Ricardo Canales, Manuel D. González, Paloma Valdés, Salvador Arias, Vicente Bañó, José Cordero, Carlos Revilla. Mercedes Mireya dubbed Ruth Roman. Other actors dubbed by Felix Acaso (Javier Escrivá), Angel Maria Baltaras (Leo Anchóriz), Eduardo Calvo (Manuel D. González), Juan Cordoba (Sebastian Canales), Marie Angelez Herranz (Paloma Valdez), Teofilo Martínez (Carlos Casaravilla). Trefilms, Spain, 1962. Winner of a Special Award at the National Syndicate of Spectacle, Spain. Also, José Buenagu for Best Music at the same awards.

Love Has Many Faces. Drama. Dir.: Alexander Singer. Scr.: Marguerite Roberts. Cast: Lana Turner, Cliff Robertson, Hugh O'Brian, Ruth Roman (Margo Eliot), Stefanie Powers, Virginia Grey, Ron Husmann, Enrico Lucero, Carlos Montalbán, Jaime Bravo, Fanny Schiller, René Dupeyrón, Patty Hobbs, Cynthia O'Neal, Dean Reed. Jerry Bresler Productions, 1965.

S.R.O. Dir.: Jerry Shafer, Rory Calhoun. Scr.: John Sanford, from the novel by Robert Deane Pharr. Cast: Rory Calhoun, Ruth Roman, Roosevelt Grier, James Mitchum, Jesse White, John Fiedler, Percy Helton. Hollywood International Productions, 1971.[2]

The Baby. Horror. Dir.: Ted Post. Scr.: Abe Polsky. Cast: Anjanette Cromer, Ruth Roman (Mrs. Wadsworth), Mariana Hill, Susanne Zenor, Tod Andrews, Michael Pataki, Beatrice Manly Blau, Erin O'Reilly, Don Malon, David Manzy, Joseph Bernard, Virginia Vincent, Ted Post. Quintet Productions, 1973.

The Killing Kind. Horror. Dir.: Curtis Harrington. Scr.: Tony Crechales (from his story), George Edwards. Cast: Ann Sothern, John Savage, Ruth Roman (Rhea Benson), Luana Anders, Cindy Williams, Sue Bernard, Marjorie Eaton, Peter Brocco, Helene Winston. Prod.: George Edwards, 1973.

Impulse. Horror. Dir.: William Grefé. Scr.: Tony Crechales. Cast: William Shatner, Ruth Roman (Julia Marstow), Jennifer Bishop, Kim Nicholas, James Dobson, Harold Sakata, Marcia Knight, Vivian Lester, William Kerwin, Marcy Lafferty, Chad Walker, Paula Dimitrouleas, Doug Hobart, Lewis Perles. Conqueror Films Inc., 1974.

A Knife for the Ladies. Horror. Dir.: Larry G. Spangler. Scr.: George Arthur Bloom, Seton I. Miller, Robert Shelton. Cast: Jack Elam, Ruth Roman (Elizabeth), Jeff Cooper, John Kellogg, Gene Evans, Diana Ewing, Derek Sanderson, Jon Spangler, Peter Athas, Phillip Avenetti, Fred Biletnikoff, Al Hassan, Pat Herrerra, Hank Kendrich, Kit Kendrich. Bryanston Pictures, Spangler, Jolley Productions, 1974.

Day of the Animals. Environmental horror. Dir.: William Girdler. Scr.: William Norton, Eleanor E. Norton, Edward L. Montero. Cast: Christopher George, Leslie Nielsen, Lynda Day George, Richard Jaeckel, Michael Ansara, Ruth Roman (Shirley Goodwin), Paul Mantee, Jon Cedar, Walter Barnes, Andrew Stevens, Susan Backlinie, Kathleen Bracken, Bobby Porter, Michelle Stacy, Michael Andreas, Jan Andrew Scott, Gil Lamb, Garrison True, Gertrude Lee, Mike Clifford, Walt Gorney. Film Ventures International, 1977.

Echoes. Mystery drama. Dir.: Arthur Allan Seidelman. Scr.: Richard Alfieri, Richard J. Anthony. Cast: Richard Alfieri, Gale Sondergaard, Ruth Roman (Michael's mother),

Nathalie Nell, Mercedes McCambridge, Mike Kellin, Sheila M. Coonan, Leonard Cro-foot, Damian Akhan, Ron Asher, Raaf Baldwin, David M. Brezniak, James Dunne, Barry Eric, Steve Cassidy, Joe Zaloom, Jan Winetsky, Dennis Wayne, John Teitsort, Paul Joynt, John Spencer, Julie Burger, Duncan Quinn, Barbara Monte-Britton, Robert Neal Marshall, Leib Lensky, Robin Karfo. Prod.: Valerie Y. Belsky, George R. Nice. Asst. Prod.: Gregg Burton, Marilyn R. Atlas. CBS, Astra Video, 1982.

Selected Stage Appearances

Dear Ruth. By Norman Krasna. Cast: Ruth Roman (Ruth), William Lundigan, Herb Anderson, Peggy Romano. At the Temple of Music, Tucson, Arizona, January 19 to 25, 1949.

Two for the Seesaw. By William Gibson. Cast: Ruth Roman (Gittel Mosca), William Lynn. National Tour, Fall, 1958 to Summer 1959. Including The Hanna Theater, Cleveland, Ohio, October 27, 1958; The Michael Todd Theater, Chicago, January 25 to 30, 1959; Geary Theater, San Francisco, May 25–30, 1959.

Appeared in a Rota of plays on tour including *Plaza Suite, The Killing of Sister George* and *The Night of the Iguana,* circa 1964–65.

Time of the Cuckoo. By Arthur Laurents, tour, including Cirque Dinner Theater, Seattle, Washington, December 31, 1964; January 1, 1965.

Candida. By George Bernard Shaw. Cast: Ruth Roman (Candida) at the Pioneer Memorial Theater, University of Utah, April 8 to 17, 1965.

Who's Afraid of Virginia Woolf? By Edward Albee. Cast: Wendell Corey, Ruth Roman (Martha), San Christopher, Erik Holland. Gallery Theater, Los Angeles, and later at the Melodyland, November 1 to 8, 1967.

Beckman Palace Cast: Ruth Roman, John Vivyan, at the Ivanhoe Theater, Chicago, August to September 1967.

Time of the Cuckoo. By Arthur Laurents. Tour c1972.

The Night of the Iguana. By Tennessee Williams. Ruth Roman, Barbara Rush. Goodman Theater, Chicago, c1977.[3]

Radio

People Are Funny. NBC Game Show. Art Linkletter (Presenter), with guests Louella Parsons, Kay Kaiser, Rudy Vallee, Walter Slezak, Ruth Roman. Circa November 1943.[4]

The Lux Radio Theatre. CBS Drama "Somewhere in the Night," William Keighley (Host), with John Hodiak, Lynn Bari, Ruth Roman (guest during intermission), March 3, 1947. "One Sunday Afternoon" Based on the play by James Hagan. Cast: Dennis Morgan, Marie Windsor, Patricia Neal, Ruth Roman, September 4, 1950. "Bright Leaf" from the novel by Foster Fitz-Simons. Cast: Gregory Peck, Ruth Roman (Margaret), Virginia Mayo, May 28, 1951. "Strangers on a Train" Cast: Ray Milland, Ruth Roman, Frank Lovejoy, Patricia Hitchcock, Ed Begley, Ted de Corsia, Martha Wentworth, et al., December 3, 1951. "The Third Man" CBS. Cast: Ray Milland, Tyrone Power, Ruth Roman, February 8, 1954. "The Blue Gardenia" NBC. Cast: Dana Andrews, Ruth Roman (as Norah), Carleton Young, Jennifer Howard, William Conrad, Herb Butterfield, Marian Richman, Charlie Lung, Jerry Hausner, November 30, 1954.

The Camel Screen Guild Theatre. NBC Drama. "Champion" Cast: Kirk Douglas, Elliott Lewis, Ruth Roman, Marilyn Maxwell, Jimmy Lydon, October 13, 1949.

Appendix

Academy Awards Program. Annual awards ceremony broadcast live from the Pantages Hotel, Hollywood. Guests including Ronald Reagan, Charles Brackett, Eve Arden, Patricia Neal, Anne Baxter, John Hodiak, Mercedes McCambridge, Broderick Crawford, Gene Autry, Ann Blyth, Leah Rhodes, Ruth Roman, Barbara Hale, Dick Powell, Bobby Driscoll, Jean Hersholt, Claire Trevor, Joanne Dru, Donald O'Connor, June Allyson, Betty Garrett, Peggy Dow, Marjorie Best, Dean Martin, Frank Loesser, Dean Jagger, Ray Milland, Ida Lupino, Cole Porter, Joseph Mankiewicz, Jane Wyman, James Stewart, Olivia de Havilland, James Cagney, et al., March 23, 1950.

Screen Director's Guild. NBC Drama. "A Star is Born" Cast: Fredric March, Ruth Roman, June 16, 1950.[5]

Bob Wells. WEBR 970 (Buffalo, New York). Interview with Ruth Roman ahead of the release of *Three Secrets,* July 26, 1950.

Stars Over Hollywood. CBS Drama. "The Templeton Case" by Victor L. Whitechurch (Tenth anniversary edition), starring Ruth Roman, September 9, 1950. "The Shining Rails" by Martin Ryerson. Art Ballinger (Host). Cast: Ruth Roman, Vic Perrin, Ted Bliss, April 17, 1954.

Easter Seals Campaign. Syndicated charity fundraiser. With guests Gordon MacRae, Lucille Norman, Ruth Roman, Phillip Carey, Phyllis Thaxter, February 25, 1951.

Hollywood Sound Stage. CBS Drama. "One Way Passage" with Ruth Roman, Frank Lovejoy, February 14, 1952.[6]

Operation Brotherhood. WBBM (Chicago). "The poignant story of wandering orphans in Czechoslovakia." Ruth Roman (Narrator). Sponsored by the National Conference of Christians and Jews in the Chicago area, January 4, 1953.[7]

The Bob Hope Daytime Show. KTBS. Ruth Roman as guest lady editor of the week, March 7, 1954.[8]

These Are My Children. KABC (Los Angeles) Broadcast. Ruth Roman (Narrator), May 10, 1954.[9]

Peter Porter. KNX (Los Angeles) Music variety show. Peter Porter (Presenter) invites star guests to select the hits. Guests: Ruth Roman, Jack Palance, Connie Russell, José Ferrer, December 18, 1954.[10]

Breakfast Club. ABC Variety Show. Don McNeill (Host), Ruth Roman (Guest), c1959.[11]

Note: A CD, MP3 and download compilation selection of Roman's radio appearances are available from the Old Time Radio Catalog (OTR.org). For details, see *Discography.*

Television

Cerebral Palsy Telecast. Charity fundraising marathon, with many guests including Jack Benny, Gene Nelson, Ruth Roman, et al., June 1, 1953.

National Tuberculosis Association Christmas Seal Sale. Syndicated nine 20-second spots and two one-minute appeals by stars, including Ida Lupino, Ruth Roman, Howard Duff, Pat O'Brien, Jane Greer, et al. Freedom Films, December 1953.[12]

Lux Video Theater. NBC, J. Walter Thompson Agency, Drama. "The Chase" Dir.: Richard Goode. Scr.: Sumner Locke Elliott, based on the novel by Cornell Woolrich. Cast: James Arness, Frances Bavier, Patrick Miller, Pat O'Brien, Ruth Roman (Lorna Gorman), Charles Watts, Margaret Lindsay, Ken Carpenter (Announcer), December 30, 1954.

The Red Skelton Hour. CBS Comedy variety show. Ruth in "Queen of Mars" skit. Cast: Jan Arvan, David Rose & His Orchestra, Reginald Denny, Ruth Roman (Queen Zodia of Mars), Billy Curtis, Bob LeMond, The Redettes, February 1, 1955.

Appendix

The Ford Television Theatre. NBC, Screen Gems. 30-minute drama. "The Lilac Bush" Dir.: Arnold Laven. Scr. Karen DeWolf from a story by Lesley Conger. Cast: Diana Christian, Marilyn Erskine, William Leslie, Ruth Roman (Connie Wilson), Leslie Matthews. A woman (Roman) plants a shrub for her son and when he dies becomes obsessed with the idea that his life was tied up with that of the tree, March 3, 1955.

The Ford Television Theatre. "Panic" Dir.: Arthur Hiller. Scr.: Karen DeWolf from a story by Forrest Kleinman. Cast: Ruth Roman (Shawn Adams), Phil Carey, George Macready, Mark Sheeler, Hal Taggart, Ike Jones. Shawn (Roman) tries to escape the persistent attentions of an obsessed man (Macready) with the help of another man (Carey) she meets in a hotel, June 14, 1956.

Producer's Showcase. NBC, Showcase Productions. "Darkness at Noon" Anti-Communist drama. Dir.: Delbert Mann. Scr.: Robert Alan Arthur adapted from the play by Sidney Kingsley, which was based on the novel by Arthur Koestler. Cast: Lee J. Cobb, Robert Gibbons, Oscar Homolka, Mikhail Rasumny, Richard Nixon, Nehemiah Persoff, Ruth Roman, Robert McQueeney, Norman Roland, Frederick Rolf, Henry Silva, Frank Sutton, Alfred Hesse, Michael Gorrin, Jimmy King, Burt Conway, Lisa Osten, Pat Perry, Steve Gray, Steve Gravers, Richard Bull, Norman Roland, Charles Rae King, Robert Gibbons, James Elward, Lois Holmes, Frank Grosso, Jerry Stiller, Joe Abdullah, Bill Lazarus, May 2, 1955.

General Electric Theatre. CBS, Revue Productions. "Into the Night" Dir.: Jacques Tourneur. Scr.: Mel Dinelli from a story by Charles Hoffman. Cast: Eddie Albert, Ruth Roman (Helen Mattson), Dane Clark, Robert Armstrong, Jeanne Bates, Wallace Clark, Bill Fawcett, Nora Marlowe, Larry Blake, Bob Bice, Jerry Mathers, Ronald Reagan (Host). A couple (Albert and Roman) on a weekend holiday away become the hostages of a pair of escaped criminals (Dane Clark and Robert Armstrong), May 8, 1955.

General Electric Theatre. CBS, Revue Studios. "The Book of Silence" Dir.: Boris Sagal. Scr.: David Karp. Cast: Whit Bissell, Eduard Franz, Jonathan Harris, Ruth Roman (Stella Krayogan), Rod Steiger, Ted Marcuse, Arlene Saxe, Celia Lovsky, Robert Gist, Ronald Reagan (Host), March 6, 1960.

The Ted Ray Show. BBC variety chat show. Guests including Ruth Roman interviewed by Ted Ray about the filming of *Joe MacBeth,* circa May 1955.

Climax! CBS Drama. "Spin into Darkness" Dir.: John Frankenheimer. Scr.: Hagar Wilde. Cast: Charles Drake, Virginia Grey, Vincent Price, Ruth Roman (Suzan Wayne), William Lundigan (Host). A woman with a gambling problem (Roman) sees an opportunity to settle all her debts thanks to the drunken promise of her employer (Price), but he then changes his mind the next day, April 5, 1956.

Celebrity Playhouse. NBC, Screen Gems. 30-minute drama. "A Letter from the Past" Dir.: James Neilson. Scr.: DeWitt Bodeen from a story by Violet Atkins. Drama. Cast: Ruth Roman, Dorothy Patrick, Jean Byron, Warren Stevens, Earl Robie, Wendy Winkelman, April 17, 1956.

Jane Wyman Presents the Fireside Theatre. NBC, Lewman Productions. 30-minute drama. "He Came for the Money" Dir.: Allen H. Miller. Scr.: Frederic Brady. Cast: Ruth Roman (Martha Benton), Wesley Lau, John Larch, Philip Pine, Jane Wyman (Host), February 13, 1958.

Confidential File: Story of a Hollywood Starlet. Short documentary including interviews. Dir.: Irving Kershner. Scr.: Paul Coates, Andrew J. Fenady, James Peck. Cast: Paul Coates, Joan Kerr, Jody Lawrence, Ruth Roman (Herself), Milt Stein. KTTV Los Angeles, 1958.

Appendix

At Random. Open-ended late-night discussion show, WBBM TV (Chicago) Host: Irv Kupcinet, with guests Sidney Poitier, Sen. Wayne Morse of Oregon, Sammy Davis, Jr., Congressman James Roosevelt of New York, Ruth Roman, February 12, 1959.[13]

Bonanza. NBC Western series. "The Magnificent Adah" Dir.: Christian Nyby. Scr.: Donald S. Sanford. Cast: Lorne Greene, Pernell Roberts, Dan Blocker, Michael Landon, Ruth Roman (Adah Isaacs Menken), Dan Megowan, Hal Smith, Victor Sen Yung, Bill Mims, Fay Roope, Mauritz Hugo, Nancy Root, Phil Bloom, Kermit Maynard, Roy Jenson, Bill Clark, Jack Perry, et al., November 14, 1959.

The Philadelphia Story. (1959) TV Movie. Dir.: Fielder Cook. Scr.: Jacqueline Babbin, Audrey Maas, adapted from the play by Philip Barry. Cast: Gig Young, Mary Astor, Christopher Plummer, Diana Lynn, Ruth Roman (Liz Imbrie), Alan Webb, Emory Richardson, Gaye Huston, Don DeFore, Leon Janney.

The Arthur Murray Party. ABC Musical Variety Show. Arthur Murray, Kathryn Murray, with guests Merv Griffin, The Four Lads, Phyllis Kirk, Abbe Lane, Ruth Roman (Herself), Ray Carter Orchestra, William Vaux, Betty Ann Grove, Judy Johnson, December 1, 1959.

The Naked City. ABC Crime series. "The Human Trap" Dir.: Lamont Johnson. Scr.: Ellis Kadison. Cast: Ruth Roman (Walda Price), Paul Burke, Horace McMahon, Jack Lord, Nancy Malone, Harry Bellaver, Zina Bethune, Gene Lyons, Marge O'Neill, Elizabeth MacRae, Bob Allen, Nicholas Saunders, November 30, 1960.

The Untouchables. ABC Crime series, Desilu Productions, Langford Productions. "Man Killer" Dir.: Stuart Rosenberg. Scr.: Sy Salkowitz, based on the book by Eliot Ness, Oscar Fraley. Cast: Robert Stack, Ruth Roman (Georgiana Drake), Bruce Gordon, Anne Helm, Paul Picerni, Nicholas Georgiade, Steve London, Mario Alcalde, Grant Richards, Jay Adler, Mario Gallo, Joe Scott, Walter Winchell (Narrator), December 7, 1961.

Bus Stop. ABC Drama series, 20th Century–Fox Television. "Turn Again Home" Dir.: Stuart Rosenberg. Scr.: Harry Kleiner, from a story by Howard Browne. Cast: Jack Albertson, Wendell Corey, Ruth Roman (Louisa), Joyce Van Patten, Angela Green, Joan Freeman, Scotty Morrow, Jack Grinnage, Rhodes Reason, George Neise, Grant Richards, Robert Rockwell, et al., January 28, 1962.

The Defenders. CBS Drama series. "The Voices of Death" Dir.: Stuart Rosenberg. Scr.: Reginald Rose. Cast: E.G. Marshall, Robert Reed, Dustin Hoffman, Ruth Roman (Martha Harrow), J.D. Cannon, Susan Melvin, Judson Laire, Donnie Melvin, Doro Merande. September 15, 1962.

The Alfred Hitchcock Hour. CBS Mystery Anthology series. "What Really Happened" Dir.: Jack Smight. Scr.: Henry Slesar, from the novel by Marie Belloc Lowndes. Cast: Alfred Hitchcock (Host), Anne Francis, Ruth Roman (Adelaide "Addie" Strain), Gladys Cooper, Steve Dunn, Michael Strong, Tim O'Connor, Gene Lyons, Charles Irving, Theodore Newton, Fern Barry, Michael Crisalli, January 11, 1963.

The Eleventh Hour. NBC, MGM Television, Drama series. "Advice to the Lovelorn and the Shopworn" Dir.: Richard Donner. Cast: Wendell Corey, Jack Ging, Harry Guardino, Ruth Roman (Clara Porter), Natalie Trundy, Robert Brubaker, Ed Prentice, Richard Donner, Ann Staunton, Ruth Packard, Matty Jordan, January 23, 1963.

Dr. Kildare. NBC Medical Drama series. Arena Productions, MGM Television. "Four Feet in the Morning" Dir.: Jack Smight. Scr.: Jerry de Bono. Cast: Jack Ging, Ralph Bellamy, Ruth Roman (Marie Quincy), Andrew Duggan, Tony Dow, Phyllis Avery, Richard Chamberlain, Raymond Massey, Marta Kirsten, November 21, 1963. (The second episode was shown on *The Eleventh Hour*, November 27, 1963, personnel as above.)

Appendix

Dr. Kildare. "A Candle in the Window" Dir.: Sydney Pollack. Scr.: Rita Lakin. Cast: Richard Chamberlain, Raymond Massey, Ruth Roman (Lily Prentice), Ronny Howard, Eddie Ryder, Eddie Firestone, Walter Burke, Isobel Elsom, Jean Inness, Jo Helton, Ed Prentiss, Pat Priest, November 5, 1964.

Sam Benedict. NBC, MGM Television Drama series. "Green Room, Grey Morning" Dir.: Abner Biberman. Scr.: E. Jack Neuman, Carey Wilbur. Cast: Edmond O'Brien, Richard Rust, Ruth Roman (Florence Haney), Frank Albertson, Tige Andrews, Sam Gillman, Joan Tompkins, Kenneth Lynch, Ralph Manza, Anthony Call, Bernadette Hale, January 19, 1963.

Route 66. CBS Drama Anthology series. "In the Closing of a Trunk" Dir.: Ralph Senensky. Scr.: Stirling Silliphant. Cast: Martin Milner, Ed Begley, Ruth Roman (Alma Hawkes), Don Dubbins, Guy Raymond, Harry Hickox, Jon Lormer, March 8, 1963.

The Greatest Show on Earth. ABC, Desilu Productions, Cody Productions. Drama Series. "Silent Love, Secret Love" Dir.: Robert Butler. Scr.: William Bast. Cast: Jack Palance, Ruth Roman (Inge Johansen), Russ Tamblyn, Robert Webber, Tuesday Weld, September 24, 1963.

Burke's Law. CBS Action-Adventure series. "Who Killed Harris Crown?" Dir.: Don Weis. Scr.: John Meredyth Lucas. Cast: Gene Barry, Gary Conway, Regis Toomey, Joan Blondell, Barbara Eden, Eva Gabor, Ruth Roman (Elinor Albrick), Lola Albright, Gene Nelson, Juliet Prowse, Don Rickles, Jackie Loughery, Than Wyenn, Eileen O'Neill, October 11, 1963.

Breaking Point. ABC, Bing Crosby Productions. Drama series. "Who is Mimi, what is She?" Dir.: Paul Wendkos. Scr.: Jay Dratler, Leonard Kantor. Cast: Paul Richards, Eduard Franz, Sylvia Lewis, Ruth Roman (Alicia Howard), Terry Becker, Hunt Powers, Sondra Kerr, Gregory Morton, Vivian Nathan, December 2, 1963.

Bob Hope Presents the Chrysler Theater. NBC, Hovue Enterprises, Morpics. Drama Anthology series. "The Candidate" Dir.: Stuart Rosenberg. Scr.: Karl Miller, Eugene Burdick. Cast: Milton Berle, Robert Webber, J.D. Cannon, Dina Merrill, Ruth Roman (Mrs. Hite), Hope Holiday, Simon Scott, John McLiam, James Flavin, Blair Davis, Isabelle Cooley, Bernard Fine, Jay Adler, Charles J. Conrad, Davis Roberts, December 6, 1963.

The Outer Limits. ABC Sci-Fi series. "Moonstone" Dir.: Robert Florey. Scr.: William Bast, Lou Morheim, Joseph Stefano. Cast: Ruth Roman (Professor Diana Brice), Alex Nichol, Tim O'Connor, Curt Conway, Harry Rhodes, March 9, 1964.

Survival! Andrea Doria. Documentary about the sinking of the SS *Andrea Doria* on July 25, 1956. James Whitmore (Narrator) interviews with survivors. Official Films, Inc., Sherman Grinberg Productions, Inc., 1964.

The Bing Crosby Show. ABC, Bing Crosby Productions. Comedy series. "Real Estate Value" Cast: Bing Crosby, Beverly Garland, Frank McHugh, Diane Sherry, Carol Faylen, Ruth Roman (Anne Rankin), Willard Waterman, Kathleen Freeman, Monroe Arnold, March 15, 1965.

Gypsy. ABC Morning Talk Show. Gypsy Rose Lee with guests Ruth Roman, Beverly Garland, Betty Furness. Seven Arts Television (San Francisco), November 19, 1965.

The Long, Hot Summer. Drama series. Dir.: Ralph Senensky. Scr.: Dean Riesner, adapted from the stories by William Faulkner. Cast: Edmond O'Brien, Roy Thinnes, Ruth Roman (Minnie Littlejohn), Nancy Malone, Lana Wood, Paul Bryar, Dan O'Herlihy, Lana Wood, Charles Lampkin, Paul Geary, et al., September 16, 1965 to April 13, 1966. Episodes: "The Homecoming" September 16, 1965. "A Time for Living" (Credited but did not appear). "A Stranger to the House" September 30, 1965. "Home is a Nameless Place" October 21, 1965. "Run, Hero, Run" November 4, 1965. "The Desperate Innocent"

Appendix

November 11, 1965. "Bitter Harvest" November 18, 1965. "Hunter to the Wind" December 2, 1965. "Nor Hell a Fury" December 9, 1965. "The Return of the Quicks" December 16, 1965. "Track the Man Down" (Credited but did not appear). "Face of Fear" January 6, 1966. "Evil Angel" January 13, 1966. "Day of the Thunder" January 19, 1966. "The Warning" January 26, 1966. "The Intruders" February 2, 1966. "From This Day Forward" February 9, 1966. "A Time to Die" February 16, 1966. "Reunion—Italian Style" February 23, 1966. "Blaze of Glory" March 2, 1966. "Crisis" March 9, 1966. "Carlotta Come Home" March 30, 1966. "Man with Two Faces" April 13, 1966.

The F.B.I. ABC, Warner Bros. Television. Crime series. "The Courier" Dir.: Ralph Senensky. Scr.: Charles Larson, from story by Robert C. Dennis. Cast: Efrem Zimbalist, Jr., Philip Abbott, Stephen Brooks, Ruth Roman (Julie Sinclair), Gene Hackman, Keye Luke, Sandra Marsh, Gene Lyons, Cherylene Lee, Noah Keen, Eddie Guardino, Dene Harens, Harold Gould, Phyllis Love, January 15, 1967.

The Girl from U.N.C.L.E. NBC, MGM Television Fantasy series. "The Furnace Flats Affair" Dir.: John Brahm. Scr.: Archie L. Tegland, Sam Rolfe. Cast: Stefanie Powers, Noel Harrison, Leo G. Carroll, Ruth Roman (Dolly X), Peggy Lee, Percy Helton, Susan Browning, Herb Edelman, February 21, 1967.

Tarzan. NBC Adventure series. "The Ultimatum" Dir.: Robert L. Friend. Scr.: James Menzies. Cast: Ron Ely, Jeff Burden, Henry Corden, Ralph Meeker, Ruth Roman (Madiline Riker), Manuel Padilla, Jr., March 31, 1967.

I Spy. NBC, 3F Productions. Espionage Adventure series. "Let's Kill Karlovassi" Dir.: Christian Nyby. Scr.: Michael Zagor. Cast: Robert Culp, Bill Cosby, Walter Slezak, Ruth Roman (Maria), Peter Wyngarde, Paul Muller, Helen Hall, Irene Prador, Giuseppe Paganelli, September 11, 1967.

The Name of the Game. NBC, Universal Television, Adventure Drama series. "Witness" Dir.: Lamont Johnson. Scr.: Dick Nelson from a story by Robert E. Thompson. Cast: Robert Stack, Joan Hackett, Ruth Roman (Bea Decker), Joseph Campanella, Jack Carter, Victor Jory, September 27, 1968.

Mission: Impossible. CBS, Paramount Television. Action-Adventure series. "The Elixir" Dir.: John Florea. Scr.: Bruce Geller, Max Hodge. Cast: Peter Graves, Martin Landau, Barbara Bain, Greg Morris, Peter Lupus, Ruth Roman (Riva Santel), George Gaynes, Morgan Sterne, Ivor Barry, Richard Angarola, Arthur Eisner, Cosmo Sardo, Marco Lopez, Charlie Picerni, Irene Kelly, Robert Board, Bob Johnson, et al. Women's Wardrobe: Sabine Molana, November 24, 1968.

Premiere. CBS Drama series. "Crisis" Dir.: Paul Wendkos. Scr.: Anthony Spinner. Cast: Carl Betz, Davey Davison, Robert Drivas, Ruth Roman (Mrs. Winters), Susan Strasberg, Joan Karr. (Scheduled for September 2, 1968, but postponed and aired September 3, 1970.)

The Outcasts. ABC Western series. "The Town That Wouldn't" Dir.: Allen Reisner. Scr.: Ben Brady, Richard N. Bluel, Leon Tokatyan. Cast: Don Murray, Otis Young, Ruth Roman (Jade Willoughby), Robert F. Lyons, Leo Gordon, March 31, 1969.

Marcus Welby, M.D. ABC, Universal Television Drama series. "Diagnosis: Fear" Dir.: Chris Christenberry. Scr.: Margaret Armen. Cast: Robert Young, James Brolin, Elena Verdugo, Ruth Roman (Dr. Margaret), John Findlater, Tom Drake, Vinton Hayworth, Vaughn Taylor, Jim S. Smith, Howard Culver, Stuart Nisbet, Ida Mae McKenzie, Janet Wood, December 30, 1969.

The Old Man Who Cried Wolf. (1970) ABC, Aaron Spelling Productions, TV Movie. Dir.: Walter Grauman. Scr.: Luther Davis, based on a story by Arnold Horwitt. Cast: Edward G. Robinson, Martin Balsam, Diane Baker, Ruth Roman (Lois), Percy Rodrigues, Sam Jaffe, Edward Asner, Martin E. Brooks, Paul Picerni, Robert Yuro, Bill Elliott,

185

Appendix

James A. Watson, Jr., Naomi Stevens, Virginia Christine, Jay C. Flippen, Pepe Brown, Jack Gordon, et al.

Mannix. CBS, Paramount Television, Crime Drama series. "The Judas Touch" Dir.: Gerald Mayer. Scr.: Merwin Gerard, Richard Levinson, William Link. Cast: Mike Connors, Gail Fisher, Robert Lansing, Ruth Roman (Victoria Parrish), James Wainwright, Brenda Benet, Don Eitner, Robert Ritchie, Wayne Heffley, Linda Chandler, Dennis McCarthy, January 16, 1971.

The Virginian. Western series. "The Angus Killer" James Drury, Van Johnson, Ruth Roman (Marjorie Worth), Dina Merrill, Stephen McNally, Slim Pickens, Chill Wills, Andrew Parks, Jon Lormer, Christopher Howell, 1971.

It Was a Very Good Year. Channel 9 Documentary Interview series. Mel Tormé salutes 1956 with guests Jonathan Winters, Ruth Roman, Bill Russell, June 11, 1971.

Incident in San Francisco. (1971) ABC, Quinn Martin Productions. TV Movie Thriller. Dir.: Don Melford. Scr.: Robert Dozier, from the story "Incident at 125th Street." Cast: Richard Kiley, Leslie Nielsen, Dean Jagger, John Marley, Phyllis Thaxter, Ruth Roman (Sofia Cianelli), David Opatoshu, Claudia McNeil, Tracy Reed, Julius Harris, Tom Nardini, Christopher Connelly, Richard O'Brien, Ken Lynch.

Ironside. Universal Television, NBC Mystery series. "Gentle Oaks" Dir.: Robert Clouse. Scr.: Collier Young, Michael Fisher. Cast: Raymond Burr, Don Galloway, Don Mitchell, Elizabeth Baur, Ruth Roman (May Joyce Skinner), John Carradine, Harry Townes, Gene Lyons, Jeff Davis, Lynn Hamilton, Jon Lormer, Barry Cahill, Jason Wingreen, Arthur Hanson, Jessica H. Jones, November 30, 1971.

The Sixth Sense. Universal Television, NBC Mystery Drama. "Once Upon a Chilling" Dir.: Sutton Roley. Scr.: Doug Ingalls, Anthony Lawrence. Cast: Rod Serling (Host), Gary Collins, Ruth Roman (Mrs. Cloister), Susan Strasberg, Robert Brubaker, Joel Fabiani, John Hillerman, David Huddleston, October 28, 1972.

Mod Squad. ABC Crime Thriller. "Belinda, End of Little Miss Bubble Gum" Dir.: Seymour Robbie. Scr.: Brynn Morgan, Buddy Ruskin. Cast: Michael Cole, Clarence Williams III, Peggy Lipton, Bob Balaban, Cathy Burns, Tige Andrews, Anthony James, Ruth Roman (Irene Morris), Dane Clark, John Karlen, Vernon Weddle, Len Lesser, Art Aragon, et al., December 7, 1972.

Go Ask Alice. (1973) Dir.: John Korty. Scr.: Ellen M. Violett, Beatrice Sparks, based on her book. Cast: William Shatner, Jamie Smith-Jackson, Ruth Roman (Psychiatrist), Julie Adams, Wendell Burton, Ayn Ruymen, Andy Griffith, Mimi Saffian, Jennifer Edwards, Daniel Michael Mann, Robert Carradine, Frederick Herrick, Michael Morgan, Gary Marsh, Mackenzie Phillips, Al Checco, Charlie Martin Smith, Michael Moore, Barbara Mallory, Jeanne Avery, Michael A. Freeman, et al. Metromedia Producers Corporation.

Cops (1973) CBS, Cherokee Productions, TV Movie Comedy pilot (30 minutes). Dir. & Scr.: Jerry Belson. Cast: Vincent Gardenia, Bruce Davison, Scoey Mitchell, Britt Leach, Pat Morita, Ruth Roman (Wanda Burke), Stuart Margolin, Vic Tayback, Little Dion, Betty Aidman, Royce Wallace, Bob Harks, Royce Wallace, Bob Harks.

Faraday & Company. Universal Television, NBC Drama series. "Say Hello to a Dead Man" Dir.: Gary Nelson. Scr.: Ken Pettus, Bert Prelutsky, Leonard Stern. Cast: Dan Dailey, James Naughton, Sharon Gless, Geraldine Brooks, Jim Connell, Howard Duff, Liam Dunn, Jerry Dunphy, Drout Miller, Ruth Roman (Paula Sandford), Craig Stevens, David Wayne, Victor Mohica, Percy Rodrigues, et al., September 26, 1973.

Hec Ramsey. Universal Television, NBC Mystery Western series. "A Hard Road to Vengeance" Dir.: Alex March. Scr.: Harold Jack Bloom, S. Bar-David. Cast: Richard Boone, Richard Lenz, Stuart Whitman, Ruth Roman (Della Redsmith), Keenan Wynn, Rita

Appendix

Moreno, Harold J. Stone, Perry Lopez, James G. Anderson, Ted Markland, Jean Allison, Judson Morgan, Harry Hickox, John Alderson, et al., September 26, 1973.

Kung Fu. Warner Bros. Television, ABC Adventure series. "A Dream Within a Dream" Dir.: Richard Lang. Scr.: Ed Spielman, Herbert Miller, John T. Duggan. Cast: David Carradine, John Drew Barrymore, Ruth Roman (Rhoda Norman), Tina Louise, Sorrell Booke, Howard Duff, Keye Luke, Philip Ahn, Radames Pera, Mark Miller, Rudy Diaz, et al., January 17, 1974.

Cannon. Quinn Martin Productions, CBS Crime Drama series. "Flashpoint" Dir.: William Wiard. Scr.: Robert Heverley, Edward Hume. Cast: William Conrad, Ruth Roman (Nora Parrow), Bob Random, Robert Reiser, Kristoffer Tabori, Ninette Bravo, Frank Maxwell, Martin West, Jesse Vint, James Lydon, Don Dubbins Heather Lowe, Olan Soule, Gordon De Vol, Tifni Twitchell, November 13, 1974.

Punch and Jody. (1974) Dir.: Barry Shear. Scr.: John McGreevey. Cast: Glenn Ford, Pam Griffin, Ruth Roman (Lil Charny), Kathleen Widdoes, Parley Baer, Susan Brown, Don "Red" Barry, Billy Barty, Mel Stewart, Cynthia Hayward, Patty Maloney, Pat Morita, Peter Ford, Billy Jean Beach, Read Morgan. Metromedia Productions.

Harry O. Warner Bros. Television, ABC Crime series. "Death Certificate" Dir.: Russ Mayberry. Scr.: Howard Rodman, John Meredyth Lucas. Cast: David Janssen, Anthony Zerbe, Ruth Roman (Ethel Martel), Norman Burton, Denise Galick, Kiel Martin, Thom Christopher, Paul Tulley, Bill Henderson, Rod Colbin, Richard Stahl, Susan Adams, Michael Alaimo, Hank Rolike, Robert Casper, April 29, 1976.

Police Woman. David Gerber Productions, Columbia Pictures Television, NBC Crime Drama series. "The Disco Killer" Dir.: Ernie Pintoff. Scr.: Robert Collins, Stanley Roberts, Edward DeBlasio. Cast: Angie Dickinson, Earl Holliman, Charles Dierkop, Ed Bernard, Ruth Roman (Adele Arnold), Jon Cypher, Taaffe O'Connell, Patricia Singer, Eddie Fontaine, Don McGovern, Guy Marks, MacIntyre Dixon, Frank Downing, Joy Bond, William Edmondson, January 25, 1977.

The Sacketts. Media Productions, NBC Western series. "Part 1" & "Part 2" Dir.: Robert Toten. Scr.: Jim Byrnes, Louis L'Amour. Cast: Sam Elliott, Tom Selleck, Jeff Osterhage, Ben Johnson, Gilbert Roland, Ruth Roman (Rosie), Glenn Ford, Mercedes McCambridge, Jack Elam, Gene Evans, Paul Koslo, Slim Pickens, L.Q. Jones, et al., May 15, 16, 1979.

Willow B: Women in Prison. (1980) ABC, Lorimar Productions, Crime Drama TV Movie Pilot. Dir.: Jeff Blackner. Scr.: Gerry Day. Cast: Debra Clinger, Trisha Noble, Carol Lynley, Elizabeth Hartman, Sally Kirkland, Sarah Kennedy, Liz Torres, Susan Tyrell, Lynne Moody, Ruth Roman (Sgt. Pritchett), Sandra Sharpe, Virginia Capers, Norma Donaldson, Jared Martin, John P. Ryan.

Fantasy Island. Comedy Drama series. "My Fair Pharaoh" Cast: Ricardo Montalbán, Herve Villechaize, Joan Collins, Michael Ansara, Ron Ely, Larry Linville, Ruth Roman (Mistress of the Harem), Carol Lynley, Chris Capen, Brioni Farrell, James Whitworth, John Davey, et al., May 10, 1980.

Knots Landing. Metro-Goldwyn-Mayer Television, Lorimar Productions, CBS 21 Episodes, January 16, 1986 to January 15, 1987. Dir.: Nick Havinga. Scr.: David Jacobs, David Paulsen. Cast: William Devane, Kevin Dobson, Julie Harris, Lisa Hartman, Michele Lee, Constance McCashin, Donna Mills, Ted Shackelford, Douglas Sheehan, Joan Van Ark, Hunt Block, Ruth Roman (Sylvia Lean), et al. "The Confession" January 16, 1986. "Alterations" January 23, 1986. "Friendly Enemies" January 30, 1986. "The Key to a Woman's Heart" February 6, 1986. "A Very Special Gift" February 13, 1986. "Distant Rumblings" March 13, 1986. "Phoenix Rising" March 20, 1986. "The Legacy" April 3, 1986. "Arsenic and Old Waste" April 10, 1986. "A Change of Heart" April 17, 1986. "His Brother's Keeper" May 1, 1986. "Thicker Than Water" May 8, 1986. "For Appearance's Sake" October 16, 1986. "All Over but the Shouting" October 23, 1986. "Pressure Points" October

187

30, 1986. "Brothers and Mothers" November 6, 1986. "Over the Edge" November 13, 1986. "A Turn of Events" November 20, 1986. "Touch and Go" November 27, 1986. "The Inside Man" December 4, 1986. "My True Love" January 15, 1987.

Murder, She Wrote. CBS, Universal Television, Mystery Drama series. "If It's Thursday, it Must Be Beverly" Dir.: Peter Crane. Scr.: Wendy Graf, Lisa Stotsky, Philip Gerson, Robert E. Swanson, Robert Van Scoyk. Cast: Angela Lansbury, Julie Adams, Tom Bosley, Antoinette Bower, Gloria DeHaven, Ray Girardin, Dody Goodman, Kathryn Grayson, Ruth Roman (Loretta Spiegel), William Windom, Sally Klein, Rick Lenz, November 8, 1987. "The Sins of Castle Cove" Dir.: John Llewellyn Moxey. Scr.: Robert Van Scoyk. Cast: Angela Lansbury, Julie Adams, Luke Askew, Frederick Coffin, Gloria DeHaven, Kathryn Grayson, Page Hannah, Ron Masak, Ruth Roman (Loretta Spiegel), Sally Klein, Will Nye, William Windom, Graham Jarvis, Rosanna Huffman, Fran Ryan, Joan Roberts, Stuart Nisbet, April 9, 1989. "Town Father" Dir.: John Llewellyn Moxey. Scr.: Philip Gerson. Cast: Angela Lansbury, Julie Adams, Orson Bean, John Considine, Gloria DeHaven, Kathryn Grayson, Ruth Roman (Loretta Spiegel), Barbara Perry, Basil Hoffman, William Lantau, Richard Paul, Ron Masak, Lee Purcell, Holland Taylor, William Windom, Sally Klein, Phyllis Franklin, Charles Woolf, Courtney McWhinney, Sheila Pinkham, December 17, 1989.

Discography

The Best of Old Time Radio—Alfred Hitchcock. Radio Spirits Smithsonian Legendary Performers Series 6 X CD Disc 6 #1 *The Lux Radio Theater* "Strangers on a Train" Cast: Ray Milland, Ruth Roman, Ed Begley, Frank Lovejoy, Patricia Hitchcock. Originally broadcast December 2, 1951, Radio Spirits 53998 (2000).

Ruth Roman Collection. CD MP3 compilation of radio broadcasts available from Old Time Radio Catalog. *Academy Awards Ceremony* (1949), *Lux Radio Theater* "Somewhere in the Night" (1947), "Strangers on a Train" (1951), "The Blue Gardenia" (1954), *Screen Guild* "Champion" (1949), *Stars Over Hollywood* "The Singing Rails" (1954). See: *https://www.otrcat.com/p/ruth-roman.*

Some Collectible Magazines

Ambiance. Cover, March 1948 (France).

The Photoplayer. Cover, February 12, 1949 (Australia).

Revista de Semana. Cover, 1949 (Brazil).

8 Otto #14. Cover April 7, 1949 (Italy).

Life. May 1, 1950, Cover and article "The Rapid Rise of Ruth Roman" pp. 51–52.

Look Magazine. Voted "The Big Time Movie Star of 1950," June 1950 & "Roman Holiday" article; Ruth Roman visits the Arrowhead Hot Springs Mineral Bath, August 1, 1950.

Screen World. Cover and article, Fall 1950.

Quick. Cover October 23, 1950; Cover, October 15, 1951; Cover and article, June 30, 1952.

Festival. Cover, January 10, 1951 (France).

ABC Film Review. Cover, February 1951 (UK).

Screen Stories. Cover, May 1951.

People. Cover with Farley Granger, May 9, 1951.

Appendix

Bis. Cover May 22, 1951 (Italy).

Filmland. Cover (shared with Janet Leigh) and article "All About Men" by Ruth Roman, July 1951.

Camara. Cover, 1951 (Spain).

Hafta. Cover, October 4, 1951 (Turkey).

Peter Noble's Picture Parade 1952. Hard cover album with dust jacket; Cover with Farley Granger and articles (Burke Publishing, London, 1952).

Al Kawakeb #41. Cover, 1952 (Egypt).

O Idilio. Cover with Richard Todd, January 1952 (Brazil).

Uge-Magasinet #16. Cover (with Steve Cochran) and story, 1952 (Denmark).

Mon Film. Cover, with Farley Granger, April 2, 1952 (France).

Picture Show. Cover with Errol Flynn, August 16, 1952 (UK).

Cinémonde. Cover, January 16, 1953; Cover with Gary Cooper, June 5, 1953 (France).

Geino Gaho. Cover, June 1953 (Japan).

Le Ore # 14. Cover and article, August 1953 (Italy).

Garbo. Cover, October 17, 1953; February 20, 1954 (Spain).

Eiga No Tomo. Cover, November 1953 (Japan).

Picturegoer. Cover, December 5, 1953; two-part interview with Dick Richards, July 9, 16, 1955 (UK).

Tempo. Cover, December 7, 1953.

Movie News Pictorial. Cover, February 1955 (Singapore).

Movie Pictorial. Cover, October 1955.

Bolero. Cover, with Van Johnson, April 22, 1956 (Italy).

Kristal. Article about the *Andrea Doria* sinking, January 12, 1957 (Germany).

Le Film Complet. Cover and contents, with Van Johnson *Le Fond de la Bouteille (The Bottom of the Bottle)* 1957 (France).

Fotogramas #637. Cover (with Rita Hayworth) and article, February 10, 1961 (Spain).

Films in Review. (Honorable mentions) 1969 pp. 455, 520.

Chapter Notes

Introduction

1. Ruth Roman interview, *The Saratogian*, May 14, 1954, 18.

Chapter 1

1. Magazine cutting circa 1954.
2. U.S. Census Records 1910, 1920, 1930.
3. Marriage certificate, Boston, Anthony Roman, Mary Gold, Oct. 6, 1916.
4. Ruth Roman birth certificate, Dec. 22, 1922, Massachusetts, Birth Records, Vol. 072 Lynn–Malden, 17 Oct.–31 Dec 1922. Anthony Roman was 25 and Mary 24.
5. "Roman History," *Photoplay* 39 (clipping).
6. *Picturegoer* clipping, July 1955.
7. Marriage certificate, Jack Flaxman, Ruth Roman, 15 May 1939, Nashua, Hillsborough, New Hampshire, Film No. 004244841. Anthony Roman died before the census was taken (April 4, 1930) at the age of about 32.
8. Julia Inman, "'Long Summer' Role Familiar to Ruth Roman," *The Indianapolis Star*, Sept. 5, 1965, 109.
9. Ruth Roman, "Miracle in Boston," *Photoplay*, June 1950, 91.
10. Cutting from *Motion Picture* circa 1951, 56.
11. "The Elizabeth Peabody House" at the West End Museum Exhibit, 2015.
12. From unnamed cutting collection in scrapbook circa 1951.
13. Phone conversation with Budd Moss, July 4, 2020.
14. "Televiewing," *The Daily Bulletin*, Dec. 4, 1959, 13.
15. "Roman Candle," *Modern Screen*, 1950.
16. Jim Goldrup and Tom Goldrup, *The Encyclopedia of Feature Players of Hollywood Vol. 2* (Albany, GA: Bear-Manor Media, 2012).
17. Unnamed newspaper cutting circa 1949.

Chapter 2

1. Ruth Roman as told to Dick Richards, "Hollywood Has Been Good to Me But...," *Picturegoer*, July 9, 1955.
2. Marriage certificate, Jack Flaxman, Ruth Roman, 15 May 1939, Nashua, Hillsborough, New Hampshire, Film No. 004244841.
3. Ruth Roman interview with Dick Richards, "You Can Soon Tell When You're a Star," *Picturegoer*, July 16, 1955.
4. Harrison Carroll, "Behind the Scenes in Hollywood," *Ogdensburg Journal*, Nov. 8, 1950.
5. Jack Flaxman died in 2001 in Las Vegas at the age of 84.
6. Hedda Hopper, *Hartford Courant*, Dec. 11, 1949.
7. "Roman Candle," *Modern Screen*, 1950.
8. Ruth Roman as told to Dick Richards, "Hollywood Has Been Good to Me But...," *Picturegoer*, July 9, 1955 (cutting).
9. Mel Heimer, "My New York," *The Logan Daily News*, Aug. 18, 1950, 4.
10. Marjory Adams, "Ruth Roman, Boston's Newest Film Star, Returns in

Triumph," *The Boston Globe*, July 18, 1950, 44.

11. Leon Cutterman, "Our Film Folk: Hard Work and Ambition Makes Boston Girl Hollywood Sensation," *The Sentinel*, July 13, 1950, 33.

12. "Ruth Roman Empire Star," *The Windsor Star*, Ontario, Canada, Feb. 23, 1952, 33.

13. Jerry Asher, "I Learned About Women from Women," *Screenland*, Nov. 1952, 66.

14. "Ruth Roman Enjoys Just Roamin' Around," *Pittsburgh Post-Gazette*, Sept. 12, 1951, 12.

15. "Joy Street Theatre: The Imaginary Invalid," *The Boston Globe* circa 1941 (press cutting).

16. *The Boston Globe*, Aug. 7, 1949, 106.

17. "Producer Guy Palmerton," *Finchburg Sentinel*, Sept. 23, 1948.

18. Jon Bruce, "When They Loved and Lost," *Screenland*, May 1950, 63.

19. Ruth Roman obituary, *The Independent*, Sept. 1999 (cutting).

20. John Todd, "In Hollywood," *Ottawa Journal*, Nov. 27, 1948, 14.

21. "Ruth Roman of Boston," *The Wisconsin Jewish Chronicle*, July 21, 1950, 8.

Chapter 3

1. Jack Quigg, "Here's How a Girl Cracks the Movies," *St. Louis Globe-Democrat*, Feb. 25, 1951.

2. *Photoplay*.

3. "Behind the Scenes," *Photoplay*, Jan. 1951, 6.

4. "Should a Woman Tell Her Past?" *Screenland*, 1950, 69.

5. Ruth Roman, "The Days I Don't Forget," unnamed clipping circa 1956.

6. Alice Pardoe West, "Ogden Red-Head Gets Headlines in Show Business Weeklies," *The Ogden Standard-Examiner*, Apr. 12, 1953, 29.

7. Harold Heffernan, "The Familiar Detours to Stardom," *St. Louis Post-Dispatch*, Oct. 18, 1949, 31.

8. Doris Lilly, "House of the Seven Garbos," *Screenland*, Jan. 1950, 65.

9. Harold Heffernan, "The Familiar Detours to Stardom," *St. Louis Post-Dispatch*, Oct. 18, 1949, 31.

10. Diane Telgen and Jim Kamp, *Notable Hispanic Women Vol. 1* (Farmington Hills, MI: Gale Research, 1993), 96.

11. Ruth Roman, "Should a Woman Tell Her Past?" *Screenland*, 1950.

12. Ruth Roman, "I Have a Ten-Year Plan," magazine cutting circa 1950.

13. "Wayne's Beard Holds Up Film," *The Spokesman-Review*, May 3, 1950, 32.

14. William C. Cline, *In the Nick of Time: Motion Picture Sound Serials* (Jefferson, NC: McFarland, 1984), 191.

15. Erskine Johnson, "In Hollywood," *Ogdensburg Journal*, June 30, 1951, 6.

16. Loose cutting from *Photoplay* circa 1951, 74.

17. The surviving portion of *Time to Kill* (1945) is available to view at the Internet Archive: https://archive.org/details/Time_to_Kill_1945.

18. Roman quoted in Boze Hadleigh, *Marilyn Forever: Musings on an American Icon by the Stars of Yesterday and Today* (Lanham, MD: Rowman & Littlefield, 2016), 62.

19. Ruth Roman, "Should a Woman Tell Her Past?" *Screenland*, 1950.

20. *Quick*, Oct. 23, 1950, 52.

21. Gladwin Hill, "Hollywood's Roman Candle," *Collier's* 127 (1951), 26.

22. John Meredyth Lucas, *Eighty Odd Years in Hollywood: Memoir of a Career in Film and Television* (Jefferson, NC: McFarland, 2004).

23. David Quinlan, *Quinlan's Film Stars* (London: Batsford, 2000), 449.

24. Reba and Bonnie Churchill, *Long Beach Independent*, Jan. 15, 1949, 14.

25. Edwin Schallert, "Slezak to Act Balzac; Taylor Opus Chosen," *The Los Angeles Times*, Jan. 30, 1947, 15.

26. Edwin Schallert, "Bankhead Movie Deal Reported on Fire Here," *The Los Angeles Times*, June 29, 1948.

27. Edwin Schallert, "Remarque Novel Eyed; McLaglen Role Heavy," *The Los Angeles Times*, Feb. 5, 1948, 63.

28. Edwin Schallert, "Donna Reed Will Play 'One Woman' Role," *The Los Angeles Times*, July 1, 1948, 23.

29. Unlabeled magazine cutting from collection of clippings circa 1955.

30. *Quick*, October 23, 1950, 52.

31. "Lundigan Will Come to City in Stage Role," *Tucson Daily Citizen*, Jan. 15, 1949, 3.

32. Ruth Roman, "Should a Woman Tell Her Past?" *Screenland*, 1950.

Chapter 4

1. Lydia Lane, "Hollywood Beauty: Glamor Isn't a Trick, Declares Ruth Roman." *The Knickerbocker News*, Albany, N.Y., May 8, 1953, 4-B.

2. Leslie Halliwell, *Halliwell's Film Guide* (London: Guild, 1983), 902.

3. Robert Herring, *Life and Letters and the London Mercury, Vol. 62* (London: Brendin, 1949), 65.

4. "Star's View on Casting," *Daily Telegraph*, Feb. 28, 1952, 18.

5. "Ruth Roman Obituary," *The Independent*, September 1999.

6. *Saturday Evening Post*, 1950, 133 (cutting).

7. Hedda Hopper, *Miami Daily News-Recorder*, Jan. 17, 1950, 23.

8. Sheilah Grahame, "Hollywood," *Calgary Herald*, May 6, 1949, 14.

9. Ruth Roman, "The Days I Don't Forget," film clipping circa 1956.

10. "Ruth Roman," *Buffalo Courier-Express*, Apr. 17, 1949, 43.

11. "Telling on Themselves," *Screenland*, Dec. 1950, 66.

12. Jimmie Fidler, "In Hollywood," *Monroe News-Star*, July 30, 1951, 10.

13. Casting for *The Breaking Point*, see Bob Herzberg, *The Left Side of the Screen: Communist and Left-Wing Ideology in Hollywood 1929–2009* (Jefferson, NC: McFarland, 2014), 225.

14. Edith Gwynn, "Hollywood," *The Cincinnati Examiner*, July 14, 1949, 12.

15. Lawrence J. Quirk, *The Passionate Life of Bette Davis* (London: Robson, 1990), 323.

16. Lane Crockatt, "Ruth Accepts New Role," *The Times* (Shreveport, Louisiana), Jan. 16, 1986, 23.

17. Sheilah Grahame, "Hollywood," *The Times-Tribune*, June 22, 1949, 44.

18. Hedda Hopper, "The Sexiest Girl in Town," *Photoplay*, 1950.

19. Lane Crockett, "Ruth Roman Accepts New Role," *The Times*, Jan. 16, 1986, 23.

20. Letter from Ruth Roman to a friend circa 1950.

21. Alan M. Wald, *American Night: The Literary Left in the Era of the Cold War* (Chapel Hill: University of North Carolina Press, 2012), 130.

22. "Ruth Roman," *The Brooklyn Daily Eagle*, Aug. 15, 1949, 4.

23. Paul A. Woods, *Martin Scorsese: A Journey Through the American Psyche* (London: Plexus, 2005), 89.

24. Undated clipping from *Modern Screen* circa 1951.

25. Leonard Nimoy interview with Karen Herman, The Television Academy Foundation, Nov. 2, 2000.

26. Edan Hughes, *Artists in California 1786–1940* (Hughes Publishing Co., 1989).

27. Henry Wilcoxon and Katherine Orrison, *Lionheart in Hollywood: The Autobiography of Henry Wilcoxon* (Lanham, MD: Scarecrow Press, 1991), 163–66.

28. Carleton Carpenter, *The Absolute Joy of Work: From Vermont to Broadway, Hollywood, and Damn Near 'Round the World* (Albany, GA: BearManor Media, 2016)

29. "Commies Blast Cvetic Movie," *The Pittsburgh Press*, Mar. 3, 1951, 4.

30. Marilyn Ann Moss, *Giant: George Stevens, a Life on Film* (Madison, WI: Terrace Books, 2004), 160.

31. Erskine Johnson, "O'Keefe Says Dollar Sign is Success Sign," *The Saratogian*, September 1, 1950, 13.

32. Edwin Schallert, "Barbara Bates to Get 20th Century Build-Up," *The Los Angeles Times*, June 10, 1949, 43.

33. "Ruth Roman Burned in Gun Battle," *The Pittsburgh Press*, June 20, 1950, 14.

34. John O'Dowd, *Kiss Tomorrow Goodbye: The Barbara Payton Story* (Albany, GA: BearManor Media, 2006).

35. "Stage and Screen," *The Knoxville News-Sentinel*, Jan. 31, 1952, 4.

36. Erskine Johnson, "In Hollywood,"

Plattsburgh Press Republic, Nov. 30, 1949, 10.

37. Erskine Johnson, "Booked Tour Brings Page of Experience," *The Saratogian*, Sept. 6, 1950, 15.

38. Rudy Behlmer, *America's Favorite Movies: Behind the Scenes* (New York: Frederick Ungar, 1982), 225.

39. "At Local Theatres," *Republican & Herald*, Oct. 23, 1950, 7.

40. Sergio Leeman, *Robert Wise on His Films: From Editing Room to Director's Chair* (West Hollywood: Silman-James Press, 1995), 94.

41. "Top-Grosses of 1950," *Variety*, Jan. 3, 1951, 58.

42. Email from Budd Moss, Aug. 8, 2020.

43. "Ruth Roman Never to Stage Rebellion," *Longview News-Journal*, Apr. 13, 1950, 4.

Chapter 5

1. "Ruth Roman," *The Times*, Sept. 14, 1999, 21.

2. "Ruth Roman Shaken Up in Bus Crash," *Pasadena Independent*, Feb. 17, 1950.

3. Frank Neil, "In Hollywood," *Endicott Daily Bulletin*, Mar. 30, 1950, 10.

4. "Entertainments: New Films in London," *The Times*, December 10, 1951, 8.

5. Patricia White, *Uninvited: Classical Hollywood Cinema and Lesbian Representability* (Bloomington: Indiana University Press, 1999), 178.

6. Edwin Schallert, "'Force of Arms' Indexed for Todd," *The Los Angeles Times*, Feb. 15, 1951, 9.

7. See Richard Todd, *Caught in the Act: The Story of My Life* (London: Hutchinson, 1986), 258.

8. "Berlinale Retrospective King Vidor," Berlinale, Feb. 26, 2020.

9. "Quota of New Faces," *Variety*, Jan. 2, 1952, 71.

10. *Motion Picture Vol. 83–84* (New York: McFadden-Bartell, 1952).

11. Michelle Ford, "Those Who Saw War Appreciate Peace of Christmas," *Waterville Times*, 1998, 48.

12. "AMVETS Pick Ruth Roman as 1951 Clover Girl," *The Los Angeles Times*, July 20, 1951, 12.

13. "In Hollywood," *Fort Worth Star-Telegram*, July 4, 1951, 10.

14. See the discussion on *Starlift* in Robert J. Lentz, *Korean War Filmography: 91 English Language Features Through 2000* (Jefferson, NC: McFarland, 2003), 330.

15. "Movie Talk: At the Dixie," *The News-Leader*, Staunton, Virginia, Nov. 23, 1951, 4.

16. Edith Gwynn, "Hollywood," *The Mercury*, July 6, 1951, 4.

17. Phone conversation with Budd Moss, July 4, 2020.

18. Ruth Roman, "A Man Would Be a Fool to Marry Me," *Screenland*, 1949.

19. See Mosley, Leonard *Disney's World* (New York: Scarborough House, 1990).

20. Undated newspaper cutting circa 1950.

21. "Hollywood He-Men Most Over-rated," *Santa Cruz Sentinel*, June 9, 1949, 9.

22. Malcolm Boyd, *As I Live and Breathe* (New York: Random House, 1969), 30. Boyd left show business and the secular sphere entirely to become an Episcopal priest.

23. See discography. See also Connie J. Billips and Arthur Pierce, *Lux Presents Hollywood: A Show-by-show History of the Lux Radio Theatre and the Lux Video Theatre, 1934–57* (Jefferson, NC: McFarland, 1995).

24. "Ruth Roman Obituary," *The Independent*, Sept. 1999.

25. See Dan Callahan, *The Camera Lies: Acting for Hitchcock* (Oxford: Oxford University Press, 2020), 167, 170–71.

26. Francois Truffaut with Helen G. Scott, *Hitchcock by Truffaut* (New York: Simon & Schuster, 1967), 148.

27. Joan Schenkar, *The Talented Miss Highsmith: The Secret Life and Serious Art of Patricia Highsmith* (New York: St. Martin's, 2010), 319.

28. Patrick McGilligan, *Alfred Hitchcock: A Life in Darkness and Light* (New York: Harper Perennial, 2004), 206.

29. Lane Crockett, "Ruth Roman Accepts New Role," *The Morning News,* Jan. 16, 1986, 56.
30. "Good Luck Charm Given Actress," *Pittsburgh Press,* Nov. 26, 1950, 69.
31. *American Lawn Tennis* 45 (1951), 15.
32. *Comparison* Issues 7–11 University of Warwick, Graduate School of Comparative Literature, University of Warwick, 1978 University of California.
33. Gerald Gardner, *The Censorship Papers: Movie Censorship Letters from the Hays Office 1934 to 1968* (New York: Dodd, Mead, 1969), 121.

Chapter 6

1. Ruth Roman, "A Man Would Be a Fool to Marry Me," *Screenland,* 1949.
2. "Actress Wed," *Albuquerque Journal,* Dec. 23, 1950, 10.
3. Erskine Johnson, "In Hollywood," *Visalia Times-Delta,* Jan. 4, 1951, 14.
4. Ruth Roman interview with Dick Richards, "You Can Soon Tell When You're a Star," *Picturegoer,* July 16, 1955.
5. *Modern Screen* circa 1951 (clipping).
6. "Movies: Hollywood Quotes," *Elmira Advertiser* (New York), June 30, 1951, 6.
7. Leslie Snyder, "Brief Marriage?" *Modern Screen,* 1951.
8. "Ruth Roman Wants to Be Hollywood's Queen of Sarong," *Madera Tribune,* June 12, 1951.
9. "Ruth Roman Fencer," *The Charlotte Observer,* Oct. 7, 1951, 70.
10. Patricia Cleary, "Wise Move Star Lists 10 Fundamentals in art of avoiding arguments," *The Niagara Falls Gazette,* Aug. 30, 1951, 18.
11. Harrison Carroll, "Behind the Scenes in Hollywood," *Lancaster Eagle-Gazette,* Jan. 26, 1951, 6.
12. Erskine Johnson, "Buddy Baer's Hair Dyed Red for Film," *The Saratogian,* June 23, 1950, 32.
13. Emery Wister, "'Show' Nuf," *The Charlotte News,* Oct. 18, 1951, 29.
14. Jerry Asher, "I Learned About Women from Women," *Screenland,* Nov. 1952, 66.
15. "Ruth Gets Idea of Being Hussy," *Buffalo Courier-Express,* Mar. 18, 1951, 17-D.
16. "Ruth Roman Has Proved She Can Stop Traffic," *Brooklyn Eagle,* Aug. 5, 1951, 25.
17. "Review Tomorrow Is Another Day," *Motion Picture Daily,* Aug. 13, 1951, 3.
18. "Studio Size-Ups," *Film Bulletin,* Aug. 13, 1951, 5.
19. "Modern romantic drama for RKO," "Busy Girl Pulls the Strings," *Prescott Evening Courier,* Aug. 13, 1951, 5.
20. "Virginia Mayo, Ruth Roman Probable Miss America," *The Los Angeles Times,* July 23, 1951, 53.
21. Ronald L. Davis, *Just Making Movies* (Jackson: University Press of Mississippi, 2005), 197.
22. *Travel Magazine Incorporated* 1952, 33.
23. "Roman Robe," *The Central New Jersey Home News,* June 1, 1952, 32.
24. Louella Parsons, "Louella Parsons Says," *Albany Times-Union,* Feb. 5, 1951, 5.
25. "Star Feature: A Girl of Many Ambitions," *MGM Press Book Young Man with Ideas* (1952), 3.
26. "Star Feature: Glenn Ford Has No Complaints," *MGM Press Book Young Man with Ideas* (1952), 5.
27. *The New York Times Film Reviews Vol. 4* (New York Times, 1949), 2618.
28. "Invitation, with Dorothy Maguire, Van Johnson and Ruth Roman," *Harrison's Reports,* Jan. 26, 1952, 15.
29. "Ruth Roman Relishes Part That Makes Her Real Meanie," *The Brooklyn Daily Eagle,* Feb. 17, 1952.
30. "Advance Story: Ruth Roman Plays a Meanie," *Invitation MGM Press Book* (1951).
31. Edwin Schallert, "Ruth Roman Will Star as Doctor," *The Los Angeles Times,* May 8, 1950, 66.
32. "Actress Prefers Not Being Alone," *Buffalo Courier-Express,* June 24, 1951, 14-D.
33. "Star Ruth Roman Prefers Competition in Everything," *The Charlotte Observer,* Aug. 13, 1950, 52.

34. "Ruth Roman Tackles Spanish," *The Pittsburgh Press*, Sept. 20, 1953, 100.
35. "Roman Travelogue," *Press & Sun-Bulletin*, Oct. 25, 1953, 36.
36. Phone conversation with Budd Moss, July 4, 2020.
37. Hedda Hopper, "Hedda Hopper's Hollywood," *Buffalo Courier-Express*, June 13, 1953.
38. "Ruth Roman Hinted as Graham Replacement," *The Los Angeles Times*, July 11, 1953, 21.

Chapter 7

1. Hedda Hopper, "Hedda Selects Her Film Stars for '50,'" *Buffalo Courier-Express*, Jan. 1, 1950, 5-C.
2. "Press Association Honors Ida Lupino," *The Pomona Express*, Jan. 29, 1951, 8.
3. Ad from a clipping in *National Geographic* 1951.
4. *Collier's* 1950, *Shortsville Enterprise*, 1949 (clippings).
5. Patricia Cleary, "Ruth Roman 1950 College Man's Ideal," *The Knoxville Journal*, Mar. 19, 1950, 15.
6. "Molecular Miss," *The Brush News-Tribune*, June 29, 1950, 39.
7. "Showbiz by the Armed Forces Press Service," *Camp Carson Mountaineer*, May 25, 1951, 12.
8. "Ruth Roman Made Sweetheart of YMCA," *The Valley Times*, Oct. 21, 1950, 15.
9. "Ruth Honored," *Battle Creek Enquirer*, Oct. 15, 1950, 8.
10. "A Good Choice," *Schenectady Gazette*, May 21, 1955, 43.
11. Maralyn Marsh, "Sultry Ruth Roman Shoulders Way to Top of Sensuous Poll," *The Herald-News*, July 28, 1950, 18.
12. Kaspar Monahan, "Show Shops," *The Pittsburgh Press*, July 26, 1950, 12.
13. Patricia Cleary, "One of World's Most Kissable Women Picks 10 Top Kissable Males," *The Journal-Times* (Racine, Wisconsin), Oct. 30, 1949, 6.
14. Frank Neill, "In Hollywood," *Long Beach Independent*, Aug. 9, 1949, 19.
15. Dr. Robert Allyn Franklin, "His Job Is to Change Faces," *The Singapore Free Press*, Oct. 1, 1949, 31.
16. "Hollywood Tattle Tales." *Archie* 52.
17. "Calls Ruth Roman's Curves Most Interesting in a Decade," *News-Journal* (Mansfield, Ohio), Feb. 2, 1951, 27.
18. Erskine Johnson, "Even Durante Looks Pugnosed to Cyrano," *The Los Angeles Times*, Dec. 26, 1950, 63.
19. Vernon Scott, "Roman Sounds Off for Slacks," *The Pittsburgh Press*, Dec. 11, 1955, 25.
20. Susan Trent, "It Pays to Be Sensational," *Modern Screen*, 1951 (clipping).
21. Walter Winchell, "Broadway," *The Charlotte Observer*, Mar. 25, 1950, 44.
22. Robert C. Ruark, "Hollywood People Are Tired," *Buffalo Courier-Express*, July 17, 1950, 10.
23. "Plot on Stars: Quitter Blown Up," *The Courier-Mail* (Brisbane), May 19, 1952, 1.
24. "Dynamite Blast Victim Says Stars Faced Blackmail," *The Fresno Bee, The Republican*, May 18, 1951, 31.
25. "Ruth Roman to Visit City Wednesday," *Buffalo Courier-Express*, July 23, 1950, 5-C.
26. Harold V. Cohen, "The Drama Desk," *Pittsburgh Post-Gazette*, July 26, 1950, 12.
27. "I'll Pose in My Own Curves Vows Actress in Bosom Row," *The Brooklyn Daily Eagle*, Jan. 2, 1954, 14.
28. Lane Crockatt, "What's in View: Ruth Roman Joining Knot's Landing," *Battle Creek Enquirer*, Jan. 16, 1986, 14.

Chapter 8

1. Leon Cutterman, "Our Film Folk: Ruth Roman Praises Movie Work's Education," *The Wisconsin Jewish Chronicle*, May 11, 1951, 34.
2. Bob Thomas, "Ruth Roman Is Leaving Studio Without Blast," *Oatland Standard*, Sept. 23, 1954, 11.
3. Edwin Schallert, "Lady Pirate Tale Proposed for Ruth Roman," *The Los Angeles Times*, Mar. 12, 1954, 59.
4. "In Hollywood," *The Los Angeles Times*, June 12, 1953, 63.

Notes—Chapter 8

5. Edwin Schallert, "Powell to Direct Wayne as Khan," *The Los Angeles Times,* Feb. 25, 1954, 56.

6. Bob Thomas, "Ruth Roman Not Bitter at Separation from Movie Studio," *The La Cross Tribune,* Sept. 24, 1953.

7. "Interview with Bruno Engler: Photographer and Mountain Man," *National Post,* Ontario, Canada, Oct. 13, 1984, 71.

8. Jimmie Fidler, "Hollywood Star Dust," *The Miami Herald,* Aug. 30, 1953.

9. Harrison Carroll, "In Hollywood," *Lancaster Eagle-Gazette,* Oct. 8, 1953.

10. "No Feud," *The Times Standard,* Eureka, California, May 14, 1955, 45.

11. Donald Dewey, *James Stewart* (Boston: Little, Brown, 1996), 356.

12. "Rogers Jr., as Sr.," *Variety,* Nov. 7, 1951, 27.

13. Sheilah Grahame, "Hollywood Today," *The Province,* British Columbia, Canada, Aug. 13, 1953, 12.

14. "Star Dust," *Valley Morning Star,* Sept. 21, 1953, 2.

15. "Ruth Whittles While Roman Works," *The Newcastle Sun,* NSW, Aug. 26, 1954, 26.

16. Jawaharlal Nehru, *Selected Works of Jawaharlal Nehru Second Series Vol. 30* (Jawaharlal Nehru Memorial Fund, 2002), 212.

17. Sidney Skolsky, "That's Hollywood for You," *Photoplay,* Sept. 1952.

18. "Studio Briefs," *The Los Angeles Times,* Sept. 28, 1953, 54.

19. "Herbert J. Yates Presents The Shanghai Story," *Exhibitors' Campaign Book* (1954).

20. Anthony Slide, *Frank Lloyd: Master of Screen Melodrama* (Albany, GA: BearManor Media, 2009).

21. Leonard Maltin, *Leonard Maltin's Movie and Video Guide 1998* (New York: Penguin, 1997), 1197.

22. "Down Three Dark Streets (1954)," AFI Catalog of Feature Films.

23. Sheilah Grahame, "Hollywood: Peck Will Be Featured," *The Times-Tribune,* Oct. 28, 1953, 40.

24. Erskine Johnson, "Wealthy Marriage Will Not Halt Ruth Roman's Career," *The Sacramento Bee,* May 12 1954, 17.

25. "Hollywood," *The Daily Clintonian,* Oct. 19, 1954 (clipping).

26. "Ruth Roman to Claim Cruelty," *Press & Sun-Bulletin,* Mar. 24, 1955, 28.

27. Thomas Wiseman, "Lady Macbeth Dons a Swimsuit," *The Singapore Free Press,* June 30, 1955, 11.

28. Emily Belser, "Ruth Roman Given Shot at Sex Appeal," *Fort Worth Star-Telegram,* Aug. 29, 1955, 17.

29. "Joe Macbeth Ban Complete," *Singapore Standard,* Feb. 22, 1956, 1.

30. Victor Valentine, "Macbeth—Culture with Curves," *The Argus,* Melbourne, Victoria, May 12, 1955, 33.

31. "The Film That Set Sparks Flying," July 1955 (magazine cutting).

32. "Wonderland Pictures," *Western Herald,* Sept. 20, 1957, 31.

33. "Man on a Bus," *The Jewish Audio-Visual Review Tenth Annual Edition* (National Council on Jewish Audio-Visual Materials, Broadway, New York, 1960), 29.

34. Harold N. Pomainville, *Henry Hathaway: The Lives of a Hollywood Director* (Lanham, MD: Rowman & Littlefield, 2016), 176.

35. *Focus on Film* 31–34 (1978), 18.

36. Allen Eyles, "Virginia Mayo," *Focus on Film* 37 (1981), 28.

37. See "Great Day in the Morning" chapter in Chris Fujiwara, *Jacques Tourneur: The Cinema of Nightfall* (Jefferson, NC: McFarland, 2015), 229–34.

38. Emily Belser, "Ruth Roman Given Shot at Sex Appeal," *Fort Worth Star-Telegram,* Aug. 29, 1955, 17.

39. Virginia Mayo, with L.C. Van Savage, *The Best Years of My Life* (Chesterfield, MO: Beachhouse Books, 2002).

40. See "Rebel in Town," *Catholic World* 183 (1956), 382.

41. See "The Screen: Twelve O' Clock is Still High," *The Commonweal* (New York: Commonweal Publishing Corporation, 1956), 492.

42. "Rebel in Town," *The Paris News* (Paris, Texas), Nov. 4, 1956, 27.

43. Michael F. Blake, *Hollywood and the O.K. Corral: Portrayals of the Gunfight and Wyatt Earp* (Jefferson, NC: McFarland, 2012), 98.

197

Chapter 9

1. Forrest Powers, "TV and Radio Chatter: Ruth Roman Wants to Laugh a Little," *The Minneapolis Star*, Dec. 7, 1959, 27.
2. Roman was announced for several television projects, including a comedy, *Dear Midge*, planned as a series of twelve episodes. Other names involved included Imogene Coca, Robert Newton and Buster Crabbe. The series did not apparently come about, but a story of that name aired on *The Loretta Young Show* around the same time. Producer Tony Owen lined up a deal for a series of 39 half hours to be made in Rome with Roman and other guest stars but that too did not bear fruit. "Hollywood," *The Daily Wisconsin Rapids*, Apr. 24, 1954, 5. "Star Dust," *Postville Herald* (Iowa), Mar. 3, 1954, 10.
3. Leonard Maltin, "The Casablanca We May Never Get to See," May 20, 2018.
4. Jack Gould, "Producers' Showcase Darkness at Noon," *The New York Times*, May 1955.
5. "In Review Darkness at Noon," *Broadcasting*, May 9, 1955, 22.
6. Forrest Powers, "TV and Radio Chatter: Ruth Roman Wants to Laugh a Little," *The Minneapolis Star*, Dec. 7, 1959, 61.
7. "Amos 'n' Andy to Try Novel TV Experiment," *The Saratogan*, Mar. 1, 1955, 19.
8. Erskine Johnson, "Mrs. Medic to Appear in TV Show Episode," *The Saratogan*, Jan. 15, 1955, 53.
9. "Bonanza," *Broadcasting*, Sept. 22, 1969, 63.
10. Irv Kupcinet, *Kup's Chicago* (Cleveland: World, 1962), 220.
11. See Carol Felsenthal, "The Lost World of Kup," *Chicago Magazine*, July 11, 2007.

Chapter 10

1. Quoted in J. Wallace Hamilton, *Horns and Halos in Human Nature* (Westwood, NJ: Fleming H. Revel Company, 1954), 85.

2. "Ruth Roman and Husband Plan Divorce," *The Times, Shreveport*, Nov. 5, 1955, 2.
3. "Ruth Roman Divorce," *The York Dispatch*, Mar. 30, 1956, 21.
4. "Ruth Roman Divorced from KLAC Head," *The Los Angeles Times*, Mar. 30, 1956, 35. "Ruth Roman Gets Divorce," *The Knickerbocker News*, Mar. 30, 1956, 8-A.
5. "Nearly All Aboard Ill-Fated Andrea Doria are Saved: About 50 Persons Missing," *Schenectady Gazette*, July 27, 1956, 52.
6. There are several books on the *Andrea Doria* sinking. See Alvin Moscow, *Collision Course: The Andrea Doria and the Stockholm* (New York: G.P. Putnam & Sons, 1959) and Pierette Domenica Simpson, *Alive on the Andrea Doria! The Greatest Sea Rescue in History* (New York: Morgan James, 2008). The author was herself a survivor of the sinking.
7. Budd Burton Moss, with Julie McCarron, *And All I Got Was Ten Percent! What It's Like to Be a (Famous) Hollywood Agent*, Vol. 1930–1970 (2012), 37.
8. Walter Winchell, "Writes of New York," *Buffalo Courier-Express*, Nov. 21, 1956, 18.
9. "Ship Ceremony Thwarted; Ruth Roman Wed Ashore," *Democrat & Chronicle*, Nov. 9, 1956, 17.
10. "Ruth Roman Remembers Who Taught Her to Fish," *Pittsburgh Post-Gazette*, Oct. 15, 1958, 6.
11. "Actresses in Venice Say Italians Are Tops as Flirts," *The Journal News*, Sept. 4, 1957, 5.
12. Jean-Luc Godard, "Beyond the Stars," *Cahiers du Cinema* 1 and "Au dela des etoiles," *Cahiers du Cinema* 79 (January 1958), 18.
13. "Bitter Victory," *Film Bulletin* (1957), 1917.
14. Moss, *All I Got Was 10 Percent*, 37.
15. See the article about Nicholas Ray by David Thompson, "In a Lonely Place," *Sight and Sound*, Oct. 1979, 216.
16. Christopher Lee, *Lord of Misrule* (London: Orion, 2004), 170.
17. "Seven for Sinners Due to Match

Roman, Horton," *The Los Angeles Times*, Aug. 10, 1957, 23.

18. Richard B. Jewell and Vernon Harbin, *The RKO Story* (London: Octopus Books, 1982), 297.

19. Erskine Johnson, "Ruth Roman's Figure Displayed in New Italian Biblical Movie," *Quebec Chronicle-Telegraph*, Feb. 1, 1955, 24.

Chapter 11

1. Kaspar Monahan, "'Two for Seesaw' Brings Fun and Pathos to Nixon," *The Pittsburgh Press*, Oct. 14, 1958, 9.

2. Moss, *And All I Got Was Ten Percent!*, 37.

3. Harold V. Cohen, "Nixon Gets Something Rare in 'Two for the Seesaw,'" *Pittsburgh Post-Gazette*, Oct. 14, 1958, 13.

4. Kaspar Monahan, "'Two for Seesaw' Brings Fun and Pathos to Nixon," *The Pittsburgh Press*, Oct. 14, 1958, 9.

5. "Drama: A View of Ruth Roman's End of the Seesaw," *The San Francisco Examiner*, June 28, 1959, 120.

6. Moss, *And All I Got Was Ten Percent!*.

7. Sheldon Cheney, "Sarah Siddons Society," *Theatre Arts* 44 (1960), 95.

Chapter 12

1. "Ruth Roman 'They Forgot My Name,'" *Intelligencer* Lancaster, Pennsylvania, Mar. 30, 1967, 14.

2. "Ruth Roman, Mate Separated," *Star Tribune*, July 12, 1960, 8.

3. Telephone conversation with Budd Moss, July 4, 2020.

4. *Ibid.*

5. Mortimer W. Hall (1924–2012) was married four times: (1) Mary Ann Parker (d. 1945); (2) Ruth Roman (1950–56) (div.); (3) actress Diana Lynn, 1956–71 (d. 1971); and (4) Penelope Coker (1972–2012). *Forbears and Descendants of Ezra Carter Gross and Phoebe Fisher Gross* (1961), 45. "Mortimer W. Hall Death Notice, Poughkeepsie, New York," *Poughkeepsie Journal*, Mar. 7, 2012.

6. "Ruth Roman Seeks Hike in Support Payment,s" *Pasadena Independent*, May 25, 1962.

7. "People," *The Pittsburgh Press*, June 9, 1962, 2.

8. Hildy Crawford, "Around Town," *Desert Sun*, Feb. 7, 1961, 23.

9. Arthur McClure, and Ken D. Jones, *Star Quality: Screen Actors from the Golden Age of Films* (New York: A. S. Barnes, 1954), 225.

10. Hedda Hopper, "Cast Virtually Certain for 'Return to Peyton Place,'" *The Los Angeles Times*, Jan. 22, 1960, 12.

11. Augusto M. Torres, *Cineastas Insolitos* (Madrid: Nuer Edicines, 2000), 129.

12. Andrew Sarris, "Alexander Singer," *The American Cinema Directors and Directions 1929–1968* (New York: E.P. Dutton, 1968), 224.

13. Quoted in "Love Has Many Faces (1965)," Leslie Halliwell, *Halliwell's Film Guide* (London: Guild, 1983), 498.

14. "Perspective '61," *Broadcasting*, Feb. 20, 1961, 122.

15. Rita Lakin, *The Only Woman in the Room* (New York: Applause Books, 2015).

16. Vince Edwards, "Ed's Easy Subjects: O'Brien, Ruth and Roman Films," *The Pittsburgh Press*, July 23, 1965, 61.

17. Mark Philips and Frank Garcia, *Science Fiction Television Series* (Jefferson, NC: McFarland, 2012).

18. Erskine Johnson, "Ruth's Shift Not Among Her Errors," *Wausau Daily Herald*, Mar. 27, 1964, 8.

19. "Ruth Roman's War on Waist," *Newport Daily News*, Mar. 18, 1964, 39.

20. "'Candida' Star Ill, Cancels U. Date," *The Salt Lake Tribune*, Mar. 28, 1965, 24.

21. "Candida," *The Daily Utah Chronicle*, Apr. 18, 1965, 1.

22. Frank Brunsman, "U's 'Candida' True to Shaw," *The Salt Lake Tribune*, Apr. 9, 1965, 19.

23. "Roman and Lucky," *Pittsburgh Post-Gazette*, July 20, 1967, 12.

24. Richard Lamparski, *Whatever Became Of... Eighth Series* (New York: Crown, 1982), 305.

Chapter 13

1. Buck Biggers and Chet Stover, "TV Tinderbox," *Times-News*, Twin Falls, Idaho, 1973.

2. In 1971, it was reported in several sources, including *Variety* and *Films and Filming*, that Roman was among the cast of a film, variously titled *Everyman* or *S.R.O,*. to be filmed in Dallas, Texas, for producer-director Jerry Schafer. The principal cast members included Rory Calhoun, Rosie Grier, Jesse White, Jim Mitchum, Tom Bosley, John Fiedler and Percy Helton. It would appear to have been based on the novel by Robert Deane Pharr published in the same year. S.R.O. stood for Single Room Occupancy. There is no mention of the film in most works of reference, but it is listed among Roman's credits on the BFI website, so I have included it among her list of feature films in the Appendix for reference. See *Films and Filming* (Hansom Books, 1971), 6, and "Hollywood Production Pulse," *Variety*, July 22, 1970.

3. Ted Post, interviewed by Jeremy Kenyon of D.G.A., Visual History with Ted Post.

4. Article in the *Hollywood Reporter*, 30 Apr. 1970.

5. For an interesting critique of *The Baby* see the chapter "Filmic Regression: The Baby and Baby Huey" in Mike Kelley and Roger Conover, *Foul Perfection: Essays and Criticism* (Cambridge: MIT Press, 2003), 11.

6. Richard Sheib, *The Science Fiction, Horror and Fantasy Movie Review*. For the best assessment on this genre of horror see Peter Shelley, *Grand Guignol Cinema: A History of Hag Horror from Baby Jane to Mother* (Jefferson, NC: McFarland, 2009).

7. See *The Gerald Fried Collection: The Baby* Caldera Records C 6029 (2019) http://caldera-records.com/portfolio/the-baby/gallery/soundtracks/ which includes an audio commentary by the composer and detailed liner notes by David Fuller and Stephan Eicke.

8. Hill Place, "Medium Cool: An interview with actress Marianna Hill," December 17, 2016.

9. "Ruth Roman," *The Killing Kind Press Book*, 1973.

10. Brian Albright, *Wild Beyond Belief: Interviews with Exploitation Filmmakers of the 1960s and 1970s* (Jefferson, NC: McFarland, 2008), 28.

11. "A Knife for the Ladies," *AFI Film Catalog.*

12. See David Quinlan, *Quinlan's Film Stars* (London: Batsford, 2000), 449.

13. Vernon Scott, "Where Are They Now? Ruth Roman Gets Offer of Series," *The Province*, Feb. 16, 1973, 46.

14. *Arts Magazine* 47 (1973), 78.

15. William Ross Wilson, Ruth Roman, Marriage Records, Clark, Nevada, April 4, 1976.

16. Ellie Schlitz, "Star Refuses to Ignore Natural Acting Abilities," *Arizona Republic*, July 30, 1974, 31.

17. Telephone conversation with Budd Moss, July 4, 2020.

18. See David R. Greenland, *The Gunsmoke Chronicles* (Albany, GA: BearManor Media, 2013).

19. See "The Sixth Sense" in John Kenneth Muir, *Terror Television: American Series 1970–1999* (Jefferson, NC: McFarland, 2013).

20. See Herbie J. Pilato, *The Kung Fu Book of Caine: The Complete Guide to TV's First Eastern Western* (Clarendon, VT: Tuttle Company, 1993).

21. "Jealous Actress Ripped Star's Fur Coat," *The Times*, Jan. 20, 1973, 3.

Chapter 14

1. Ellie Schultz, "Star Refuses to Ignore Natural Acting Ability," *Arizona Republic*, July 30, 1974, 31.

2. Tom Lisanti, *Carol Lynley: Her Film & TV Career in Thrillers, Fantasies and Suspense* (Albany, GA: BearManor Media, 2020).

3. "What's in View: Ruth Roman Joining Knot's Landing," *Battle Creek Enquirer*, Jan. 16, 1986, 14.

4. See James Robert Parish, *The Unofficial Murder, She Wrote Casebook* (New York: Kensington Books, 1997).

5. "Film Fax," *Film Review* (1991), 50.

6. Buck Biggers and Chet Stover, "TV

Tinderbox," *Times-News*, Twin Falls, Idaho, 1973 (clipping).

7. Phone conversation with Budd Moss, July 4, 2020.

Epilogue

1. Edwin Schallert, "Matrimony, Motherhood Revive Ruth's Career," *The Los Angeles Times* 1953 (cutting).

2. "Ruth Roman Accepts New Role," *The Morning News*, Jan. 16, 1986, 56.

Appendix

1. See David Quinlan, *Quinlan's Film Stars* (London: Batsford, 2000), 449.

2. See "S.R.O. (1971)" at BFI (bfi.org. uk).

3. *John Willis' Theater World* 34 (1977–78), 36.

4. Art Linkletter, *Women Are My*

Favorite People (New York: Doubleday, 1974), 93.

5. "Fredric Marches Eyeing Legit Scripts for Fall," *Variety*, May 31, 1950, 2.

6. "Radio Highlights," *The Brooklyn Daily Eagle*, Feb.14, 1952, 12.

7. "Radio and Television," *The Journal-Times*, Racine, Wisconsin, Jan. 3, 1953, 8.

8. "Ruth Roman Is Bob Hope's Lady Editor of the Week," *The Times*, Mar. 7, 1954, 11-D.

9. "Radio Round-Up," *Daily News-Post & Monrovia Daily News-Post*, May 10, 1954, 6.

10. "Radio," *The Valley Times*, Dec. 18, 1954, 24.

11. *Breakfast Club Album* (1959), 25.

12. "National Tuberculosis Assn," *Broadcasting*, July 27, 1953, 51.

13. Irv Kupcinet, rv *Kup's Chicago* (Cleveland: World, 1962), 220.

Bibliography

Basinger, Jeanine. *Anthony Mann*. Middletown, CT: Wesleyan University Press, 2007.

Bergan, Ronald. *The United Artists Story*. London: Octopus Books, 1986.

Billips, Connie J., and Arthur Pierce. *Lux Presents Hollywood: A Show-by-Show History of the Lux Radio Theatre and the Lux Video Theatre, 1934–57.* Jefferson, NC: McFarland, 1995.

Bowers, Ronald L. *The Selznick Players*. New York: A. S. Barnes, 1976.

Cameron, Ian Alexander, and Elisabeth Cameron. *Dames*. New York: Praeger, 1969.

Carpenter, Carleton, *The Absolute Joy of Work: From Vermont to Broadway, Hollywood, and Damn Near 'Round the World*. Albany, GA: Bear Manor Media, 2016.

Cottom, J.V. "Ruth Roman: L'Ambition Comme Sa Beaute." *Les Immortels du Cinema* (1976).

Edwards, Paul M. *A Guide to Films on the Korean War*. Westport, CT: Greenwood Press, 1998.

Films in Review 38 (1987).

Halliwell, Leslie. *Halliwell's Film Guide*. London: Guild Publishing, 1983.

Harris, Robert A., and Michael S. Lasky. *The Complete Films of Alfred Hitchcock*. Secaucus: Carroll, 1993.

Hirschhorn, Clive. *The Universal Story*. London: Octopus Books, 1983.

Hirschhorn, Clive. *The Warner Bros. Story*. London: Octopus Books, 1979.

International Motion Picture Almanac. Quigley Publications, 1951.

Jewell, Richard B., and Vernon Harbin. *The RKO Story*. London: Octopus Books, 1982.

Kaufman, David. *Doris Day: The Untold Story of the Girl Next Door*. New York: Virgin Books, 2008.

Leeman, Sergio. *Robert Wise on His Films: From Editing Room to Director's Chair*. West Hollywood: Silman-James Press, 1995.

Linkletter, Art. *Women Are My Favorite People*. New York: Doubleday, 1974.

Moscow, Alvin. *Collision Course: The Andrea Doria and the Stockholm*. New York: G.P. Putnam & Sons, 1959.

Moss, Budd Burton, with Julie McCarron. *And All I Got Was Ten Percent! What It's Like to Be a (Famous) Hollywood Agent*. Vol. 1, 1930–1970. CreateSpace, 2012.

Moss, Marilyn Ann. *Giant: George Stevens A Life on Film*. Madison, WI: Terrace Books, 2004.

Pym, John. *Time Out Film Guide*. London: Penguin, 2000.

Quinlan, David. *Quinlan's Film Stars*. London: Batsford, 2000.

Raborn, George. *George Raborn Presents: How Hollywood Rates*. New York: B. Nelson, 1955.

Rainey, Buck. *Sweethearts of the Sage: Biographies and Filmographies of 258 Actresses Appearing in Western Movies*. Jefferson, NC: McFarland, 1992.

Bibliography

Shelley, Peter. *Grande Guignol Cinema: A History of Hag Horror from Baby Jane to Mother.* Jefferson, NC: McFarland, 2009.

Simpson, Pierette Domenica. *Alive on the Andrea Doria! The Greatest Sea Rescue in History.* New York: Morgan James Publishing, 2008.

Torres, Augusto M. *Cineastas Insolitos.* Madrid: Nuer Edicines, 2000.

Weldon, Michael. *The Psychotronic Video Guide.* London: Titan Books, 1996.

Index

Numbers in **_bold italics_** indicate pages with illustrations

Index

Index

Index

209

Index

Index

Index

Index

Index